BLACK SUFFRAGE

A NATION DIVIDED: STUDIES IN THE CIVIL WAR ERA
Orville Vernon Burton and Elizabeth R. Varon, Editors

Black Suffrage

Lincoln's Last Goal

PAUL D. ESCOTT

UNIVERSITY OF VIRGINIA PRESS

Charlottesville and London

University of Virginia Press
© 2022 by the Rector and Visitors of the University of Virginia
All rights reserved
Printed in the United States of America on acid-free paper

First published 2022

9 8 7 6 5 4 3 2 1

Library of Congress Cataloging-in-Publication Data

Names: Escott, Paul D., author.
Title: Black suffrage : Lincoln's last goal / Paul D. Escott.
Description: Charlottesville : University of Virginia Press, 2022. | Series:
   A nation divided: studies in the Civil War era | Includes bibliographical
   references and index.
Identifiers: LCCN 2021054643 (print) | LCCN 2021054644 (ebook) |
   ISBN 9780813948171 (hardcover) | ISBN 9780813948188 (ebook)
Subjects: LCSH: African Americans—Suffrage—History—19th century.
   | Racism—United States—History—19th century. | White suprem-
   acy movements—United States—History—19th century. | African
   Americans—Social conditions—To 1964. | Political parties—United
   States—History—19th century. | United States—Race relations—History.
   | United States—Politics and government—1861–1865.
Classification: LCC JK1924 .E83 2022 (print) | LCC JK1924 (ebook) |
   DDC 324.6/208996073—dc23/eng/20211214
LC record available at https://lccn.loc.gov/2021054643
LC ebook record available at https://lccn.loc.gov/2021054644

Cover art: "The National Colored Convention in Session at Washington,
D.C." (Sketch by Theodore R. Davis, Harper's Weekly, 6 Feb. 1869; Library
of Congress, Prints and Photographs Division, LC-USZ62-100970)

Para Candelas
más que nunca

❖ CONTENTS ❖

❖ PREFACE ❖

This book examines the attitudes toward Black suffrage that surfaced in the North immediately after the end of the Civil War. The victory of the Union Army over Confederate forces meant that the nation would remain united. But the war had not only been about the extension of slave territory or the South's secession. Beneath these issues lay the question identified by Alexander Stephens of Georgia: "the proper *status* of the negro in our form of civilization."[1] What did Union victory mean for Black rights? Would African Americans gain full liberty, equality under the law, or the right to vote? After the war ended, victorious northerners had to face those questions. Underlying issues of racism and white supremacy became more visible and central than they had been before.

The Civil War was such a significant event in U.S. history that interpretations of it have often been polemical, contrasting, or misleading. Defeated southern whites invented their narrative of a sacred Lost Cause. Northern perspectives on the war changed over time. Fifty years ago respected scholarly interpretations of the period were positive, even celebratory. They emphasized the great advances in human liberty that the United States achieved by ending slavery and preserving the nation. Decades later, as global and domestic affairs changed, citizens' perspectives evolved, and historians began to pay more attention to what was not accomplished by the Union victory. At this moment in the twenty-first century, unsolved racial problems—and their roots in the Civil War era—appropriately demand attention. Police killings of unarmed Black men, threats by armed white supremacist groups, and racist comments from the White House all have made clear that the nation's racist past is not past. For that reason Americans need to recognize that white supremacy has deeply infected the culture.

More than a decade ago when I turned my research toward the North and Abraham Lincoln, I focused on racism as opposed to emancipation, on stubborn problems as opposed to satisfying achievements. My guiding assumption has been that an accurate knowledge of the roots of contemporary problems is essential to addressing them effectively. Therefore, I analyzed Lincoln's record as a great emancipator but not a great egalitarian. For most of his life he promoted colonization—the removal of African Americans from the nation—and his priority as president was not emancipation but preservation of the Union. Many of his policies implied a greater concern for southern whites than for enslaved African Americans. I also investigated important, engrained elements of racism in the Republican Party. Unfortunately, for many in Lincoln's party and for many more in the society of his day, racial equality was unthinkable. My most recent book, *"The Worst Passions of Human Nature": White Supremacy in the Civil War North*, explored the imposing breadth and strength of racism and white supremacy in the North during the Civil War. That project took me more deeply into the newspapers, magazines, and partisan propaganda of the war years.[2]

It therefore seemed logical to extend my research into the months of 1865 that followed Abraham Lincoln's assassination. Quite a few outstanding works have laid bare the dynamics of Reconstruction policymaking in 1866, 1867, and later, but similarly detailed studies of northern public opinion and attitudes in the last eight or nine months of 1865 are few or lacking. Once I pushed my research into that period, with a focus on Black suffrage, I found that there was much worth noting. Andrew Johnson's policies were not the only influence at work. Racism that flourished in the Democratic Party contended with arguments that the end of the war required a new status for African Americans. The activities of abolitionists, Black leaders, and pro-suffrage Republicans were energetic and prominent, and the events affecting public attitudes had important implications for subsequent years. Accordingly, this book traces and analyzes public discussion and debate on Black suffrage in the North. Because Congress was not in session, the emphasis falls mainly on newspapers, magazines, public celebrations or meetings, public speeches by political figures, and organizing efforts and agitation by abolitionists and Black leaders. The presentation of evidence is both thematic, as suggested in chapter titles, and chronological, as indicated in the early pages of each chapter. The last eight or nine months of 1865 showed both the continuing power of racism and white supremacy in the northern population and the increasing strength of equalitarian ideals within the Republican Party.

A final note: I regret that some readers may be troubled by the evidence of racism in the period as well as by the occasional appearance in quotations of the offensive N-word. Working with the press, I have tried to minimize or avoid its use, but such blatant racism was, unfortunately, deeply characteristic of the time. As citizens, we need to be aware of ugly facts as well as progress in U.S. history. It would be a mistake to sanitize the record so completely as to lose an accurate sense of the past.

I gratefully thank Dr. Jeffrey Crow, my good friend since graduate school, for his advice and comments. I also am indebted to Professor David Goldfield and an anonymous reviewer for the University of Virginia Press for helpful and well-considered comments and suggestions. All errors or omissions are, of course, my own responsibility.

Lincoln's Last Goal

S pring was coming to the nation's capital. Flowers began to open, and barren trees sprouted new leaves of lambent green. Spring is usually a hopeful time, but this was especially so in Washington, D.C., in 1865, because there was news of imminent victory. At last, after four years of unprecedented death, destruction, and uncertainty, the Union armies were about to prevail over the rebellious Confederacy.

On April 2 Jefferson Davis and his Cabinet abandoned Richmond. On April 3 northern soldiers took control of the Confederate capital. Abraham Lincoln and his son Tad then walked the city's streets, visiting the rebel White House and the Virginia State Capitol. On April 9 Robert E. Lee surrendered his army to Ulysses S. Grant. This cascade of long-awaited news brought "immense gatherings" into the streets of the Union capital. During a week of joy and relief, "flags were flying from every house and store," and bells were ringing, "men laughing, children cheering; all, all [were] jubilant." On April 13 an immense illumination celebrated Lee's surrender, as residents lighted candles in every house and every part of the city.[1]

Victory had finally arrived. It was a victory that most northerners had expected to be easy in a war they had assumed would be short. It was a victory coming after dispiriting reverses, painful sacrifices, and enormous change—vast and sweeping innovations that neither civilians nor elected leaders had foreseen. Many of the changes would not have happened except that an encompassing wartime emergency had overtaken the North and transformed people's thinking in many ways. Compelled by events, the Union adapted to emergency conditions by adopting revolutionary measures—conscription, taxation, extraordinary spending, martial law, and, most especially, emancipation. Slavery, an institution much older than the republic and anchored by deep roots that reached far into every aspect of society, at last was to end. Transformative change had been the means to success, the price of victory.

But now, what would victory mean? Was the Union preserved or changed? As the end came for a war that had been revolutionary, would the revolution end as well? Would emancipation lead to full freedom or give way to "oppressions akin to slavery."[2] Would the North revert to old habits or confirm new goals? Would citizens seek relief or embrace more change, regress or continue to progress? Did victory mean a "new birth of freedom" leading to a "more perfect" Union, or merely an escape from tension and sacrifice?

In April it seemed that a return to the prewar Union might be impossible. Perhaps four years of violence and demonization of the enemy precluded any fraternal reunion with "erring brothers." During the conflict many northerners had grown bitter toward the rebel South. Looking back over the past, they often viewed slavery as the cause of the war and the slaveholding South as the source of all the nation's problems. Many became convinced that selfish slave masters had dominated the republic for generations, that an antidemocratic aristocracy of wealth and privilege controlled southern society, and that the lords of the lash had turned their barbarism upon Union prisoners and Black Union troops. Reconciliation with such enemies seemed impossible and undesirable. Perhaps victory required continued revolutionary change to create the "more perfect Union." Emancipation—never planned by Abraham Lincoln or his administration in 1861—should lead to meaningful, complete liberty, many believed. Victory should democratize the South and bring full citizenship to former slaves.

Yet it also was undeniable that the wave of change which rolled over the wartime North had not obliterated all habits or patterns of thought. Emancipation had come about as a controversial means to preserve the Union, not because northerners agreed that it was morally right and necessary. Racism had deep roots in society, and racism had colored the policies of Republican leaders and the Republican president.[3] Surely, too, ordinary people wanted relief from crisis and the comfort of old routines. The years of emergency and unexpected change had been exhausting, and revolutionary initiatives always demanded great expenditures of energy. What, then, should victory mean?

Abraham Lincoln was ready to answer that question with a singular, transformative vision. This vision became fully evident only in the last months of his life. It was one that he had come to slowly amid the accumulating grief of a terribly destructive war. As a decent, caring man who had presided over immense bloodshed and sorrow, Lincoln now longed for a better society and a new start for the nation. Aware that emancipation was a historic advance, he hoped that the nation would draw closer to its founding ideals. Through 1864 he had augmented his tireless pursuit of reconciliation with southern whites by gradually embracing a new but significant desire for broader racial justice. In the final months of the conflict his hopes vaulted forward, and he dreamed of a nation not just reunited but redeemed. Forgiveness between enemies and justice for the oppressed were remarkably optimistic and idealistic goals. Lincoln's last goal revealed the depth of his empathy, generosity, and moral greatness.

The Great Emancipator had not been an abolitionist but a politician who helped to build a new party opposed to slavery's expansion. His Republican Party contained a spectrum of views, from abolitionists through colonizationists and racists. The crisis of war had pushed Lincoln and the Republicans toward emancipation and other racially progressive measures. Part of his vision—the part centered on reconciliation with southern foes—was long established. In his first inaugural address he repeated previous declarations that he had "no purpose, directly or indirectly, to interfere with the institution of slavery in the States where it exists." He declared that he had "no objection" to a proposed constitutional amendment that would prohibit federal interference with slavery forever. Then for almost two years Lincoln scrupulously kept his promise to respect the rights of southern slaveholders. Rather than undermine slavery, he lagged far behind Congress and much public opinion in taking action against the sin of human bondage. He repeatedly and consistently invited reconciliation with white southerners while moving slowly to address the hopes of the enslaved.[4]

When Lincoln announced his policy of emancipation in September 1862, he believed that this new, stronger action had become indispensable. He justified it as a necessary war measure, and most Republicans insisted that saving the Union, not abolition, remained their goal. Lincoln's Preliminary Emancipation Proclamation gave the rebellious states one hundred days in which they could return to the Union and retain their slaves. By holding elections in which a majority of their voters selected representatives to Congress, they could be deemed *not* to be in rebellion. Before those one hundred days were over, he went further. To encourage a return to loyalty, he quietly relaxed the level of participation that he desired and renewed his proposals for a very gradual, completely voluntary emancipation that would be compensated by the federal government.[5]

Through most of the war Lincoln offered freed slaves and African Americans much less than an equal place in American society. For example, in December 1861, when the disrupting events of war had already brought practical freedom to thousands, he recommended colonizing African Americans in some foreign land where the climate was "congenial to them." In 1862 he urged a group of Black leaders to promote colonization, saying that opposition to the idea was "an extremely selfish view of the case." In 1863 and 1864 Lincoln continued to pursue an impractical interest in colonization and made new efforts to reassure white southerners of his goodwill. In December 1863 he presented a plan for reconstruction that offered pardon to most rebels if they would acknowledge the end of slavery. If only 10 percent of the voters in any rebel state would reassert their loyalty, he would allow them to form a new government. Lincoln wanted southern whites to make some provision for the education of former slaves. But to encourage the "deeply afflicted" rebels to "be somewhat more ready to give up the cause of their affliction," slavery, he offered to let them define the immediate postwar status of the freed people as a "temporary arrangement" for a "laboring, landless, and homeless class." One year later he affirmed that he had granted special pardons to some Confederates and that "no voluntary application has been denied."[6]

But Lincoln had always hated slavery and its violation of the ideals articulated in the Declaration of Independence. He also responded gradually to pressure from Radical Republicans, the abolitionist minority within his party. Two days after the Battle of Bull Run, Senators Charles Sumner of Massachusetts and Zachariah Chandler of Michigan visited the White House and argued that emancipation was a military necessity. Sumner, along with Representative Thaddeus Stevens of Pennsylvania and Senator Henry Wilson of Massachusetts, kept up the pressure and lobbied Lincoln every chance they could. Those three, said Lincoln, "simply haunt me with their importunities" about emancipation. The president also developed respect for Black leaders like Frederick Douglass and began to think more deeply about the rights of Blacks in the South. In secret in March 1864 he wrote to Michael Hahn, the governor of the small but loyal government that had been established in occupied portions of Louisiana. "I barely suggest for your private consideration," said Lincoln, "whether some of the colored people may not be let in" to the ballot. He specifically mentioned "the very intelligent, and especially those who have fought gallantly in our ranks." Although this was "only a suggestion," Lincoln felt it might help "to keep the jewel of liberty within the family of freedom."[7]

Then in the last months of the war Lincoln's moral vision grew. His actions and words showed that he was idealistically driven to lead the nation onto a new path of peace, reconciliation, *and* greater racial justice. He broadened his overtures to southern whites and proclaimed a significant new concern for the rights and future of southern slaves. First, he appealed to Congress to approve the Thirteenth Amendment, send it to the states, and thus write the end of slavery into organic law. He called on the lawmakers to act immediately, rather than wait for the seating of a new Congress that would propose the amendment. Vigorous efforts by his allies helped bring that to fruition. Then at the beginning of February 1865 he met with Confederate commissioners at Hampton Roads and did all he could to induce them to return to the Union. Promising generosity in pardons, he suggested that they might make a transition to emancipation by delaying its effective date by five years. He also held out the possibility of a $400 million indemnity to slaveholding states, an idea that he promptly drafted and presented to his shocked and disapproving Cabinet. Overcoming four years of bitterness toward wartime foes would not be easy, but that was part of Lincoln's hope.[8]

The moral imperative shaping Lincoln's longing for a better Union was evident in his second inaugural address in March, one of the shortest and most remarkable orations of any president. It was a solemn but moving presentation by a leader keenly aware of war's tragic costs. In paragraphs whose content and cadence had the character of a sermon, Lincoln identified slavery as "somehow" the cause of a vast war that neither side had anticipated. While they were killing each other, both sides "read the same Bible, and pray[ed] to the same God, and each invoke[d] His aid against the other." In the end, Lincoln said, the purposes of "the Almighty" were fulfilled. If God gave "this terrible war" to Americans because it was "His appointed time" to remove slavery, surely God's judgment was "true and righteous altogether." That was so even if it meant that "all the wealth piled by the bond-man's two hundred fifty years of unrequited toil shall be sunk, and . . . every drop of blood drawn with the lash, shall be paid by another drawn with the sword." Then Lincoln challenged his countrymen to learn from the carnage, to put rancor aside, to "judge not that we be not judged." He challenged them to "achieve and cherish a just and lasting peace" by acting "with malice toward none; with charity for all." Although his address did not specifically mention freed Blacks, its moral focus had clear implications. The gift of charity, the absence of malice, and the embrace of justice would logically apply to the division between North and South and between the races.[9]

Lincoln spent much of the last three weeks of his life near the Virginia battlefields. He was eager to escape from Washington and witness in person the coming of peace. Talking with Union soldiers was a pleasure for him, and he shook hands with patients at an army hospital for "several hours." But it was not only Union soldiers that were in his thoughts. Lincoln also made "a point of shaking hands with the hospitalized Confederates." Speaking with General Grant and others on March 28, he discussed offering generous terms of surrender to Confederates in order to get the "deluded men" of the rebel forces "back to their homes." Once there, he was certain, "they won't take up arms again. Let them all go, officers and all, I want no more bloodshed." The terms of a future peace settlement, he made clear to Grant, must remain in the president's hands. At this point, writes the historian David Donald, Lincoln was determined that peace "would ensure his war aims of Union, Emancipation, and at least limited Equality."[10]

On April 4 he went to see Richmond, the captured rebel capital. On the way a Black workman recognized him, shouted "there is the great Messiah!" and fell to his knees. As Lincoln urged the man to stand, a crowd of Black people quickly gathered around the president, shouting, "Bless the Lord, Father Abrahams Come." In the fashionable part of Richmond, wealthy rebels closed their blinds and drapes, but African Americans and working-class people greeted him enthusiastically. In the Confederate White House he met with John A. Campbell, the rebellion's assistant secretary of war, who wanted to talk about peace. To hurry that peace, Lincoln even came close to taking the false step of legitimizing the existing, rebel legislature of Virginia by allowing it to assemble, on condition that it would take that state out of the Confederacy. Before he sailed away from City Point, he told an army band to play "Dixie," because it was "now Federal property" and he wanted the rebels to know that "with us in power, they will be free to hear it again."[11]

But defeated southern whites were not the only people in Lincoln's thoughts. He returned from Virginia "with a new sense of urgency about reconstruction," and he did not shrink from challenging the nation's deeply entrenched racism. His resolution sprang from a growing desire for greater racial justice. During the war he had drawn closer to a number of Black Americans. He forged a friendship with Frederick Douglass and met with free Black leaders, with freedmen, and with escaped slaves. Often he had stopped at a "contraband" camp near the capital to visit, talk, and sing hymns with "Aunt" Mary Dines and other former slaves. He also developed friendly relationships with leading Republicans who had fought most vigorously for equality. Lincoln called on Massachusetts's Senator Charles Sumner to accompany him and Mary Todd Lincoln to the inaugural ball, and he told Sumner that he did not understand why most people viewed William Seward as the president's closest advisor. "I have counseled with you," he told Sumner, "twice as much as I ever did with him." Lincoln also had discussed with the Radicals in his party the idea of requiring Black suffrage in the recognition of returning southern states.[12]

Now he wanted the war to end and a better nation to come into being, for Blacks as well as whites. Despite his awareness of the inveterate racism in society, Lincoln made a significant, new commitment in the last public speech of his life. On April 10 happy serenaders gathered in front of the White House and called on their victorious president for a speech. He replied that he was not ready to speak that night but on the next evening Lincoln delivered a prepared address. In that speech he argued that differing, legalistic theories ought not to slow the practical challenge of bringing seceded states back into the Union. He defended the progress made in Louisiana under his 1863 plan and urged building on it. Then he told his audience not only that the Thirteenth Amendment must be ratified but that the "colored man" should have the ballot. Many had been advocating this measure, he noted. At that moment Lincoln announced that "I myself would prefer that it were now conferred on the very intelligent, and on those who serve our cause as soldiers."[13]

This was farther than the cautious president had ever gone. It aligned him, for the first time, with his party's advocates of equal rights. Black suffrage would authenticate the rights of African Americans and confirm their

Frederick Douglass, the noted abolitionist who had more influence on Lincoln than any African American, continued to fight for Black suffrage. (B. F. Smith & Son Photographers, Portland, Maine, 1864; Liljenquist Family Collection of Civil War Photographs, Library of Congress, Prints and Photographs Division, LC-DIG-ppmsca-69250)

status not as aliens but as citizens in a multiracial democracy. Although less than a formal proposal to Congress, these words were a public declaration that defined his position as chief executive and established a basis for future policy initiatives and debates. Lincoln's record showed that he moved cautiously and slowly, but once he arrived at a conclusion, he did not retreat from it. He now had endorsed Black suffrage, at least for some African American men, and thereafter he would put his talents to work toward reaching that goal. The president committed his voice and influence to support Black suffrage in the weeks and months to come.

Thus Lincoln looked toward the Reconstruction period in a spirit of generosity, forgiveness, and justice that would encompass both returning rebels and aspiring African Americans. He had defined an ambitious agenda, one that would require not just change but moral renovation. In the minds of many whites, Black suffrage and reconciliation with rebels did not seem compatible. Embracing southern whites seemed to imply accepting their hostility to Blacks. Adopting Black suffrage—an unpopular measure—might depend on a willingness or desire to punish rebels. Only through a high-minded personal renewal of citizens, North and South, did both seem possible.

Lincoln's last hope grew out of idealism and morality, rather than down-to-earth, practical politics. But Lincoln was also a practical politician, one who did not give up easily and who knew how to find a way forward amid difficulties. His leadership through a multitude of crises had saved the Union. In victory he was looking not for rest but toward the building of a better society—one that would, as he had put it earlier, "elevate the condition of men" and "lift artificial weights from all shoulders."[14] His hope for reconciliation and Black suffrage, if successful, would produce a new Union of broader freedom and greater justice. Lincoln had defined an idealistic agenda for 1865.

1

Shock, Grief, Disorientation

O n April 14 everything changed. John Wilkes Booth fired a bullet into Abraham Lincoln's brain while the president was enjoying a play at Ford's Theatre. Three doctors rushed to Lincoln's box but quickly saw that his condition was hopeless. His body was carried to a room across the street where Cabinet members and political leaders quickly gathered. Senator Charles Sumner was one of the first to arrive. The abolitionist senator pushed his way into the small and crowded bedroom and for more than eight hours held the president's hand while sobbing "with his own head bowed until it almost touched the pillow." Mary Lincoln entered the room almost every hour but promptly was overcome with emotion. Just before 7:30 in the morning, Secretary of the Navy Gideon Wells was among those who witnessed the end of a "good and great man."[1]

Powerful emotions rocked the North. At first, some felt that "the atmosphere of Washington" was "charged with terror." Then an "air of gloom" hung over the capital, and "almost every house was draped and closed." Author Edward Everett Hale recalled that for nearly two weeks, "all things stood still" and "no word was read or written that had not reference" to Lincoln. The young Henry Cabot Lodge, then only fourteen years old, remembered waking to "the horror, the dazed surprise, [and] the shock of the announcement" of the president's death. Lincoln's body lay in state in the East Room, where "great crowds" pressed in to take "their last look at the President's kind face." Welles wrote that "strong and brave men wept when I met them," but he felt that the deepest mourning was visible in "several hundred colored people," standing in "a cheerless cold rain . . .

in front of the White House." Their numbers did not "diminish through the whole of that cold, wet day." Women as well as men, and little children too, "thronged the streets," perhaps wondering "what was to be their fate since their great benefactor was dead."[2]

Newspaper headlines struggled to express people's shock and grief. "Abraham Lincoln Assassinated! The country is struck dumb, nerveless with horror," cried the *Vermont Watchman and State Journal.* Other Republican papers from New York through Chicago to Kansas and beyond wailed over "The Great Calamity," "The Great Tragedy," "Horrible Scene in his Bedchamber," "Horrible Tragedy," "the appalling news," or the "atrocious crime." From the "exhilaration" of victory, "the nation throughout its length and breadth, became as a house of mourners," wrote an Ohio editor, and a Pennsylvania paper struck a common theme when it honored "The Martyr President." A conservative Unionist paper in Maryland declared that the assassination had covered "the whole land . . . with the mantle of gloomiest and direst woe." "The bullet that pierced the head of President Lincoln touched the heart of the nation," editorialized the *Cincinnati Commercial.* "No event since the death of Washington has so filled the land with sorrow."[3]

Democratic newspapers voiced dismay and sorrow as fervently as their Republican counterparts, even though many of them had savagely attacked Lincoln during his life. From Illinois the *Ottawa Free Trader* regretted that some of its criticisms may have been "intemperate," for now it felt "horror and dismay" and declared, "There is no name for the crime." A Pennsylvania journal that had been extremely harsh throughout the war now called the murder "so astounding as to seem almost incredible." It was a "great national calamity" that brought "universal gloom and sorrow." Other Democratic editors deplored "the great National Tragedy" and judged it "the greatest calamity that could have befallen" the country. A previously hostile editor in Indiana denounced Booth's "Deed of Blood" and said that "the loyal people of the United States have been astounded, surprised, and saddened beyond measure." For the nation it was a "humiliating fact that the President . . . had been basely, cowardly, and brutally assassinated."[4]

Editors and individuals praised Lincoln's humane character and kind spirit. The Democratic *Daily Ohio Statesman* now recalled that "his purposes were good . . . he was naturally a pure-minded, moderate man." The Republican *New York Tribune* marveled that he "was never provoked to the exhibition of one trace of hate, or even wrath," toward the rebels who tried to destroy the country. The *Independent* from Oskaloosa, Kansas, re-flected that "his great care, caution and prudence have sometimes led the people to think he was too slow, but afterwards, the wisdom of his course has generally been seen." A Democratic editor in Illinois claimed never to have "doubted the goodness of heart, or honesty of intention of the President." The wife of Vermont's governor observed, "There is a sense of personal loss," and Philadelphia's Sidney Fisher, a wealthy lawyer, land-owner, and essayist, also "felt as tho I had lost a personal friend, for indeed I have & so has every honest man in the country." Another northern aristo-crat, Charles Francis Adams, who felt that the president was no "gentleman" and doubted Lincoln's "capacity for reconstruction," nevertheless believed that "the loss of Lincoln is hardly reparable."[5]

Northerners of either party had many reasons to feel lost and vulner-able. Suddenly they confronted multiple shocks: the violence of Lincoln's death, the sudden loss of the country's wartime leader, and the uncertainty of what lay ahead in Reconstruction. Naturally they reached out for some means of reassurance. One impulse was to draw together, to unite as Amer-icans, to find strength in a shared nationality and in trusted institutions. The *New York World*, a leading Democratic paper, counseled "just men of all parties and shades of opinion" to "bury all bitterness and extravagances born of political conflict" and "love our country as well as he [Lincoln]." The *Philadelphia Bulletin* judged that the assassination had ended "all parti-san feeling" and brought about "perfect unanimity." The *Cincinnati Gazette* assured its readers that the Constitution made provision "against any con-tingency by which a collapse of Government might occur."[6]

Another reaction was to look for comfort in the character of the new president. In 1861, when most southern leaders were renouncing their loyalty to the nation, Tennessee's Andrew Johnson had proved himself a staunch Unionist by refusing to secede. That record reassured many. Ver-mont's *Burlington Free Press* called him "an independent and fearless man, an earnest patriot and an unflinching friend of liberty." The editor was will-ing to overlook Johnson's drunkenness at his swearing-in as vice president and believed "he will not fail the country now." Other papers noted his humble origins, recalled his hostility to aristocrats, and took heart that he was "emphatically a self-made man—a man of the people." If a few Demo-cratic journals pointed out that he had been a Democrat through most of his life, other Republican papers took his Unionism as proof that he would "manfully grapple with the difficulties of his position, and, God helping and preserving him, master them all."[7]

The *Chicago Tribune*, a major Republican journal, looked for continuity from the new president. It agreed with Wisconsin's Senator James Doolittle that Johnson "will undoubtedly pursue the same policy as Mr. Lincoln," and in fact, after being sworn in, the new president told members of his cabinet that his policy would "be the same as that" of Lincoln. The full content of that policy could not be known in April, but Johnson seemed to strike the right tone and avoided missteps in his first days in office. He called for church services throughout the land on the day of Lincoln's funeral, and he spoke of his attitude toward the rebels.[8]

In the painful aftermath of the assassination, there was fierce anger over all the suffering brought on by secession, and Johnson reflected that feeling. He spoke of "condign punishment" for southern leaders, saying, "The American people must be taught . . . that treason is a crime and must be punished." Such comments encouraged a Radical like Michigan's Zachariah Chandler to think that Johnson would have stronger policies than Lincoln. But Johnson's early statements also balanced punishment and forgiveness in a way that seemed acceptable to many. Johnson met with several state delegations, and to a group from Massachusetts he reportedly said "*that traitors should be punished by death,* but that discrimination should be made between their ignorant tools and the intellectual leaders." He told Iowa's Governor William Stone that he would "deal kindly and leniently with the mass of the people of the South" while punishing only "the guilty authors of the rebellion." Leniency toward supposedly deluded masses seemed to incorporate much of Lincoln's hope of reconciliation. To some ardent but pious abolitionists, like Martha Coffin Wright, forgiveness seemed a "genuine Christian sentiment." On the other hand, many Democratic newspapers called shortly after the assassination for the execution of those who had plotted Lincoln's death.[9]

The idea of "condign punishment" for the rebellion's leaders was consistent with widespread rancor over the long, destructive war and might hold important implications for Black suffrage. Abolitionists and a minority of Republicans sought equal rights for Black men. But northern racism was a formidable barrier to Black suffrage; it was deeply rooted and had surfaced constantly and intensely in partisan contests and anti-Republican rhetoric. Many racists were likely never to change their views on African American character or status, but burning resentment of southern traitors could fuel support for Black people's interests over the interests of rebels. To empower or reward Black southerners was one way to penalize white southerners. James Freeman Clarke, the Massachusetts theologian and author, told his congregation that Black suffrage and disfranchisement of slaveholders was "the revenge we take for the murder of Lincoln." Such revenge had the potential to teach a painful lesson to prominent southern leaders who wanted to continue their control over the people they had enslaved. Hostility toward the South thus could translate into support for former slaves. However, a goal of conciliating rebels *and* protecting the freed people entailed contradictory mindsets that could be extremely difficult to reconcile.[10]

Beneath the North's feeling of unity that sprang from grief and the need for reassurance lay a history of sharply divided attitudes. Before long, as emotions became less acute, Republicans and Democrats began to diverge on the need for measures of punishment. Both sides began to speak out in turn. For many pro-administration or Republican editors, the assassination was proof that policies toward the South must be severe.

Under a headline "The Rebellion Responsible," the *New York Sun* called Lincoln's murder "the result of a deliberate and consummately planned conspiracy." The *Sun* suggested that high-ranking southern leaders might have been involved. If anyone doubted that "the conspicuous rebel chiefs were accessory to the assassination," wrote the popular and widely read *Harper's Weekly*, that person "should remember that the crime is no more atrocious than many of which they are notoriously guilty." The *Chicago Tribune* agreed and charged that "undoubtedly arson and murder were the 'new means of warfare' contemplated by Jeff. Davis and his confederate congressmen." Two months later the *Tribune* was still calling for Jefferson Davis's execution and labeling as "chicken-hearted" those who disagreed. The *New York Herald*, reliably conservative if not officially Democrat in its views, declared that the assassination "must and will stimulate us to go on against rebellion until it has exterminated the very spirit in which their damnable atrocities originated."[11]

A belief that strong measures must be imposed on the South tended to unite Republicans and lent support to Lincoln's hope for Black suffrage. Righteous anger over the assassination fed into a bitterness toward the South that had grown during four years of bloodshed and sacrifice. The *Chicago Tribune*, for example, favored Black suffrage and "*castigation*" of rebels until "the pride and arrogance of these assumed aristocrats" were broken and they respected "northern opinions and courage." These emotions convinced some Republicans that suffrage reforms and other major changes were necessary in Reconstruction. If the defeated South remained a hardened, inveterate enemy, any compassionate reconciliation would be a mistake. The deeper the hostility toward rebels and traitors, the more likely a conviction developed that Black suffrage was necessary.[12]

Congress had adjourned on March 4 but some Radical Republican leaders like Charles Sumner sounded out the new president before they left Washington. These Radical Republicans were pleased to hear Johnson speak about treason as the highest of crimes. A Republican newspaper in Indiana argued that "Rebel Barbarity" justified execution for Jefferson Davis and some others, and its editor added that lower-ranking officials should "be forever disfranchised, and have their property confiscated." In Pennsylvania a Republican journal warned that "conciliatory measures" could never make "good Union citizens" out of Confederate leaders. "Kindness is thrown away upon such men." They must be treated "as a conquered people" whose lives "depend upon the mercy of the Government." A conservative Unionist paper in Maryland judged that rebel leaders had lost "the ordinary instincts and feelings of humanity." That meant that although the rebellion was crushed, "*its venom is not.*" Even Horace Greeley's *New York Tribune*, which shared and promoted Lincoln's hope for *both* reconciliation and Black suffrage, described the assassination as part of "a comprehensive plot, whereto the rebel leaders were privy." Those men also were guilty of mistreatment of U.S. prisoners, refusal to exchange troops, and "frequent butcheries of our colored soldiers." Therefore, "Let Us Forgive Slowly," for the rebels were not "perfectly conquered or converted."[13]

Northern Democrats had a different perspective. They condemned the assassins in April but their approach to the seceded South was far closer to Lincoln's desire for a generous reconciliation between South and North. A large section of the Democratic Party had blamed abolitionists for secession, defended the South's right to hold slaves, and criticized Republicans for failure to accept the Crittenden Compromise and thus avoid an unnecessary war.[14] From the moment of Lincoln's death, some editors now worried that his "conciliatory policy so recently begun" might be abandoned. A Pennsylvania editor hoped that Johnson would "be governed by moderate councils" and guided by Lincoln's final address, which "promised so much hope for the early pacification of the country, and healing of the wounds of the rebellion." In Ohio another Democratic editor wrote that "in his last days, Mr. Lincoln showed signs of a wise moderation. If the same spirit can prevail, we shall have peace again. But some bad men are striving to prevent it."[15]

Lincoln's death was "the greatest calamity that could have befallen" the country, said the *Daily Ohio Statesman*, because "no man had, or will have, the power and influence that he possessed to bring Peace" through his "measures of wisdom and moderation." A Dayton editor agreed that Lincoln "had in contemplation" the measures that were needed and would have defied "the threats of radical men." The *New York World* lamented that "the day which preceded his death was passed in employments more full of promise than any other in the calendar of this momentous year." Its editor could only hope that Johnson "will pursue the healing policy on which his deceased predecessor had entered." From Indiana an editor voiced deep regret that death came "when the President himself had set his heart on mercy, and seemed intent on winning back to the Union the affections of the misguided South, instead of obdurately punishing them." Democratic papers like these had argued that every severe wartime measure only made reunion more difficult. There could be no reunion, they believed, without conciliation and respect for southern rights.[16]

Such contrary views—expressed in many quarters during the North's greatest period of grief and disorientation—indicated that ordinary citizens were not feeling the idealism and moral inspiration that drove Lincoln in his last weeks of life. Those who embraced one part of Lincoln's vision often rejected the other element. Reconciliation *and* racial justice comprised a highly ambitious agenda. How many northerners were ready to write a new page in the nation's history, to end division and bring the government closer to its founding ideals? The intensity of April's powerful emotions might fade as northerners emerged from crisis and the routines of peacetime returned. Could political opponents then put partisan divisions aside? Were the two parts of Lincoln's last hope compatible—could Americans embrace both Black suffrage and "charity" for rebels? The remaining months of 1865 would provide an answer.

That outcome was uncertain, its contents still to be determined, and for several weeks it was not the central part of northerners' thinking. More mundane events claimed people's attention as they began to put the war behind them, and questions of policy were not the first thing on citizens' minds. Lincoln's assassination continued to dominate the newspapers for the rest of April as his funeral cortege slowly wound its way toward Illinois. Thousands turned out along the route to say their goodbyes to the slain president. Then the first, practical steps toward reestablishment of peace began to receive attention. In late April and May many citizens focused not on the future but on immediate and welcome progress away from a war-time way of life. Ordinary citizens were tired of crisis and loss.

There was exciting, joyous news that many soldiers would be returning home, for the government made plans to demobilize its vast army quickly. The War Department halted purchases of arms and ammunition, horses, mules, wagons, and many other types of supplies and gave priority to the honorable discharge of "all soldiers in hospitals who require no further medical treatment." Soon headlines announced that "The Troops Start Homeward," and many fathers, mothers, wives, and children began to count the days in expectation of emotional reunions. Governors urged the War Department to speed discharges, and in just seven months the government released over 800,000 men. Prior to those homecomings, however, a celebration for the mass of the army would take place in the nation's capital. The War Department on May 17 announced that a Grand Review "of the gallant armies now assembling around Washington will take place" on May 23 and 24. Proudly the victorious troops would march in immense columns through streets thronged by cheering crowds, and all could celebrate the nation's victory and power.[17]

There also was excitement about the revival of normal channels of trade and commerce. On April 29 President Johnson lifted restrictions "upon internal, domestic and coastwise commercial intercourse" with almost all of the Confederacy. For businesses this meant that former commercial relationships could resume, and for many private citizens it signified the mail would flow freely once again. "The pacifying power and influences of commerce and prosperous trade cannot be over estimated," enthused one Pennsylvania newspaper. "This alone will invigorate the industry of the whole country and give the people everywhere opportunity to cultivate the arts of peace, so that they may forget the employments and passions of war." At the same time some editors pointed out challenges that must be met in the conversion to a peacetime economy. The New York Herald reported that young men, discharged from the army, now were anxious for jobs, either new positions or posts they hoped to reclaim. The New York World was more worried. It predicted that economic issues might be central to future months, as "hundreds of thousands" would be thrown out of employment by the end of the war. Its editor also feared high prices and a redundancy of labor as the soldiers returned.[18]

People also paid attention to the arrest of Jefferson Davis and leading Confederates and read about the final acts of surrender. On April 18 Confederate general Joseph Johnston signed surrender terms with U.S. general William Tecumseh Sherman near Durham Station, North Carolina. There was cause for rejoicing that the last major southern army thus had given up the fight. Soon, however, problems surfaced. Sherman had agreed to terms that would guarantee to "the people and inhabitants" of Confederate states, "so far as the Executive can, their political rights and franchises, as well as their rights of person and property." The agreement also spoke of recognition "of the several State governments" once their officers and legislatures took oaths "prescribed by the Constitution of the United States." It appeared that Sherman was recognizing rebellious governments, Confederate officials, and probably even the human property of enslavers.[19]

The negative reaction was swift. President Johnson and his Cabinet immediately recognized that such terms must be rejected, and General Ulysses S. Grant traveled south to inform Sherman in person that he must demand new terms limited to military matters only. A Vermont editor wrote that Sherman's terms "strike us, and must strike the Country, with the utmost astonishment . . . almost incredible." The *Chicago Tribune* criticized Sherman's "grave mistake" and called him "one of the worst negotiators of whom we have any knowledge." Even a fiercely Democratic paper from Illinois lamented that "Gen. Sherman has committed a *faux pas*—in plain English, made a blunder, which may cost him much of his military reputation."[20]

But once the agreement had been rejected and new terms accepted, Democratic editors began to rally to Sherman's defense. They knew that his political opinions favored many Democratic positions, and some thought of him as a possible future presidential candidate. By May 6 the critical Democratic editor from Illinois had changed his tune and maintained that Sherman's critics and the War Department "did the hero of the Carolinas a great injustice." A Pennsylvania Democratic paper argued that the surrender's initial text was not excessively lenient—it "was only that which Mr. Lincoln foreshadowed to General Sherman at the[ir] City Point meeting." Other editors defended Sherman, or, like the *New York World*, criticized Secretary of War Edwin Stanton's behavior toward the general. The feisty Sherman vigorously defended himself, and before long Democratic editors argued that he had "come out all right."[21]

Another issue that gained currency in the month after the assassination had been important to Democrats during the war years: the question of using military commissions, instead of civil courts, to try traitors or those suspected of disloyalty. At first there was a furious reaction against any who had been involved in Lincoln's assassination, and conservative or Democratic newspapers took a hard line. The *New York Herald* early in May claimed that Jefferson Davis's complicity in the assassination was clear, and an aggressively Democratic editor in Pennsylvania wanted Johnson to "punish with severity the instigators and leaders of the rebellion." But military commissions—like the one that would try and condemn the suspected assassins of Lincoln—were a violation of civil rights, Democrats believed. They demanded that such military trials quickly stop and gleefully publicized any Republican who agreed with them. Therefore, an Ohio newspaper spotlighted Edward Bates, who had been Lincoln's attorney general, for undertaking in Missouri a series of articles assailing martial law and arrests by provost marshals. A Conservative Unionist paper in Maryland praised Illinois's Senator Lyman Trumbull, who had declared that "a Union forced by arbitrary power . . . is not the Union I am struggling for."[22]

Within a month after the assassination Democratic newspapers were united in giving strong support to one part of Lincoln's vision—the desirability of a conciliatory and generous approach to white southerners. The *Daily Ohio Statesman* said that Johnson should "temper his administration with the same mercy and generosity that it was understood President Lincoln" had planned to use. Newspaper colleagues from that state agreed that "wisdom and moderation" were the "only elements by which that commonwealth [Virginia] could be restored to her allegiance," and they pointed out that even the "notorious rebel General Forrest" had urged his troops to "lay aside all feeling animosity and revenge." The *Philadelphia Ledger* advocated reuniting the nation by "mak[ing] the situation for our 'wayward' sisters as pleasant as possible," and the *Albany Evening Journal* hoped to see the South "regenerated and redeemed" and readmitted to the Union "without humiliation." Democratic support was strong for a conciliatory and merciful approach to rebellious southerners.[23]

What of Lincoln's desire for Black suffrage? Would it encounter a fair-minded reception or meet with partisan conflict? Was the renewed and redeemed Union that Lincoln hoped for—a nation closer to its founding ideals—possible?

2

Hopeful Signs

B lack suffrage had a substantial and surprising amount of support in the spring of 1865. Although racism continued to be widespread in the North, the enormous and unexpected changes brought by the war had made a difference. Previously Black men had been able to vote in only a few northern states—in parts of New England and, with a property qualification, in New York.[1] But the wartime emergency had begun to alter the legal and mental landscape. The conflict brought an end to slavery, defeated the politically powerful southern aristocracy, and put Black men from the North and South into U.S. Army uniforms. A freer, more powerful nation was taking the place of the old Union, and many northerners—carried along by the war's unprecedented events—were adjusting to new realities. In that context Black suffrage was newly conceivable, and the support that emerged was notable both for its extent and for some of its sources.

The *New York Herald*, for example, had hewed to a conservative point of view, even though it was not an avowed Democratic journal. Now, however, the *Herald* endorsed Black suffrage, reasoning that "the exclusion of free negroes from the right of suffrage is a necessity of negro slavery, but where slavery does not exist there is no such necessity. Give the emancipated negroes of the rebel States, then, in the reconstruction of those States, the right to vote along with the whites." The *Herald* went on to dismiss the potent and common objection that suffrage would lead to social equality with whites. "There need be no fear," said the paper, "that this concession will lead to negro social equality. Negroes vote in New York, and yet in

New York there is no approach to negro social equality. Society will take care of itself in the matter, as it does in everything else affecting its peace and harmony."[2]

Within a few weeks the *Herald* developed additional, specific rationales to justify giving the ballot to former slaves, despite objections in the North that they were uneducated and unqualified. The *Herald* favored suffrage for "four classes of Southern negroes." These included "every negro who has borne arms in the cause of the United States; . . . every negro who owns real estate; . . . every negro who can read and write; . . . [and] every negro who had belonged to any religious organization or church for five years before the war." Noting these arguments, the Republican *Cleveland Daily Herald* added another cogent point: "There is not an objection to negro ballots that does not apply to a large minority of our present voters. In intelligence, loyalty, and property interest in the government, the colored population are the equals with the great mass of legal voters." Moreover, through their service in the army they had gained a "moral right" to vote.[3]

Despite the fact that racism was nearly ubiquitous and often virulent in the North, the attitude of the *New York Herald* was neither entirely surprising nor out of season and discordant with the new postwar realities. Emancipation was about to extinguish, in practice and in the Thirteenth Amendment, the legal structures that countenanced holding human beings in bondage. Free men—in American practice and law, dating back to seventeenth-century Virginia—had typically been viewed as citizens, invested with rights. Free Black men in North Carolina had enjoyed the right to vote until 1835. If the people formerly held in bondage were slaves no longer, was it not inevitable that they become citizens? Black southerners, in addition, had fought in large numbers for the Union or had aided Union troops in various ways, all expressive of a loyalty deserving recognition. If the slave South was defeated unconditionally, wasn't a new status natural? Thus there was an evident logic in accepting a new status for African Americans, given the legal and structural changes brought on by the war. At the beginning of the postwar period, some white northerners—and even some Democrats—were able to contemplate what had previously been unthinkable.

The *New York World* was one of the nation's most prominent Democratic newspapers, yet it too adopted an unaccustomed perspective. The issue of suffrage, said the *World*, was a policy question "of the very first magnitude," and then it looked to the future and argued that Black suffrage would be necessary: "If, after order and stability are restored in the South, the Southern people shall see fit to admit the freedmen to a participation in the elective franchise, it may be wise and politic for them to do so. . . . We are of opinion that the *next generation of negroes will either have the suffrage or perturb the State.*" In the North the African American population was small, and "the question might be decided either way without peril to the public tranquility." In fact, northern states had a variety of rules about Black suffrage, and all had proved workable. But in southern states the Black population was very large, and "we do not believe that . . . the colored population, when possessing freedom and *the means of education can be permanently excluded from the elective franchise.*" The *World* thus accepted both emancipation and the necessity of Black suffrage, though it wanted southern states to make that decision. One of its rivals, the local *Daily News,* also "c[a]me out for Negro suffrage." Its stance was particularly surprising because some staunch Unionists regarded it as "the organ of Seceshdom in this city."[4]

A Republican editor in Pennsylvania commented that these views were "an instance of the astonishing progress made" by New York newspapers which had been "strenuous advocates of the 'divine institution.'" Previously, stoking "fears of amalgamation and miscegenation" had been a priority, especially for the *New York World.* Now the *World* itself commented with "wonder" on the change of feeling in the city. Black troops marching in Lincoln's funeral procession received "one continued ovation . . . for miles," yet only a short time before, in the riot of 1863, "for one entire week it was as much as a negro's life was worth to be seen in the streets." Horace Greeley's *New York Tribune* likewise saw remarkable progress in the fact that Blacks had gained the right "to be carried in all public conveyances" in the city. Greeley felt that there was no "community where a greater proportion of citizens hate their Black fellow-citizens than New-York, but even in New-York this blind prejudice could make no resistance to the conviction of the majority that negroes had the same right as whites" to public transportation. Greeley himself shared Lincoln's desire for reconciliation and Black rights. He long had contended for "conciliation and kindness toward the defeated Rebels" along with the core "principle of Democracy, of equal rights before the law." The "reciprocation of kindly feelings between the Abolitionists and their lifelong, deadly Southern antagonist" would "do much" to open "the path of the nation toward genuine peace and durable prosperity."[5]

The *Chicago Tribune,* one of the North's most important Republican papers, wanted the votes of "the intelligent freedmen, now citizens" to help reconstruct the South. It recognized that racial prejudice was still widespread but saw great progress toward Black suffrage. "The sentiment of the country," declared the *Tribune,* "has already set in so strongly in favor of negro suffrage in some form as one of the elements of reconstruction in the South, that the only practical question seems to be to what extent and with what conditions, if any, shall it be granted." A Republican journal in Kansas also perceived major changes in racial attitudes: "There was a time when any proposition in favor of negro suffrage could be silenced simply by cursing the negro, and wishing him in some hot climate. That time is past. . . . A mighty change has been going on in the public mind . . . and men who were bitterly opposed to the Emancipation Proclamation, now are warmly in favor of negro suffrage."[6]

Serious magazines joined in calls for Black suffrage. Their readership consisted of educated, civically engaged people whose views could influence public discussion. The *North American Review* backed Black suffrage in a way very similar to the spirit that had motivated Lincoln. "Our duty," it declared, "is not to punish, but to repair. . . . Once rid of slavery, which was the real criminal, let us have no more reproaches." It was important both to bind the wounds "of our Black brother . . . [and] not [to] harden our hearts against our white brethren." The *North American Review* disapproved of "any general confiscation of Rebel property" but wanted the "great slaveholders" rendered "powerless for mischief." Then it made three strong arguments for Black suffrage. Armed with the ballot, former slaves would gain the "power of self-protection," something essential "which no government can so safely, cheaply, and surely exercise in their behalf." Moreover, "Unless we make the Black a citizen, we take away from the white the strongest inducement to educate and enlighten him." As for the specter of social equality, this article agreed that equal social status depended on an individual's character. "If he is capable of it, his title is from God, not from us." African Americans deserved "a fair chance."[7]

The *Atlantic Monthly* spoke out for suffrage as "Fair Play." An article noted that the war had brought a change in terminology from "slaves" to "contrabands" to "freedmen," and the next step would be to "drop the *d*" and call the former slaves freemen. White freemen had rights, and despite fears that slavery had demoralized and degraded its victims, "it is almost universally admitted that the 'freedmen' are industrious, intelligent, self-supporting, soldierly, eager for knowledge," and more manageable than white refugees. Asking "whether we of the North are ready to do our" part, the *Atlantic* concluded that "the essential thing . . . to give them is justice." A period of "preparation" was inferior to "fair play. Preparation is apprenticeship, prescription. . . . Fair play is . . . to recognize the freedman's right to all social and political guaranties, and then to let him alone."[8]

Harper's Weekly had a wide circulation and influence, and it argued that justice and liberty were as important as peace: "If we ought not to punish deluded rebels, neither ought we to betray true men." Emancipation was profoundly important, but it only partially took care of "political regeneration. . . . The only remedy is to not simply free but also to enfranchise the negroes. Give the negroes a vote and they will most certainly be courted by both parties at the South." Support from *Harper's Weekly* for Black suffrage ran strong through April and May into June. Declaring that "The Right Way [Is] the Best Way," this journal opposed any racial qualification as "in direct conflict with the fundamental principle of the Government." Educational requirements would be "unfortunate," since they would "exclude the most trusty citizens of the State. . . . Let all loyal freemen vote in reorganizing the States."[9]

Another magazine, the *New Englander*, had advocated for "Universal Suffrage" from the beginning of 1865. Its views provided an early glimpse into the possibility that hostility to rebels could justify Black suffrage. The *New Englander* argued that the Union could exert "the governing power . . . of the conqueror," because no less an authority than the Supreme Court had ruled that the Civil War was "to be prosecuted according to the laws of war." Southern rebels therefore had become "public enemies," and this piece warned that southern whites would reestablish a harsh control over African Americans if they could: "Slavery is abolished, but peonage, or some other plan of forced labor" would be "hardly less unjust or dangerous to the nation." The North had a duty to "discriminate between leaders and followers and the loyal," and for "Blacks, who are loyal . . . impartial suffrage is right."[10]

Littell's Living Age publicized a meeting organized by prominent Bostonians at Faneuil Hall in June. One speaker after another advocated strongly for Black suffrage and developed reasons bearing on abstract rights as well as national self-interest. No one should "be expelled from voting because of their race or color," declared a resolution approved by the meeting. Concern for the freed people led one speaker to argue, "If we withhold from them all political right, we withhold from them all power of self-protection and self-defence." White southerners then could "keep them down on that dead level of ignorance and debasement to which slavery sank them." Another speaker argued that "our security" depended on "freedman suffrage." Because slavery was ending and the three-fifths formula for counting slaves no longer applied, the South was going to enjoy increased representation in Congress. That raised the danger that former rebels would repudiate the national debt and take "control of our national legislation and all our foreign and domestic policy." The stability of the government, as well as racial justice, depended on Black suffrage.[11]

Several well-known voices connected with New England, abolitionism, or Republican reform also attracted attention as they promoted the values in Lincoln's last address. The well-known poet John Greenleaf Whittier turned to prose to advocate for Black suffrage in a Massachusetts newspaper. Against popular sentiment for "hanging leading traitors," Whittier advised, "Let them live," if mainly in exile. As for "the misguided masses of the South," Whittier maintained that they deserved forgiveness, aid, and patience. "Our sole enemy was Slavery, and Slavery is dead." Therefore, he urged northerners to be "magnanimous" and to do "good to those who have hated us." But equally important was the need to root out prejudice, for John Wilkes Booth had been prejudice's instrument. "Wherever God's children are despised, insulted and abused on account of their color," wrote Whittier, "there is the real assassin of the President still at large." The former slaves represented "4,000,000 . . . unmistakably loyal people of the South, the patient, long-suffering, kind-hearted victims of oppression." They must stand "equal before the law" and have "the same rights of citizenship, which are to be accorded to the rank and file of disbanded Rebels."[12]

Henry Ward Beecher, the North's most famous minister, attracted considerable newspaper coverage in the spring. Speaking in Charleston, South Carolina, on April 14 at the raising of the stars and stripes over Fort Sumter, Beecher urged his audience to "pray for the quick coming of reconciliation and happiness under his common flag." "Black clouds full of voices of vengeance," he knew, threatened punishment of the leaders of the rebellion, "but for the people misled, for the multitude drafted and driven into this civil war, let not a trace of animosity remain." Beecher added that the war had revealed "the capacity, moral and military, of the Black race," a people who "have been patient, and gentle, and docile, and full of faith and hope and piety." He challenged southern whites to "educate the Black man, and by education make him a citizen."[13]

On Black suffrage, Beecher had already made his position clear. In February in his church in Brooklyn, the minister had advocated plainly for "the giving to all men, black and white, the right of suffrage." He demanded "faith in our own national principles" and the full recognition of "the natural rights of men . . . without regard to race, or color, or condition." Black men had earned the ballot through their loyalty and military service and had "given evidence that they will make good use" of that right. Without universal suffrage, Beecher warned, "we cannot have peace . . . because no question is ever settled that is not settled right."[14]

Beecher was not the only prominent northerner to advocate reconciliation. In Ohio the conciliatory views of Henry Stanbery attracted notice, particularly from Democratic editors friendly to the South. Stanbery had been Ohio's first attorney general, and his prominence in the legal community of Cincinnati gave him a national stature that would lead to his confirmation as U.S. attorney general in 1866. With the end of the war, Stanbery delivered a speech declaring, "In this great day of jubilee, *nothing short of a general amnesty will*, in my poor judgment, *meet the occasion*." Southerners had suffered "far more" than northerners, he maintained. "Send them help. Give them bread instead of a stone." In victory the goal should be "reconciliation," and to any who felt that retribution was needed, Stanbery answered, "There is my oldest son, maimed for life by a rebel bullet. No, fellow citizens, the struggle is over. . . . Let the reign of good will return also." The *Daily Ohio Statesman* happily pointed out that Stanbery's counsels of conciliation were matched by men like Horace Greeley and New York's Gerrit Smith.[15]

Among abolitionists and reform philanthropists, few were better known than Gerrit Smith. To the surprise of Democrats, Smith wrote to President Johnson and advocated "universal pardon and forgiveness." Smith and many other abolitionists had long opposed capital punishment, and now he recalled Jesus's spirit on the cross and wrote, "If possessed of this spirit, we shall forgive and forget the wrongs done the North, and shall feel that the South has suffered enough, and that she deserved to be soothed, and comforted, and no more afflicted by us." A few weeks later he delivered a speech in New York City in which he opposed the execution of any rebels for treason. But he also called for Black suffrage, arguing that the ballot box should belong to the loyal, and that political and civil rights should not depend on race or origin. Smith added other proposals, such as repudiating the southern debt and giving to the poor lands that formerly had been part of great estates, but much of his speech echoed Lincoln's last address.[16]

Other abolitionists put their emphasis on the necessity of Black suffrage and insisted on the full range of equal rights for African Americans. When the Massachusetts Anti-Slavery Society met in April, Wendell Phillips condemned the policies in Louisiana of General Nathaniel Banks, who restricted the mobility of former slaves and tied their labor to the plantations. To Frederick Douglass, Banks's policy "practically enslaves the Negro, and make the [Emancipation] Proclamation of 1863 a mockery and delusion." Douglass went on to demand the "'immediate, unconditional, and universal' enfranchisement of the black man, in every State in the Union. [Loud applause.]" Denying that such progress was "premature," he insisted that "now is the time" to act, when "the American people are in tears" and feel the need "to learn righteousness."[17]

One month later a schism among abolitionists impaired their cooperation but focused attention on the issue of Black suffrage. William Lloyd Garrison scheduled the annual meeting of the American Anti-Slavery Society for May 9 and announced his proposal to dissolve the organization. To continue to operate, he claimed, would be to "stultify" the society "by superfluous action." Since slavery had "received its death-wound," the purpose of the organization was fulfilled, and there was no "occasion to continue . . . a moment longer." Evidently believing that racial attitudes had changed greatly, he claimed that the organization had no "special importance," now that it was "swallowed up in the great ocean of popular feeling against slavery." Garrison denied that he intended "to retire from the field of labor" of "putting down prejudice," but, he said, now "we have the million with us" and should "mingle . . . with the great mass of our fellow citizens. I have only to go before any loyal audience . . . and assert the right of the colored man to vote," he asserted, and the verdict would be strongly in favor.[18]

Many of his colleagues did not agree. Charles Lenox Remond undoubtedly spoke for the North's African Americans when he objected. If Garrison were to "go out upon the highways and byways," Remond countered, and say that it was time for "anti-slavery work" to cease, he would be "utterly overwhelmed with opposition" from Blacks. By a margin of ten to one the American people would oppose the "full recognition of the colored man's equality in this country." Despite the immense gratitude that Remond expressed to numerous white colleagues in the Anti-Slavery Society, he asserted that "it is utterly impossible for any of our white friends, however much they may have tried, fully to understand the Black man's case in this nation." "Hatred of the colored man in the North" was rampant, and Remond had encountered it personally on his way to the meeting.[19]

George T. Downing, a Black businessman and leader from Rhode Island, argued that the work must continue "to secure to the colored population of the United States all the rights and privileges which belong to them as men and as Americans." Frederick Douglass pointed out that the society had previously done "good *anti-slavery* work" fighting against suffrage restrictions in the North. Douglass knew that winning the ballot remained a challenge in both sections. "Slavery," he insisted, "is not abolished until the Black man has the ballot." He also quoted the well-known abolitionist

Charles Lenox Remond, a free Black man from Massachusetts, was an eloquent abolitionist lecturer, recruiter of Black troops, and advocate of equality. (Photographed by Samuel Broadbent, ca. 1851–56; Boston Public Library)

editor Edmund Quincy, who had said, "While a Black man can be turned out of a car in Massachusetts, Massachusetts is a slave state."[20]

Many white abolitionists agreed that the ballot was essential. Wendell Phillips proposed that since the Thirteenth Amendment was not yet ratified, "fresh and untiring diligence" was required to finish the society's work and put "the liberty of the negro beyond peril." Securing rights for African Americans was not "incidental," as Garrison phrased it, to the society's original work. Phillips endorsed the view that "there should be no peace and no reconstruction that does not put land under the foot of the negro, and a ballot in his hand." To reach those goals he believed that the society, with its accumulated prestige, should work to influence public opinion. Parker Pillsbury blamed slavery for Lincoln's assassination and declared, "Our work is not done . . . nor will my work be done until the blackest man has at least all the rights which I myself enjoy." After much discussion, Pillsbury successfully offered resolutions committing the organization to convince the nation that "color or race is no test of fitness for citizenship," and that African Americans should enjoy *"the same privileges"* and *"exercise the same prerogatives"* as whites. In the end, Wendell Phillips won election as president of the society, and Garrison retired. The American Anti-Slavery Society would fight on for Black suffrage.[21]

Political leaders who welcomed abolitionist support found themselves in an anomalous position that made it harder for them to influence opinion that spring. Congress had adjourned until December, so no legislation could be advanced and no debates reported from the House or Senate. Consideration of Black suffrage would have to move forward in the public sphere alone, through newspaper opinions, reports on events, publications, or speeches delivered on public occasions. Promptly some Republicans seized on opportunities to speak about Black suffrage and the treatment of southern rebels.

As politicians addressed these subjects, a change in the character of arguments began to be more visible. Accustomed to dealing with troublesome realities, Republican officeholders were aware of both anti-Black prejudice in the North and bitterness toward southerners for causing the war. These two widespread attitudes pointed in opposite directions. Racism tended to promote understanding and generosity toward white southerners. Black suffrage, on the other hand, could be a deserved castigation for rebels as well as a means to safeguard emancipation and ensure loyalty.

Where racial idealism often was weak, bitterness and rancor toward Confederates frequently were strong, and advocates of Black suffrage realized that abandoning conciliation could open the path to Black suffrage. As discussion and debate unfolded in the months ahead, such motives would play a larger role.

One of the first Republican officeholders to speak out was Congressman William Kelley, Republican of Pennsylvania, who joined others in addressing freedmen in Charleston as the war ended. Prominent abolitionists and Radical Republicans like Garrison and Senator Henry Wilson limited themselves to praising the end of slavery and urging the former slaves to practice virtue and work conscientiously. But Kelley went farther. He declared that "every man upon our soil shall enjoy all the rights of men," and that northerners must learn that "these are to be our fellow-citizens." Unlike Gerrit Smith or Henry Stanbery, Kelley had no faith in southern whites and asserted, "We have not altered the spirit of the rebels." Unless Black men gained the right to vote "in the revolted States," Kelley predicted that the South would send to Congress "believers in the doctrine of secession" and demand payment of the Confederate debt. At the end of May Kelley told Boston's Emancipation League that "prejudice" was now the "subtle and powerful enemy, which lurks in our own households, the prejudice against the negro in which we have been trained from infancy." Only by doing "full justice" to African Americans, he declared, "can we obtain salvation to ourselves."[22]

Benjamin Butler also was prompt that spring to advocate Black suffrage and a stern approach to defeated rebels. Distrust of southern whites furnished many reasons to demand Black suffrage, and this Massachusetts politician and political general was quick to denounce "the malice and hate of the rebels." To those ready to treat Confederates "as brothers," Butler declared in mid-April that Lincoln's assassination *"prevents us from making a too precipitate peace,* and from forgetting our vow that these national paracides should be punished." They were "not yet fitted" for readmission because "the soul of the rebellion" was not extinguished. "Perfidy, murder and treason," said Butler, "were not the insignia of 'erring brothers' or 'wayward sisters.'" Offended by some people's praise of Robert E. Lee, Butler asserted that West Point graduates who "betrayed the country, forfeited honor, [and] struck down the flag" deserved the penalty given to deserters. "Military traitors" deserved "condign punishment," and Confederate law-givers merited disfranchisement, but Butler urged "fellowship for the misguided and deceived victims of the rebellion, and equal rights for the Black man." This was "The Right Kind of Talk," judged a Republican newspaper.[23]

The chief justice of the United States, Salmon Chase, vigorously committed his prestige to the cause of Black suffrage. Putting his judicial robes aside, the naturally political Chase made a tour through the South, speaking to various audiences in southern cities. His trip prompted him to warn President Johnson of "how little" southerners understood the war's change in "political relations." Chase's most widely reported address came in Charleston, South Carolina, to a predominantly Black audience. After commenting that throughout his career he had wanted to see "every man, of whatever complexion, protected in all his natural rights," he praised the wartime contributions of African Americans. Then he challenged them to prove themselves worthy of freedom and restated his long-held support for Black suffrage. Chase acknowledged that not everyone agreed with his view, but he told the freed people, "If you are patient, and constantly show . . . that you can be safely trusted with the right of suffrage, . . . you will get it." Reportedly he predicted that freedmen could gain the ballot "in a very short period." In New Orleans he declined to make a public address but publicized his views in a letter to a committee of Black leaders. Former slaves were citizens, Chase affirmed, "and consequently entitled to the rights of citizens." They should claim their rights persistently and prove their worth "by economy, by industry, by sobriety." "Universal suffrage" would be the "best reconciler" of public security and the revival of prosperity. A few weeks later Chase delivered the commencement address at his alma mater, Dartmouth College. There his language was unqualified: "No reorganization of the country will be complete and permanent until every man in it, of whatever color, is allowed to vote. The right of suffrage is a right of freedom and citizenship, and it must be granted to all."[24]

The substantial advocacy for Black suffrage by well-known individuals encouraged Republican newspapers to address the subject. Horace Greeley's popular *New York Tribune* consistently took its stand with Lincoln's last address—in favor of both Black suffrage and a generous, forgiving policy toward southern whites. It saw an advantage in the fact that Lincoln's successor was a southerner. When rebels gain amnesty from the new president, "there will be a very general disposition to acquiesce" in his policy, since Andrew Johnson "knows what is necessary in the premises." At the same time the *Tribune* called for "Equal Rights" and was adamant in supporting "the principle of Democracy, of equal rights before the law." After "fighting for four years to maintain that principle all over the continent, what a ludicrous inconsistency it is to deny it at our own doors." Black citizens had "the same right as the whites" to vote and to enjoy other rights such as access to streetcars and "all public conveyances."[25]

The *Civilian and Telegraph* of Cumberland, Maryland, faced the question frequently asked during the war: "What shall we do with the negroes?" Its editor called on his readers to discard their "preconceived ideas and prejudices. . . . He is a man, though degraded and demoralized by years of slavery and ignorance, held and forced into circumstances which made many a white man a beast." The fact that slavery had not destroyed African Americans was "the best evidence of their manhood and their susceptibility of improvement and elevation." The editor urged "improv[ing] them" through education and compensated labor, "and they will become as useful as the white man. Place before them the reward of the elective franchise and they will become as faithful in the field of politics as they have in the field of battle." Despite these progressive opinions, the traditional views of a former slaveholding state emerged when this paper affirmed that the "Almighty Creator" had forbidden "miscegeneation or social equality."[26]

The *Pittsburgh Gazette* believed that establishing loyal governments in the Confederate South would require admitting "all the colored men to the ballot-box, but it would exclude many white." Loyalty should be the chief criterion, even "in all the border States," and to exclude Black men as a class would be "nothing but . . . a blind and slavish prejudice." This journal backed Black suffrage in the state of Pennsylvania as well. It was, the editor wrote, "the spirit of slavery" that had restricted suffrage to whites in past decades, and that law now needed to be changed. "A large portion" of Pennsylvania's African Americans were "worthy, intelligent, honest men," yet such character was not always expected of naturalized foreigners. Anti-Black prejudices should be "among the cast-off barbarism and follies of a by-gone era."[27]

Ohio's *Ashtabula Weekly Telegraph* was "aware that there are many prejudices among good and loyal people against investing negroes with political rights." Its editor even shared the view that "the great mass of the colored people are unfitted to exercise intelligently the right of suffrage" as were "many of the poor whites." But "it would be unjust to give the right to vote to those who have been endeavoring to overthrow the government for four

years past, and deprive those of the privilege who, tho' in a humble capacity, have done all they could to sustain it. Fighting for freedom covers
the right to vote for it when secured," and as "the negro has established
his *military* status, he is now entitled to his *political.*" The editor rejected
fears of social equality with the same argument that Black leaders and many
Republican officials used. Social status, he declared, "can never be established by law" because it "is a matter of choice, taste and preference." On an
optimistic note, this newspaper observed that the prejudice against Black
military service had largely "been overcome," and in like manner hostility
to Black suffrage will be "speedily overcome."[28]

The *Chicago Tribune,* one of the nation's most important Republican journals, began its advocacy of Black suffrage by asserting that white southerners remained bitter and would revolt tomorrow "if they believed it possible
to make headway against our armies." As long as they remained uncoop-
erative, it would be necessary to make progress "in spite of them." That
meant turning to the 4 million "colored American citizens, of undoubted
loyalty, in the Southern States." A few weeks later the *Tribune* argued that
South Carolina could not have a republican government if it excluded the
Black majority. Noting the supportive views of Black suffrage taken by
the *New York Herald* and the *New York World,* the paper claimed that public
sentiment was already "strongly in favor of negro suffrage in some form" for
the South.[29]

The *Chicago Tribune's* editor was aware, however, of the power of racism and white supremacy. He warned against "intemperate" demands for
"an indiscriminate suffrage without regard to intelligence or other qualification," which he believed would be "defeated . . . without doubt, and for the
present at least, without remedy." Black suffrage should not be "*the main
basis* of reconstruction" in states where uneducated freedmen would "rule"
the white minority. The *Tribune* felt that hostility toward voting by uneducated Blacks was greater in the North than the South. Therefore, the paper
favored a literacy qualification and felt that "every prudent and intelligent
Black man" in either section could meet that requirement "within one year
at the farthest."[30]

The *Boston Commonwealth* expressed the attitudes of many Republicans
who were more concerned about practical results in Reconstruction than
about abstract principles or moral right. If southern whites could not be
trusted, then the freedom of Black southerners would be in danger and the
security of the Union would be uncertain. The possibility that northern

Copperheads were eager to assist and support recalcitrant rebels increased these dangers. Political control and northern interests could be imperiled. A headline in the *Boston Commonwealth* therefore read, "Negro Suffrage the Only Security for Permanent Peace." Unless freedmen won the ballot, southern whites would cause them "only to be 'hewers of wood and drawers of water.'" Such intransigent southern whites would unite with northern Democratic allies to "control the legislation of the country" once more.[31]

For that reason a Republican newspaper in Vermont advocated strong measures against southern whites supplemented by Black suffrage. "Punish the leaders," demanded a contributor to St. Johnsbury's *Caledonian:* "Disfranchise forever every man of a certain rank. Disfranchise for a term of years, every man who has borne arms under, or sworn allegiance to, the rebel power. Let every loyal man at the South vote, regardless of color." That was the only way to "obtain security for the future." It was a mistake to show cordiality to "southern rebels and murderers" before "they repent." The right of suffrage was "an act . . . of justice" to loyal Blacks and whites, but more important was the motive of "no compromise" with "traitors" and "murderers."[32]

From Wisconsin came arguments for Black suffrage in newspapers from two of the larger cities. The *Madison Capitol* reasoned logically that the destruction of slavery had to lead to citizenship and equal rights. Its editor declared, "We are pretty clear in our own minds that suffrage will be extended to negroes sooner or later. . . . Let us look at the question in the light of common sense, and let the negro get along as fast as he can, while we labor to . . . restore the rule of law and order, and to inaugurate peace throughout the land." The *Milwaukee Daily Sentinel* agreed and felt that it was useless for politicians to stand in the way and "again jeopardy all the interests of the white race, in order to keep the black race under."[33]

The citizens of Boston who met at Faneuil Hall in June had a comprehensive view of the challenges of Reconstruction. They took a stand for the rights of African Americans but also anticipated from southern whites a stubborn resistance that would require strong measures. Eschewing any partisan motives, these Bostonians soberly judged the whole direction of southern society to have been aristocratic, antidemocratic, and anti-Black. "Slavery and oligarchy" would not disappear easily, nor would the South's desire to control the national government. Force defeated the rebellion, and force would be needed to secure the victory. Before readmitting states that would revert to their past practices, it was necessary to "secure . . . complete and veritable freedom" to the slaves, irreversibly prohibit slavery, and make southern states "republican." To achieve those goals, "military occupation" should continue, with no hasty readmission, until change had taken place. No rebel state should be readmitted until its constitution gave "to the freedmen the right of suffrage" in a manner that was "impartial" and "reasonably attainable by intelligence and character." The freedmen must have "the right to be educated, to acquire homesteads and to testify in courts" as a matter of "political justice and safety, and not of social equality."[34]

In these issues and in the future of the freedmen, the nation had a deep interest. An experiment of speedy restoration might command "earnest wishes for its success" but also careful scrutiny. The process of reconstruction should produce an "educated, industrious, landholding, . . . voting, self-protecting" and productive ex-slave population in a secure republic. One of the speakers at the Faneuil Hall meeting, Richard Henry Dana, acknowledged that the regeneration of the South would not be easy. He argued that it was necessary to hold each defeated southern state "in the grasp of war until the State does what we have a right to require of her." Conferring the ballot on former slaves "is a revolution," he said. But "if we do not secure that now, in the time of revolution, it can never be secured, except by a new revolution."[35]

Thus considerable support for Black suffrage emerged, even from some conservative or Democratic newspapers. The *New York Evening Post* commented in surprise on the strength of the position taken in July by that city's *News*, which had been considered "the southern organ in this city." The *News* wrote, "The right to vote belongs to each male citizen of twenty-one years of age. It is his by birth. . . . Nothing stood between the slave and full citizenship but . . . involuntary service—that impediment is gone thro' the actual operation of the war. . . . If the abstract right inheres in every citizen, why not in the native black man?"[36]

Progressives like Richard Henry Dana grasped the importance of keeping the "revolution" going. Republican support seemed widespread, an indication of notable progress not only during the war but also once victory became assured. Some Republicans desired both Black suffrage and a generous reconciliation, while others viewed Black suffrage as a necessary defense against a hostile, unrepentant white South. The latter motive would be at least as important as abstract principle. Would northern Democrats in this spring of 1865 be tolerant of Black suffrage now that slavery was ending, or would they oppose the "revolution" described by Dana?

❖ 3 ❖

Democratic Opposition

In the weeks after Lincoln's assassination, many ordinary citizens did not focus their attention on the war's revolutionary changes. For some, personal priorities and practical challenges were understandably more important than future political issues. Much of the daily news dealt with the end of the long conflict, for newspapers were full of stories about the surrender of Confederate armies, the arrest of Jefferson Davis and other Confederate leaders, and investigation of the assassination conspiracy. Stories about John Wilkes Booth and his death gave way to detailed, daily dispatches about the trials of his associates. These events accompanied the end of the war and suggested the end of the revolution as much as its advance. In addition, there was a natural and undeniable desire to move away from the stressful times of war and return to normal life.

Political partisanship—often intense partisanship—had been a staple of daily experience during the conflict. Even while the war was underway, controversy over Reconstruction had grown. Partisan conflict would inevitably be part of the return to normal, but the process was gradual at first. In the first days after the assassination many Democratic leaders and editors had spoken of unity and offered comforting words about the future. The shock of Lincoln's death had been so great that people felt a need for mutual support and reassurance. Still, a lasting unity based on the "malice toward none" and "charity for all" that Lincoln had hoped for was not to develop, at least not without his aid. Before long, indications began to appear that the deep divisions of wartime politics were not over and thus that the content and goals of Reconstruction would be hotly contested.

The Democratic Party of the North had faced a serious dilemma with the outbreak of war. Pressures to support the nation and rally to the stars and stripes were intense, but a sizeable portion—if not a majority—of the Democratic Party fundamentally disagreed that war was necessary or justified. These Democrats had supported the Crittenden Compromise as a solution, favored a comprehensive recognition of slaveholders' rights, and criticized abolitionists for persecuting the South. The dismay of these unhappy partisans grew as the government adopted unprecedented measures to carry on the conflict. So-called War Democrats broke with their party to support the nation in its time of crisis, and their efforts proved helpful to the Republican Party, which renamed itself the Union Party. But prominent War Democrats often announced that they were only suspending their political principles during wartime and promised to return to orthodoxy in peace.[1]

The core beliefs of Democrats dated to the administrations of Thomas Jefferson and Andrew Jackson. Devoted to states' rights and always wary of the central government and any tendencies toward centralization, most Democrats believed that the South had a constitutional right to hold slaves and defend its oppressive institution. Virulent anti-Black racism promoted sympathy for southern whites, even if northern states did not allow slavery. The sectional conflict, most Democrats decided, had been caused by despicable abolitionists, who had in their fanaticism hounded and persecuted the South. The war itself could have and should have been avoided through adoption of the Crittenden Compromise. Former president Franklin Pierce of New Hampshire exemplified these ideas when he denounced "THE MADNESS OF NORTHERN ABOLITIONISM." He stood with northern Democrats "*who respect their political obligations,*" and he felt "intense exasperation" at Republicans who allowed "FANATICAL PASSION" to carry them away. Pierce even predicted in 1860 that if war came, there would be fighting "WITHIN OUR OWN BORDERS, IN OUR OWN STREETS," between loyal Democrats and "THOSE WHO DEFY AND SCOUT CONSTITUTIONAL OBLIGATIONS." After the fighting began, Pierce wrote that he could "never justify, sustain, or in any way or to any extent uphold this cruel, heartless, aimless unnecessary war."[2]

In the fall of 1864, when Union victory was becoming more certain, Democrats had difficulty accommodating themselves to the passage of the Thirteenth Amendment. In Congress they "worked assiduously to keep visions of 'negro equality' and 'amalgamation' hanging over the congressional proceedings" and "labelled all Republicans miscegenationists." All but four

Democrats opposed the amendment when it first came up for a vote in the House. Yet it was undeniable that slavery was going to end, and realistic Democratic legislators accepted that fact. To compensate, their party "made white supremacy the only issue, substituting it for any further defense of slavery." Defending "white purity" became a better strategy than defending slaveholding rights.[3]

The first sign of enduring Democratic viewpoints in the postwar period was an overriding emphasis on the desirability and importance of conciliation with southern whites, with no hint of concern for former slaves. Since the South had been wronged, Democrats believed that southerners must be welcomed back into the Union rather than punished. The *Daily Ohio Statesman*, for example, on April 17 mourned the loss of Lincoln's "wisdom and moderation" and two days later headlined, "President Johnson to Be Merciful to the People of the Rebel States," even though he might punish some leaders. The new chief executive needed to "temper his administration with the same mercy and generosity that it was understood President Lincoln would temper his." As for making treason odious, this newspaper believed that defeat had accomplished that and nothing would be gained by "vindictive or barbarous measures." An Indiana newspaper quoted parts of a sermon by a New York minister who urged "conciliation" to solve the "Great Problem" of "restoring fraternal feeling throughout the land." The *Louisville Journal* declared that "The Cultivation of Kindly Feelings" was now "a matter of the greatest importance. . . . Haven't we had war enough?"[4]

A Democratic editor in Illinois was glad to see that Gerrit Smith and some abolitionists, all of whom had tried "to degrade the southern white man," now favored "a magnanimous policy in the treatment of the South." Another Illinois journal approved of "mak[ing] the situation for our 'wayward sisters' as pleasant as possible." It was deplorable that papers in New England—viewed as the center of moralistic fanaticism—were "famished for blood." "Wisdom and moderation," said Ohio's *Columbus Crisis*, were the only way to restore the commonwealth. Another Ohio editor criticized "New England fanatics" and argued, "Force is ended. It has played its part." The way to reconciliation was through "brotherly kindness and mutual interests." An Indiana Democratic paper warned against policies of "vengeance" and noted hopefully that during the secession crisis Andrew Johnson had called on the North to "approach what the south demands."[5]

The emphasis on conciliation supported Democrats' critical perspective on the trials of those who had conspired to kill Lincoln and on other military trials. Use of a military commission to try the assassins was ir-regular, unconstitutional, and part of "The Machinery of Despotism," said the *Plymouth Weekly Democrat*. Its editor quoted relevant sections of the Constitution as well as two New York newspapers to prove that such a trial violated "the spirit of our institutions." It constituted an "open and insolent defiance of the Constitution." Another editor objected to "the profound se-crecy" that cloaked the trials of Booth's conspirators. An Ohio Democratic newspaper took this opportunity to denounce the 1864 military trial of Lambdin Milligan and three other wartime dissenters, a proceeding that ended in scheduled execution for three of the men. Although their sen-tences were commuted to life imprisonment, the key point again was that such trials were unconstitutional because the civil courts were open and functioning. (The Supreme Court later agreed.)[6]

A great deal of Democratic thinking remained unchanged from the war years. An Indiana editor was proud that Democrats remained loyal to the "sacred truth that local self-government, or the rights of the separate States," was the best means to secure a citizen's rights. The *Ashland Union* in Ohio joined another Ohio paper in ridiculing reformist Republicans like Horace Greeley. With slavery ending, "Greeley will have to fall back upon Fouri-erism, bran bread, or some other of his favorite topics" because "the Ab-olition party falls to pieces." Most importantly, the Democratic Party had been right about all its wartime stands. Victory merely brought about "what could have been done four years ago without the loss of life or the expen-diture of a single dollar, had the counsels of the Democracy been heeded" and the Crittenden Compromise adopted. State rights and the principles of Jefferson and Madison remained "the true doctrines of our system of gov-ernment." When a Republican editor demanded to know if Democrats now would consider the war a "failure," as their 1864 platform had declared, the *Urbana Union* replied, "Not entirely." With heavy sarcasm its editor listed Republican accomplishments—they "have made three thousand millions of debt—destroyed two thousand millions of property in slaves—four thou-sand millions in dwellings and farm improvements," undermined the bank-ing system, and vitiated the courts in both the South and the North.[7]

Racism was a vital, core Democratic belief that had not changed from the war years. Democratic newspapers proved highly consistent in their use of scare tactics and vicious racism against African Americans. Lincoln's hope for Black suffrage seemed to be unnoticed or forgotten, as racist com-mentary emerged quite early. Less than two weeks after the assassination

Ohio's *Urbana Union* charged that "Negro Voting" was a tool to offset Irish support for the Democrats. On the same day a Pennsylvania editor explained that his opposition to emancipation was based only partly on the conviction that it was a repugnant violation of the Constitution. Democrats "believed, and still believe," he wrote, that emancipation would lead to "the elevation of the negro to a position of social and political equality with the white man." Such an outcome would "prove a curse instead of a blessing to the black as well as the white race."[8]

Black people were a curse and a danger to society in the views of many of these Democratic editors. In the first week of May Indiana's *Jasper Weekly Courier* claimed that Black U.S. troops in Charleston had plotted "to kill their white officers, take possession of the city and put the white people to death." The plot fortunately was discovered, but "this is one of the fruits of arming the negroes in the South," and "it will not be the last." One week later this paper was describing an "Outrage" in a nearby town. A white woman was walking down Main Street, asserted the editor, when she "was seized by a negro, who insulted her in a gross manner by kissing her." White citizens, he declared, "will not permit such outrages by insolent negroes to go unpunished." Shortly thereafter a letter to the newspaper complained that Blacks in Washington, D.C., "don't give way on the sidewalks to white people" and should be sent to another country. This correspondent warned that "there is a party which would elevate the negro above the white man."[9]

In Ohio one Democratic newspaper claimed that Black troops stationed in Memphis had hatched "a plot to murder every rebel" in the town "in revenge for the Fort Pillow massacre." That was not the only reason African Americans were dangerous to the republic. Racial equality would lead to race-mixing or violence and to inevitable degradation of society. The editor argued that General William Sherman and "a large majority of the army and its bravest and ablest officers" were deservedly hostile "to the whole doctrine of negro suffrage and equality, and to its natural and necessary but unclean corollary, *miscegenation*." The example of Mexico and other racially mixed republics "forbids political equality to the negro," and Thomas Jefferson had rightly concluded that "the two races, *equally free*, cannot live in the same government." Democratic doctrine, said this editor, was the right doctrine and had always supported white supremacy.[10]

Alluding to the supporting views of a war hero was one strategy to confirm the validity of racist dogma. William Tecumseh Sherman's anti-Black attitudes were as well-known as his military contributions, which one

Democratic newspaper characterized as "a thousand times more" important than the efforts of "all the negroes from Maryland to Texas." General
Sherman received an "enthusiastic greeting" in June when he spoke at a
Sanitary Fair in Chicago. The time for war had "passed," he told the audience, and then he defended the racial attitudes of his former foes. "*Instead of insulting, you must encourage,*" he declared. "You cannot expect the
people of Louisiana to feel as you do, nor those who live in the Carolinas.—
[Cheers.] All parties have their prejudices, and you must . . . respect them
as thy respect yours." In another address in Chicago Sherman asserted that
"he did not think [Blacks] were fitted to take part in the legislation of the
country." His words fueled appeals by Democrats who reminded army
veterans that "your invincible commander, old Tecumseh Sherman," knew
that "the Negroes are not fitted for the exercise of the elective franchise.
I want them to get a fair price for their labor," he had explained, "but I do
not think they are fit to take a part in the legislation of the country."[11]

The *Daily Ohio Statesman* warned against claims "that the colored men are
in reality the only Unionists in the South." Such "trumped up statement[s]"
were "a pretext for giving suffrage" to worthless Blacks. Military authorities
"all through the southern country . . . have promptly interposed to save the
inhabitants from being devoured by the throngs of negroes who flocked
into the principal towns and cities." These Blacks were "in a Pitiable Condition" because they would not work. "Doubts will naturally arise in some
minds, whether the freedom that has so suddenly been thrust upon the colored population is, after all, an unmixed good." The *Cincinnati Commercial*
reported that planters wanted the freedmen "removed from their midst . . .
and some openly declare they will not live in a country where the blacks are
allowed the right of suffrage." A Democratic journal in Indiana publicized
the view that in freedom Blacks would only be "an intolerable nuisance." It
was best to colonize them abroad and "be well rid of an element that, in our
midst, would always be a terrible annoyance."[12]

The *Hartford Times* defended white supremacy and rejected Republican claims that Black soldiers had provided the margin of victory in
the long war. Any such statement was "not at all complimentary to the
white soldiers." Even worse, it was part of the program of "fanatics" who
were bent on "elevating the African race above the Caucasian race." An
Indiana newspaper reminded its readers that white supremacy was one of
the core principles of the Democratic Party. It quoted Stephen Douglas's

prewar declaration: "I hold that a negro is not and never ought to be a citizen of the United States. I hold that this Government was made upon a white basis, by white men for the benefit of white men and their posterity forever, and should be administered by white men and none others. I do not believe that the Almighty made the negro capable of self-government."[13]

A Democratic editor in Mount Vernon, Ohio, warned that Republicans were planning to campaign for " 'Wolly head[s]' . . . 'Nigger's Rights,' 'More Plunder,' and 'Higher Taxes,' " goals offensive to northern troops who *"fought for the Union, and not for the nigger!"* The *Cincinnati Enquirer* did not hesitate to defend the rightness and desirability of slavery. "Four years ago," it claimed, "there were not four millions of people as happy and contented as the negroes of the South, upon the face of the earth; now there is not a people so miserable." The Black "parasites" of the South were sure to suffer without the protection formerly provided by their owners.[14]

Noxious racist language and degrading assertions quickly surfaced. The *New York Express* objected to the very idea that "half barbarized Southern Africans" could be made voters. One Ohio Democratic newspaper copied a claim that in the southwestern states Blacks were "incline[d] to become semi-savages" who would not work and lived by stealing. An Indiana newspaper proclaimed that the African "is still a ferocious cannibal, running naked in the woods," and since "the curse of God" is "upon the race," Blacks in the United States "can never compete with the white race, either in intellectual or in the agricultural field of labor.—Wherever the two races have come in competition the negro has gone down. . . . God has so ordained it." The *Chicago Times* complained that Africans "afflicted" Chicago and that their "odor . . . stifle[s] us . . . the Afrite dominates on earth, and the country is asphyxiated with unclean odors." How could one escape them "in the pulpit, on the street cars," invading the North?[15]

The *Chicago Times* as well as newspapers in Indiana and Pennsylvania complained that "darkies" were "inundat[ing] us" or "pouring into" northern states and southern cities. These journals claimed that they were "idle" and "expect[ed] to be fed and clothed and have nothing to do." Some hoped that U.S. soldiers would "tak[e] measures to rid the country of the negro population" and thus remove what an Illinois editor called a "lazy, do-less, thriftless negro population." Blacks must "leave the country" to avoid degrading it. The so-called " 'apprentice system' in the West Indies, or the 'Peon' system in Mexico" were unacceptable in the United

States. Apprenticeship or peonage or, even worse, equality before the law would result in "the country suffered to go to ruin and decay, and the negro to revert to barbarism."[16]

Thus there was ample evidence that northern Democrats planned to fight against Black suffrage. An important question that was less clear for them was the attitude they should take toward President Andrew Johnson. By refusing to secede, Johnson had proved he was a staunch and determined Unionist, and then he accepted appointment as Lincoln's wartime governor in Tennessee. Elevation to the vice presidency seemingly had cemented his identification with Lincoln's political party, and now he was the leader of the postwar Republicans. But Johnson's background and past history caused some to wonder if he might be susceptible to Democratic ways of thinking. After all, he was a southerner, he once had owned slaves, and he had been a lifelong Democrat before siding with Lincoln. For most Democrats there was insufficient reason to trust him or count on his support, but a few, even in the early days of the spring, saw reason to hope.

The *Cadiz Sentinel* as early as April 26 focused attention on Johnson and the Crittenden Compromise. Like many other unbending Democrats, this paper's editor believed the compromise had been "a satisfactory adjustment of the difficulty between the North and South. The Republican Radicals," however, "were opposed to this or any other compromise." They wrongly believed the Union needed "some bloodletting." Nonetheless, the *Cadiz Sentinel* pointed out, the "Hon. Andrew Johnson, the new President of the U.S., had voted for the Crittenden Compromise in 1861," and that fact was far from discouraging. In Michigan another Democratic paper took heart from Johnson's support of the compromise. Similarly, in Indiana a Democratic journal printed Johnson's appeal for compromise in 1861 and noted that he voted "for the 'Peace conference propositions' along with Crittenden, Douglas and others."[17]

At the beginning of May a Democratic editor in Pennsylvania asked, "What's to Come," and indicated that he feared a centralized government instead of a state-centered federation. Within a week he devoted his lead editorial to Andrew Johnson. After reviewing the president's humble origins, the editor credited Johnson with "wonderful business abilities" and skill as an orator. In an article on "The Future," he suggested that the issue of how to treat the rebels was "probably safe" in Johnson's hands. Moreover, this newspaper was pleased that the new president had voiced "sound constitutional doctrine" to members of an Indiana delegation. Johnson showed that he respected the states and rejected the idea that rebellious areas had lost "their character as States . . . their life breath has been only suspended." Then Johnson declared that just as he opposed dissolution of the Union, "I am equally opposed to consolidation or the centralization of power." These words were reassuring to Democratic ears.[18]

Hopeful Democrats would not have long to wait before they could assess the new president. As spring came to an end and summer approached, speculation about him and the future began to give way before public discussion about policy. Although Congress was adjourned, Andrew Johnson began to make clear what his approach to Reconstruction would be.

Johnson Announces
His Policy on Reconstruction

As the month of May advanced, northerners began to look for a major announcement from President Johnson. A new declaration of policy for Reconstruction would update and replace Lincoln's "ten percent" plan, which had been issued back in December 1863. Not all the attention, of course, focused on politics. Tributes to Lincoln and reminiscences about the martyred president continued to appear. Newspapers reported on the progress of Sherman's troops, heading toward Washington for the Grand Review. P. T. Barnum contacted Secretary of War Edwin Stanton and offered the government five hundred dollars for the "petticoat" that Jefferson Davis supposedly had worn as he tried to escape capture in Georgia. The first reports also began to arrive of a "political revolution" that had taken place in Haiti, and news about the fighting there would continue to claim some column inches in subsequent weeks.[1]

But interest in Johnson's policy was growing, and many observers and editors could not resist speculation. Most Republican congressmen and senators had confidence in Johnson at this point, although Charles Sumner and others were worried. Among Republican newspapers, a number desired a strong policy, contrary to Lincoln's preference for charity for all. They looked for stern measures to punish traitors and guarantee loyalty in the South. The *Ashtabula Weekly Telegraph* claimed to see signs of a "firm yet liberal" policy from Johnson. That firmness should include "inflexible justice" meted out to "the leaders of the Rebellion." The *Cincinnati Gazette* informed its readers Johnson had told the British ambassador that "traitors must be taught that they are criminals," and that his responsibility was to teach that lesson as the nation's "earnest agent." Another Republican editor shared rumors that "President Johnson's forthcoming amnesty proclamation . . . will exclude the officers who were concerned in the starvation of our prisoners, and also those who ordered the Fort Pillow massacre." The *Chicago Tribune* was encouraged that the president recognized Francis Pierpont, the wartime leader of Virginia's "restored" government, as the governor of Virginia because that action "sweeps away" the "rebel State and Confederate Governments" at Richmond.[2]

Other Republican editors had high hopes for Black suffrage. The *Cleveland Leader* remained hopeful that suffrage would be part of the reconstruction of the South. It denied reports from other sources that "the forthcoming proclamation by the President will not permit loyal negroes to vote." Two Illinois journals called attention to the support for Black suffrage that had come from the Democratic *New York World,* and one Illinois editor and a colleague in Vermont argued that "the only question is whether intelligence shall be required in the voter, of any color, and how much." More than one Republican newspaper recalled that during the war, Johnson had spoken in an inspiring way to an assemblage of Black people in Nashville, Tennessee. After damning the aristocracy that had oppressed them and challenging his audience to be virtuous, he had predicted a Moses would arise for the freed people. When the ex-slaves then called on Johnson to be their Moses, he accepted the role, declaring that he would be their Moses to guide them "through the Red Sea of war and bondage to a fairer future of liberty and peace."[3]

More conservative papers offered speculations leading in the opposite direction. The *Philadelphia Ledger* headlined one article with the words "Andrew Johnson Shows No Leaning toward the Radicals." It believed his terms would be "generous" to former rebels and warned the Radicals that Johnson would resist them because he had "more of Jacksonian firmness" in his "little finger . . . than there was in Mr. Lincoln's whole hand." The Maryland editor of a conservative Unionist paper predicted that Johnson would adhere "to his original political creed" and exclude "the fanatical Abolitionists" from policymaking. He then noted that in 1859 Senator Johnson had declared in one of his speeches that "Negroes are not included in the Declaration of Independence." The *Pittsburg Post* criticized Radicals who were complaining that Johnson's policy might be too mild. "Let us confide in him and act with him," urged the paper.[4]

Democratic editors were uncertain what to think of Johnson at this point, but they continued to press the case for leniency toward the South. Ohio's *Urbana Union* anticipated with regret that the president's approach to amnesty would be "more strict" than Lincoln's 1863 plan. Another journal in that state asked, "Would conferring suffrage on the slaves" while taking "it away from the white men" and "cutting up their estates . . . cause a Union feeling among the Southern people to grow rapidly?" In Indiana a Democratic editor publicized a sermon urging "conciliation" as the tool to reclaim former enemies and make them "our Christian brethren" once more. The *New York Sun* worried that Radical Republicans were planning an "informal meeting" in Washington to press their "views upon the new President." Johnson would have to decide whether to "be President, or . . . a mere puppet."[5]

In a more optimistic vein, a Democratic editor in Illinois saw "many indications" that Johnson "is preparing to give the extreme radicals a wide berth." Racial issues entered the picture a week later and delighted this editor, because when the president met with a delegation of "contrabands," he "gave them a lecture, rather than smooth words." Johnson stressed that they must labor and avoid both indolence and public charity. Supposedly he also "'trusted in God' they would soon be scarce in this country, and gathered by themselves in a clime and country better suited to their constitution and habits." A Democratic paper in Rock Island, Illinois, declared early in May, "An examination of the record of president Johnson's public life is refreshing to democrats and all other conservative men." The new chief executive seemed to be a true Jacksonian. Several days later this paper identified, with pleasure, "a noticeable feature in his administration thus far." Johnson's effort "has been directed for the benefit of white men, and his speeches have uniformly been upon topics connected with the interests of white men." Evidently he had "not forgotten his democratic training" and was "looking first, as being most important, to the questions affecting his own race."[6]

One major newspaper came close to the mark in its speculation or investigations. James Gordon Bennett's *New York Herald* published a dispatch toward the end of May that was copied fairly widely. "The *Herald's* special," noted a Republican paper in Indiana, had found that within the Cabinet "there is considerable diversity of opinion on several important details" regarding the question of "re-construction. . . . Secretary [of War Edwin] Stanton is understood to differ decidedly from the President, and some of

his colleagues, in regard to the proper course to be pursued. . . . He is supported by one, at least, and perhaps by two of the Cabinet while the other
side is with the President." This analysis then identified the major source of
controversy: "The question of negro suffrage is the great stumbling block
in the way of harmony. There is reason to believe that the President is dis-
inclined to take the responsibility of extending the suffrage to the colored
citizens until he has had an opportunity of ascertaining the sentiment of
Congress upon the subject."[7]

The division in the Cabinet was precisely over Black suffrage, and that
division reflected a diversity of racial attitudes in the Republican Party
which dated to its origins. As battles over the extension of slavery into the
territories intensified, longstanding political allegiances had splintered for
a variety of individuals. Some who had been Whigs and others who had
been Democrats abandoned their old loyalties to join first the Free Soil
Party and later the new Republican Party. Although a determination to stop
the expansion of slavery united them, these Whigs and Democrats brought
different viewpoints into their new party. Whigs generally had been open
to reform and willing to embrace a positive role for the central government,
whereas most Democrats believed in states' rights and limited government
as the way to promote liberty. Racism, despite being widespread among
northerners regardless of party, was stronger in a Democratic Party that
was suspicious of reformers, fads, and fanatics. This difference was rooted
in the DNA of the new party, and the revolutionary changes of the wartime
emergency had not extinguished it.

Gideon Welles, Lincoln's secretary of the navy, continued in his post
under Andrew Johnson, and his diary sheds light both on the Cabinet's
divisions and on Republican conservatism and racism. Welles was from
Connecticut and had sterling antislavery credentials—he had supported the
Free Soil Party in 1848 and joined the Republican Party at its founding
in 1854. His father, however, had been a devoted Jeffersonian, and Welles
himself had been an influential Jacksonian Democrat with national connec-
tions over two decades before he left that party. But some of its principles
had not left him, and his racial views were miles away from those of a Republican like Charles Sumner.

On May 9 Welles recorded in his diary that Johnson's Cabinet had split
evenly on the question of Black suffrage in the returning states: "Stanton,
[Postmaster General William] Dennison, [Attorney General James] Speed
were for negro suffrage; [Secretary of the Treasury Hugh] McCulloch,

[Secretary of the Interior John] Usher, and myself were opposed." With that vote Johnson determined to move forward with a wholly white electorate. For Welles, the protection of states' rights seemed most important, for he immediately added that he was opposed to "further subversion of the laws, institutions, and usages of the States respectively." He wanted no more "federal intermeddling in local matters than is absolutely necessary in order to rid them of the radical error [secession] which has caused our national trouble." In reestablishing civil governments in the South, he believed that "all laws, not inconsistent with those of the conquerors" should "remain until changed to [by] the conquered." Clearly, his states'-rights views put him against any thorough recasting of southern governments.[8]

Welles then addressed the issue of "negro suffrage," which he felt had been complicated by "the conflict through which we have passed and the current sympathy for the colored race." Agitation for the rights of African Americans evidently disturbed him, on grounds of states' rights, strict construction of the Constitution, and racial status. "The demagogues will make use of [the issue of Black suffrage], regardless of what is best for the country," he feared. They would disregard "organic law, the rights of the State, or the troubles of our government." To Welles it was "fanaticism" that some "persuade themselves that the cause of liberty and the Union is with the negro and not the white man." Among those who claimed that southern whites were tyrants was "Senator Sumner [who] is riding this idea at top speed. There are others, less sincere than Sumner, who are pressing the question for party purposes."[9]

Welles was strongly against Black suffrage, and his views were tainted by a social prejudice that only narrowly evaded racism, if at all. He acknowledged that "there may be unjust prejudices against permitting colored persons to enjoy the elective franchise, under any circumstances." But the circumstances that could justify Black voting were entirely absent in his view, and Black suffrage "should not be a Federal question. No one can claim that the blacks, in the Slave States especially, can exercise the elective franchise intelligently," Welles asserted. He noted that most northern states did not allow Black men to vote and denied that it would be "politic, and wise, or right even . . . to make so radical a change—provided we have the authority, which I deny—to elevate the ignorant negro, who has been enslaved mentally as well as physically, to the discharge of the highest duties of citizenship, especially when our Free States will not permit the few free negroes to vote." The founding fathers had left decisions on suffrage to the states, and Welles did not believe that either the president or Congress could "legitimately" give freedmen the right to vote in the South.[10]

Welles's elitism and identification with whites came out in his final comments on the Cabinet's action. He admitted that "the negro can take upon himself the duty [of voting] about as intelligently and as well for the public interest as a considerable portion of the foreign element which comes amongst us." But "each will be the tool of demagogues," Welles believed. He felt that Blacks should be educated before gaining the ballot, and "even if the government were empowered to act," voting should not "be precipitated when he is stolidly ignorant and wholly unprepared." To require Black suffrage would go against "the constitutions, laws, usages, and practices of the States which we wish to restore to fellowship." Welles's desire to reestablish that "fellowship" was evidently more important and more pressing in his mind than a consideration that went unmentioned—the fact that southern Blacks had fought to save the Union whereas southern whites had sought to destroy it.[11]

Philadelphia's Sidney George Fisher was another example of a staunch Republican limited by racism. A member of an elite, privileged family, Fisher scorned his brothers-in-law who had favored the "slave power" and had been "partizans of the South in all of its most extravagant claims." But he also denounced the idea of enfranchising "the abject and degraded negro population" and condemned universal suffrage as "the chief source of danger to our government." It merely empowered "the ignorance and recklessness of the mob," which consisted of Irish immigrants, African Americans, and other impoverished groups. Fisher viewed Black people as "docile" and lacking the "permanent capabilities of race" that would enable them to maintain and defend themselves. He wanted "moderate" Reconstruction policies, knew the war had begun only to "preserve the Union," and believed northerners "hate the idea of negro equality."[12]

On May 29 President Johnson issued two proclamations that set forth his plan for Reconstruction, thus providing some initial information for Republicans and Democrats alike. Putting the question of suffrage aside, many saw that Johnson's ideas incorporated elements of Lincoln's plan of December 1863. Johnson's first proclamation offered amnesty and pardon to southerners who would take an oath of future loyalty to the Constitution and Union. That oath would allow them to retain their property except for slaves, but some were denied an opportunity to take the oath, at least for the present. Johnson excluded high-ranking Confederate officials, civil and military, along with other categories such as federal officials who had renounced their allegiance to the United States; those who had mistreated prisoners of war; men who had been educated at West Point or the U.S. Naval Academy but fought for the Confederacy; and northerners who left their homes to fight for the rebellion. In a move that seemed aimed against the South's aristocrats, Johnson also excluded rebels whose taxable property was greater than $20,000. But they and others could make a special application to the president, who then would decide if a pardon was consistent with "the peace and dignity of the United States."[13]

A second proclamation that focused on North Carolina was the model for proclamations covering the remaining rebel states. To launch the process of restoring them to the Union, Johnson decided to appoint provisional governors, who would be responsible for renewing a republican form of government in each state, especially by calling a convention to alter and amend the state's constitution to abolish slavery. Only loyal voters were to be allowed to participate in choosing delegates to the convention. To qualify as loyal, a person had to have taken the amnesty oath and be a qualified voter under the rules of the state that were in force before secession. The elected delegates to the constitutional convention then would make necessary amendments and prescribe voters' qualifications for the future.[14]

Those rules, of course, excluded African Americans, whether they had been free or enslaved at that time. They meant that voters in the reconstructed South would all be white, not only in 1865 but very likely for years to come. Johnson's decision on policy also meant that the nation's chief executive would not be a persistent and influential supporter of Black suffrage, as Lincoln might have been. Without a change in policy, for the next seven months the cause of Black suffrage would lack strong advocacy from the White House. The nation's chief executive would not be using his influence to advance the voting rights of African Americans in statements to southerners, political negotiations, or popular discussions. Thus the proclamations were a blow to the chances of Black suffrage. Johnson defended his decision, declaring that the process he created was respectful of a constitutional power that the states "have rightfully exercised from the origin of the Government to the present time."[15]

Abolitionists were bitterly disappointed and troubled. Martha Coffin Wright believed that the amnesty proclamation "meant that slavery was 'not abolished & never will be.'" Wendell Phillips proclaimed that "the

reconstruction of rebel states without Negro suffrage is a practical surrender to the Confederacy." He saw in Johnson's policy a capitulation to
whites in North Carolina and the likelihood that, without Black suffrage, "a
century of serfdom" would replace centuries of slavery. The New England
Anti-Slavery Society condemned Johnson's North Carolina proclamation,
and abolitionists worried that his policy would be applied to the rest of the
South. Many abolitionists hoped, with Phillips, that Johnson's proclamations were "adopted as an experiment, not as a finality."[16]

Some Republican editors raised objections to Johnson's suffrage policy
from the beginning. A Pennsylvania newspaper immediately identified
"The Universal Suffrage Question" as the most important issue before the
nation, one likely to determine the next presidential election. Calling on its
readers to consider this question "without prejudice, without that repulsive
feeling toward a different race that so frequently controls us," the editor
pledged to share a variety of opinions on suffrage. But in a spirit similar to
Lincoln's last hope, he also wrote, "Let magnanimity, patriotism and the

Wendell Phillips, the
brilliant orator and rival
of William Lloyd Garri-
son, enraged Democrats
with his insistence
on Black suffrage and
equal rights. (Mathew
B. Brady, photographer,
ca. 1853–60; Library of
Congress, Prints and
Photographs Division,
LC-USZ62-129165)

best interests of our country prompt our actions." Looking ahead, he accurately predicted, "The Copperheads will blindly and fiercely oppose the enfranchisement of the negro. They have advocated the enslavement of the whole race with a persistency worthy of a better cause, and now . . . they will throw every obstacle in the way of the elevation of these unfortunates." This editor expected to see appeals "to the low predjudices of the masses" and efforts "to create greater hatred." But, he asked, should disloyal traitors be allowed to vote "while the loyal colored man, who at the call of his country rushed to the field . . . be disfranchised?" This paper also warned that efforts were underway to preserve slavery "in the modified form of caste or serfdom." A week later this journal argued that the central government should regulate voting just as it had abolished slavery. The facts of war and Union victory had discarded and nullified constitutional provisions that protected slavery: "If one part of the state constitution is to be ignored or disregarded, why not, with the same necessity existing, disregard another."[17]

Cumberland, Maryland's *Civilian and Telegraph* agreed that "Negro Suffrage" was now the key question in reconstruction policy. Those who held Black people "as the beast of the field, and degraded" would try to get their power back. "We must labor earnestly and honestly to place all men on an equality in the political point of view," this paper argued. By their military service Black men had earned the right to "the ballot box." It was clear that "ignorance is the great plea" against Black suffrage, and education was desirable, but the paper asked how many immigrants "know a single principle contained in the Constitution of the United States or the State where they locate?" Loyal Black men, it concluded, had the better claim. Two weeks later this paper followed up these points with an appeal to "*principle.*" A nation of freedom had finally ended slavery, but "our mission is yet incomplete; though freedom is acknowledged, *equality* is denied."[18]

A Kansas editor was pleased Johnson planned to exclude part of the rebel population and wished that more had suffered that penalty. Then he copied an article from the *Boston Commonwealth* titled "Negro Suffrage the Only Security for Permanent Peace." National interest was as important as principle in considering Black people's rights. Without Black suffrage the freedmen would again become "only . . . 'hewers of wood and drawers of water,'" and rebels would unite with "Northern Copperheads" to "control the legislation of the country." A Republican paper in Ashtabula, Ohio, warned that without "Negro Suffrage" the colored people of the South "will stand a poor chance for their rights." This paper acknowledged that "there are many prejudices among good and loyal people against investing negroes with political rights." It admitted that "the great mass of the colored people are unfitted to exercise intelligently the right of suffrage." But that was "true likewise of many of the poor whites," and "it would be unjust to give the right to vote to those who have been endeavoring to overthrow the government for four years past, and deprive those . . . who . . . have done all they could to sustain it." As for racist alarm about social equality, that "can never be established by law. . . . Society is a matter of choice, taste and preference."[19]

The *Cleveland Leader* initially commented that Johnson's amnesty proclamation was "meeting with approval on all hands," but soon it began to report on meetings elsewhere that called for "equal suffrage to white and black." One Vermont paper declared that the policy limiting suffrage to whites "has created regret, and perhaps dissatisfaction, among many of the Northern people." Although Blacks faced prejudice even in Vermont, they had "respected the privilege of citizenship as highly as have the whites" and had proven "the capacity of the negro for the duties of citizenship." Another journal in the Green Mountain State had no objection "to entrusting the elective franchise to men who have fought so well, and . . . proved themselves so thoroughly loyal. In fact we believe that this will be our only safety in the reconstruction of the rebellious states." This paper also quoted the *Chicago Tribune*'s report that General Grant saw a "political necessity" in conferring Black suffrage. Without it, Grant believed that the government might have to station 100,000 troops in the South to support "the [loyal] white minority . . . against the white rebel majority."[20]

Yet Republican newspapers were not united in favor of Black suffrage, and many reacted favorably or with little criticism to Johnson's proclamations. Vermont's *Burlington Free Press* reported on the terms of the amnesty proclamation and described the excluded classes as "eminently proper ones." Its editor was satisfied that slavery was not "to be resuscitated" and concluded, "Under this proclamation we may look to see the people of the Southern States returning to their fealty to the United States Government, and peace and order restored speedily over the land." A conservative Union paper in Maryland characterized Johnson's suffrage policy in a telling way—describing it as leaving the decision "with the people." Evidently only southern whites deserved to be considered "the people" when loyal governments were formed once again. That same paper reported that Blacks in South Carolina refused to work and were "stealing everything they can lay their hands upon," and did not criticize President Johnson's refusal to allow Blacks to celebrate the upcoming Fourth of July on the White House's grounds. For a Kansas editor it was enough that Johnson had a harsh policy toward "all the worse cases of the rebels"; that fact seemed to show that his "head is right."[21]

The *Chicago Tribune* reacted to the proclamations by calling the problem of reconstruction "one of the most difficult that was ever presented to human intellect." It was pleased by Johnson's provisions against traitors and aristocrats, but this important Republican journal conceded much to northern prejudice. The exclusion of Blacks from voting "does not disappoint public expectation," it said. Still, many would view this as "a step backward. . . . Even we who have advocated negro suffrage, with many and important limitations . . . wish that the door had been so far left open that colored men able to read and write and the possessors of a small amount property, might have exercised the right of self-protection that there is in the ballot. But throughout the North there will undoubtedly be a reasonably unanimous, if not complete acquiescence" in Johnson's policy. The *New York Times* also commented approvingly on the proclamations and predicted that the "chief interest" would focus on any future presidential pardons. "Unquestionably," it believed, Johnson would exercise his pardoning power "with judicious, and at the same time liberal regard both to the character of individual offenders, and to the welfare and peace of the nation at large." Black suffrage, in the judgment of the *Times*, was not "practicable" because "the *loyal* [white] men of the South will not give it; and, second, the present Constitution of the United States cannot make them give it."[22]

Why was there not more of an outcry from Republican journals over a process of reconstruction that omitted all southern Black men as voters? It was clear that the revolutionary changes of wartime had altered and advanced the views of many northern Republicans. A growing number embraced Black rights not only as a means to battlefield victory or political success but also as a matter of moral justice. The party was moving toward the vanguard of progressive thought on race. Still, most Republicans were far from being insistent, principled Radicals, and many chose to go along with the president in June. Ambassador Charles Francis Adams favored "rehabilitation" of rebels and felt that "retribution should 'extend only to a few.'" The wartime sense of revolutionary change was fading, and advocates for Black suffrage had not yet intensified their efforts. But a major reason many Republicans accepted Johnson's proclamations was the persistence of racial prejudice throughout the North. Significant elements of the party—as represented by former Democrats like Gideon Welles—opposed Black suffrage themselves. Widespread racism among the electorate induced a good deal of political caution, and northerners in general desired a peaceful political settlement after years of crisis.[23]

There were additional, and potent, political reasons. The Republican Party was little more than a decade old, still almost a fledgling organization. Given the diversity within its ranks and the resolute, strong opposition of northern Democrats, Republicans naturally felt that unity was essential to success. Although Andrew Johnson had been a Democrat for most of his life, he ascended to Republican leadership with his nomination as vice president. He became the head of the party after the assassination of Lincoln—its most visible symbol, and a force with whom all other Republicans would need to cooperate in order to have the most success. Republicans therefore were reluctant to oppose Johnson, especially before opposition might prove absolutely necessary. They hoped to work cooperatively with him, and at this point they seemed to have been overly inclined to believe that cooperation was possible.

The Springfield *Republican* revealed many of these motives in a substantial editorial that appeared shortly after the amnesty proclamation. Entitled "Treat the President Fairly," it addressed itself to all Republicans as well as to "patriotic men." The nation was entering a period of "exciting" discussion with "wide differences of opinion" over "great principles and interests." Unity, the paper urged, "was never more essential than now." What was needed were "candor and calmness." Any division "among the friends of liberty" would allow "the forces of rebellion and slavery" to advance their goals in politics, "where all their former successes were won." Differences of opinion should be tolerated and factions avoided so as not to "throw away all that has been won in so many years of sacrifice and death."[24]

The Springfield *Republican* also made a case for respecting Andrew Johnson as an individual and decision-maker. The policy that he announced was "consistent with his frequently declared principles," as well as with his actions in Tennessee, actions "approved by President Lincoln" and "known and understood by the republican party when they nominated him for vice president." Therefore, "common political comity forbids that the party should break with him for being consistent with himself." It was legitimate for advocates of Black suffrage to try to "persuade the President" and white northerners, but they should "forbear reproaches and abuse." If Johnson asserted that he had no constitutional power to enfranchise the freedmen and "would violate his oath to the constitution if he undertook it, they are bound to hold him honest in his opinion, and to honor him for his fidelity" to principle. Had the president been elected by another party, "instead of being the man of our own choice, we could hardly accord him less than this."[25]

The price of disunity and rancor, warned this paper, would be success for the Democrats, delay in reunion, and "a period of reaction." Aware of the difficulty in establishing Black suffrage, its editor argued that caution and unity were the best means to reach that desirable goal: "What we want is steady progress in the direction in which all affairs now tend. Universal suffrage is certain to come, North and South, and it will come soonest by legitimate and reasonable efforts in its behalf." In the ensuing discussion the Springfield *Republican* expressed faith that Americans ultimately would honor "their own theory of government. The suffrage will be eventually bestowed on all men capable of using it, without regard to race or color." It was best for that end to be reached through "free action" rather than "by the bayonet at the decree of the central government."[26]

In addition to these reasons there was a lack of clarity, a deceptive ambiguity, about Johnson's goals, and that ambiguity muddled Republican reactions. No congressional Republican was more dedicated to Black suffrage than Senator Charles Sumner of Massachusetts, yet Sumner apparently misunderstood the president's views. One day after the Cabinet's split vote scuttled Black suffrage in the initial stage of Reconstruction, Sumner came to talk with Gideon Welles. They discussed the trip to the South that Chief Justice Salmon Chase was about to take "to promote negro suffrage." Sumner told Welles not only "that President Johnson is aware of his [Chase's] object in behalf of the negroes" but also that Johnson "favors the idea of their voting." Welles had reason to doubt that point, and he told Sumner that Johnson merely "would not oppose any such movement, were any State to make it." Sumner seemed to be aware of this difference in interpretation, but Welles sensed that it did not greatly trouble the senator.[27]

Other Republicans and attentive observers believed that Andrew Johnson was not inveterately hostile to Black suffrage. The *Boston Commonwealth* reported that New York's Daniel Dickinson had an interview with Johnson "on the subject of extending the right of suffrage to the blacks." Dickinson assured the president that "in doing so he would be sustained by an overwhelming majority in all the Northern states," and Dickinson went away from the meeting without feeling that Johnson's attitude was negative. The *Commonwealth* went on to assert, "Individually, *the President is in favor of negro suffrage*, and will give the weight of his official position for it." *Harper's Weekly* reported that Johnson assured "a deputation of colored men" that their rights should be protected "in the fulfilment of all the relations of citizens exactly as other men are." To *Harper's Weekly* this meant that suffrage was understood not as a privilege but as a right of citizenship.[28]

The *New York Tribune* similarly reported in mid-June that Johnson met with "a fine-looking body of" freedmen from Richmond, Virginia. They voiced their hopes and requests and presented data on their community's ownership of property and faithful church attendance. In response Johnson told them "he should do all he could to have justice done them in their new condition." The *Tribune* wrote that these Black Virginians had made a "profound impression" and heard Johnson say he would protect "them and their rights." About the same time Johnson advised a committee of African Americans from the District of Columbia to press Congress for the vote. Reportedly he told his visitors that he was leaving to states the decision on suffrage there but that "he will give his whole moral influence to the extension of the right of franchise to colored persons."[29]

Republicans also presumed that the president's initial policy was not the final word on Reconstruction, for Congress would play a large role in the outcome. It seemed obvious to members of Congress, who had substantially shaped policy during the war, that the legislative branch of government must have a large impact on the Reconstruction of the Union. Ohio's Senator John Sherman recalled that Congress discussed many ideas for Reconstruction during the war, and always "the supreme power of Congress to change, alter or modify the acts of the President and to admit or reject these states . . . were recognized." Perhaps for that reason Republicans assumed too much about the cooperation they would receive from Johnson. In any case there was a belief, from an early date, that the policy announced in May was an experiment. The rather conservative *New York Times*, for example, supported Johnson's policy but argued that he might revise it as necessary. The *Times* asserted that the president would have the right to "reject" the new constitutions that North Carolina and Mississippi were framing. A correspondent of a Philadelphia paper made the same argument.[30]

No less an abolitionist than Samuel May supported Johnson's proclamations but explained his reasons to William Lloyd Garrison. Placing the decision on Black suffrage in the hands of white southerners, May said, "is eminently well calculated to bring the rebel States *to book*, to a full development of their present purposes and future designs." All would be pleased if they "lay the axe at the root of their old social barbarism, break down caste and aristocracy, . . . and give all men equal rights as citizens." It was "far better" that the southern states should establish right principles "themselves," instead of under compulsion. "But if they don't, the President, the People, and Congress will understand it; and nobody is bound to accept their action." Military rule could continue "until the true light dawns upon them," and May was confident that Congress would act against "any State presenting a Constitution excluding the freed people from citizenship and suffrage."[31]

The reaction from Democratic newspapers was quite different, both more conservative and increasingly racist. Initially there was criticism of Andrew Johnson focused on the idea that his amnesty proclamation was too harsh. Loyal Democrats, wrote an Ohio editor, expected a "free pardon" for southerners, but instead the president combined "Amnesty and Christian Ferocity." His amnesty proclamation would exclude "every man at the South who in any way enjoyed a prominence in life," and therefore Johnson had turned his back on conciliation. The *Urbana Union* likewise objected to a policy that would "doom the men who prove rich enough to be guilty" of owning $20,000 in property.[32]

But within a couple of weeks this paper focused on Black suffrage and took an interesting position that distinguished between South and North. Allowing a few African Americans to vote in Ohio might not do much harm; the paper even admitted that "many persons now excluded by color are as well qualified to vote as many who do." Black suffrage in the South, however, would be "a flagrant usurpation" of states' rights and would deliver to venal politicians "a mass of ignorant voters wholly incapable . . . and unprepared for exercising the right of voting intelligently." Forcing "repulsive" measures on defeated southern whites could not restore peace.[33]

Johnson's decision to allow the southern states to decide on Black suffrage won praise from many Democratic newspapers. The *New York World* labeled that decision "eminently satisfactory." The *Ottawa Free Trader* said that Johnson was "conforming to Democratic ideas long ago maintained." Another Illinois editor declared, "President Johnson All Right." A Pennsylvania newspaper appreciated his respect for "the reserved rights and domestic institutions" of the states, which made the Union a "mighty protector" rather than a "usurping, oppressive master." The Democratic background of the president could keep him on the correct path. "Negro Suffrage," on the other hand, was an astonishing demand from "radical abolition papers," because "the States alone can confer the right of suffrage. It is time that free white men were looking out after their rights."[34]

The dangers of Black suffrage and social equality soon became a dominant theme for many Democratic newspapers. Republicans, "niggerworshipping preachers, and gaunt, ill-favored, petticoated philanthropists" were demanding suffrage for Blacks who were "unfit to be citizens" and "would become barbarous if left to themselves." The great danger was "political and social equality with the white race," and the Democratic Party must "nip in the bud the infamous project of amalgamation, for that, and nothing short of it is the end and aim of the leaders of the abolition party." Other Democratic papers revived the racial scare tactics that had been used during the war. The *Ashland Union* attacked Republicans as "Negro Equality Abolitionists" and as "abolition radicals and negro-voting advocates." The *New York World* joined the attack on Radicals who were pressuring the president to "violate his own convictions of duty, and the principles of the Constitution!" A Radical like Charles Sumner, it said, "holds that one negro is more than equal to ten white men!"[35]

Several Democratic editors compared Andrew Johnson favorably to dangerous abolition fanatics and Radicals. The *Ottawa Free Trader* warned that there was "Radical Warfare Upon President Johnson," and thus came over to his side. The *Cadiz Sentinel* singled out Wendell Phillips as dangerous and warned that Washington, D.C.'s Radicals "are preparing to war on the President because he has squelched Negro Suffrage in the South." It agreed with the *Cincinnati Enquirer* (whose views it described) that Johnson's proclamations sorely disappointed "the ferocious and blood-thirsty demands . . . of the exterminating radicals," who looked "in vain for the establishment of negro suffrage." The Radicals' "completely unreasonable and unjust" demands for Black suffrage, wrote the *Wheeling Register*, "excite the disgust of all reasonable men." The "white people of the North will never agree" to Black suffrage, so what right do Radicals have "to even recommend it to the South?" The *Cadiz Sentinel* warned that "the Abolitionists are determined to confer suffrage upon the Black Man" in the North as well as the South, an act that the *New York World* declared would be "brazen and preposterous." An Indiana newspaper called Wendell Phillips "the negro-lover and amalgamationist" and declared that Republicans aimed to "elevate the negro above the white man." Radicals "think they can make President Johnson come to terms."[36]

These opinions signaled a growing support for Johnson among northern Democrats. The Jacksonian, states'-rights background of the president had given them cautious reason to hope. The *Daily Ohio Statesman* rejoiced that Johnson's proclamations blocked tendencies toward "consolidation." They also "pretty effectually settle[d] the question of colored suffrage in the South," for as long as Johnson's policy guided the reorganization of southern state governments, Black suffrage was totally implausible. "Johnson deserved the thanks of the Conservatives," for his decision to exclude Black men from voting in the South sanctified a states'-rights approach while also strengthening white dominance and white supremacy. Many of his reported comments betrayed a wide emotional distance from African Americans and former slaves. More and more it appeared that Lincoln's successor would be a Democratic conservative, and for that reason he won the backing of Democratic newspapers. By late May or early June almost 80 percent of the journals tracked in this study had become positive about Andrew Johnson or were aligning themselves with him as an ally against abolitionists, Radicals, and Black suffrage. Democratic support for Johnson arrived quickly.[37]

The growing support of Democratic editors for Johnson also showed beyond doubt that Black suffrage would encounter fierce resistance from the Democratic Party. Republican or abolitionist advocates of the rights of former slaves and other African Americans faced a challenge. If they wanted to advance their agenda in the remaining six or seven months of 1865, they would have to be energetic and persuasive and recover lost momentum.

❖ 5 ❖

Republicans Advocate for Black Suffrage

As spring turned into summer, a different emotional, social, and political climate was emerging—a new but inevitably different "normal." The initial shock of Lincoln's assassination was behind northerners, many thousands of soldiers were returning to their homes, and citizens were beginning to pursue personal goals designed for peacetime. New events crowded in, calling for people's attention. Newspapers reported on the growing production of petroleum in Pennsylvania's oil fields. Stories about "The Haytian Rebellion" continued to crop up, with reports either that the rebels had "gained ground" or that both sides claimed success. In New York City P. T. Barnum's museum burned to the ground in mid-July.[1]

In competition with these events and a myriad of local concerns, political issues also were gaining prominence—both those associated with the war and those looking ahead to Reconstruction. The Grand Review had given northerners abundant reason to feel pride in their nation, its democratic processes, and its power. Spectators saw, in the words of navy mathematician Simon Newcomb, the "greatest military display of the Western Hemisphere," or "in the world" according to a Washington minister. The Union had prevailed, and the nation had demonstrated that it could field what was probably the most formidable army on earth. Anger at Confederates remained strong, as many newspaper stories detailed the abuse of Union soldiers at Andersonville. The trials of those accused in the assassination of Lincoln ended on June 30, with all eight defendants found guilty. In July four went to their deaths by hanging, including Mary Surratt, whom many

Democratic editors defended. Boston's Anna Lowell viewed the executions as "a sanguinary tribute to the merciful Lincoln," and Sarah Browne considered it "too merciful" in view of what had happened at Andersonville. But New York's George Templeton Strong thought the executions might "shock public feeling" and predicted Democratic criticism, especially of the treatment of Surratt. Attention to President Johnson's policy on Reconstruction was increasing, and so was the debate on Black suffrage.[2]

The attitudes of Strong exemplified the challenges confronting advocates of Black suffrage. Few civilians had a better record as a determined Unionist and energetic supporter of the war, for Strong was a founder of both the U.S. Sanitary Commission and his city's Union League Club. He had used his personal wealth to support a Union Army regiment. Yet Strong's views on Black suffrage and the South's freedmen were uncertain and contradictory. Although well informed about national events, he had little knowledge of and no familiarity with African Americans. The fact that freedmen had "always helped the national cause to the utmost of their ability, at risk of their lives," was an argument for what he called "Darkey Suffrage." They "should have political rights at least equal to those of the bitter enemies of the country who are about to resume those rights, sullenly and under protest." But Strong also regarded this abstract consideration as "mere nonsense" since "the average field hand would use political power as intelligently as would the mule he drives." Strong gleaned from stories in the *New York World* that some freed "Africo-Americans" had the "delusion" that they no longer needed to work. That seemed understandable to Strong since, after all, they had been "systematically assimilated to brutes . . . generation after generation, for so many years." He appeared to be unsure of the proper policy. On the one hand he wrote, "Were I President, I should aim at securing political rights to property-holding Ethiopians and to such as could read and write." Yet on the other hand he had "faith in the President's judgment and honesty."[3]

Racist feelings persisted even among some committed abolitionists. Albert Browne, a rope manufacturer from Salem, Massachusetts, was a committed activist, along with his wife. During the war he worked for the U.S. Treasury Department by "taking charge of abandoned enemy property in South Carolina, Georgia, and Florida." Browne favored Black suffrage and equal rights, yet "common strains of northern racism [were] fully on display in his letters" home. He wrote of African Americans' "repulsive features" and said that all men were lazy but "the negro man emphatically so." Browne could not "fancy the negro" as some of his abolitionist friends did. "I don't love 'niggers as niggers,'" he told his wife, although "I support their rights as men, or loyal citizens."[4]

Aware of such racist attitudes and the barriers to Black suffrage throughout the North, Radical Republicans knew they had to coordinate their efforts and advocate effectively. One of the most ambitious initiatives came from George L. Stearns, the abolitionist and manufacturer from Medford, Massachusetts. Stearns believed that "the organization of the anti-slavery men of the country" would be necessary in order "to act more effectively in regard to all measures" that might arise during Reconstruction. Therefore, he set out to use his contacts, his wealth, and the postal system to create a list of two thousand activists, along with their full addresses and titles. The initial response was so encouraging that he expanded his project to aim for eight or ten thousand names. Once this directory was complete or nearly complete, Stearns pledged to "furnish every person named, with a

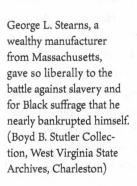

George L. Stearns, a wealthy manufacturer from Massachusetts, gave so liberally to the battle against slavery and for Black suffrage that he nearly bankrupted himself. (Boyd B. Stutler Collection, West Virginia State Archives, Charleston)

copy, free of expense," and in that way advocates of Black rights would be able to correspond and communicate with each other. By May and June copies of Stearns's circular describing this project were moving through the mails. At the same time he prepared to distribute ninety thousand copies of a pamphlet containing speeches by Wendell Phillips, Frederick Douglass, and William Kelley in favor of Black suffrage.[5]

Others began to act individually to promote support for Black people's rights and progress. Angered by President Johnson's "fatal policy," someone, possibly Charles Schulz of Boston, sent a letter of protest to Washington and then contacted Pennsylvania's Representative Thaddeus Stevens. "There must be as many voices as possible to arrest" the "fatal" course that Johnson had marked out, he told Stevens. Then he urged the Radical legislator to "make a speech" and go see the president. "The North was ready for the true doctrine and practice," Schulz believed. Within a month he told Stevens that "Massachusetts is moving" and that "never before was the unanimity so great" in his state.[6]

Among other letters Stevens received was a report from Cornelius Cole, a retiring Union Republican congressman from California. Urging Stevens to "keep a stiff rein on those rebels," Cole declared that Congress needed to "*help* the President" as soon as it reconvened. He summarized current activities in the West by other like-minded Republicans. Schuyler Colfax, Speaker of the House, was in Oregon and getting a warm reception. Ohio's James Garfield was "coming over land"; his colleague James Ashley was "in Idaho, or some other territory." All visits from eastern leaders like these were helpful and welcome, Cole added.[7]

Illinois's Elihu Washburne, another Radical Republican and supporter of Black suffrage, was also receiving mail critical of Johnson's policy. In June Secretary of the Interior James Harlan sent Washburne a letter, marked "Private," containing information about future policy. Harlan's predecessor in the Cabinet, John Usher, had opposed Black suffrage. Harlan now informed Washburne that the decision against Black suffrage was likely to be permanent. "Prest Johnson has planted himself on the North Carolina Proclamation as his platform," he wrote. That meant that Black suffrage would be lacking in "all other similar Proclamations. In my opinion," predicted Harlan, "no other [policy] can be secured except through the action of the two Houses of Congress." Although he knew that Washburne would disapprove of Johnson's policy, Harlan was supportive rather than critical of the president. He believed that Johnson was "as firm as a rock" and resistant to "Copperhead flattery." He went on to say that Johnson was "as inflexibly right on all the main points involved in the great struggle as the most ardent could desire." The future role that Congress could play might have reassured Harlan or Washburne about the prospects for Black suffrage.[8]

Other letters reached Washburne from constituents who were more alarmed about African Americans' rights. An acquaintance from Rockford, Illinois, voiced his fear that Johnson was close to restoring the rebel states "without prefixing proper terms & conditions," and that millions of northerners were not aware of "the impending crisis." Enclosing newspaper reports and letters from the South that showed the unchanged hostility of rebels, this man warned that loyal southerners, the "Poor whites, or darkies," would suffer "systematic oppression." Since Johnson was "hurrying" the return of southern states, he called on Washburne "to exert all your influence upon the President, to speedily call together the Representatives of the people" as the "only certain method" to save the situation. He feared that "if Congress does not meet before Dec[ember]," unrepentant southerners could join with northern Democrats to control Congress and possibly to repudiate the Union debt or incorporate the Confederate debt. In a second letter this man observed that Lincoln seemed to have escaped "*overpowering prejudices*" against Black people, whereas Johnson came from a class that "cherished very degrading opinions" of the "servile race" and still "may hold almost unconquerable prejudices against the African races."[9]

No doubt other personal letters of this type crisscrossed the North, and those members of the Republican Party who favored Black suffrage shared with each other ideas on what to do. Both citizen advocates and members of Congress, however, were handicapped by the fact that the legislature was not in session in Washington. There would be no news reports of debates in Congress or of legislation proposed to advance equality. To promote freedmen's rights, therefore, they had to seize opportunities to speak out in public and champion the cause. In a variety of venues they continued to do so—in meetings of Unionists, in public celebrations, or in dedications of monuments. From an early date their speeches developed an expanding range of arguments for Black suffrage—arguments based on justice for Black soldiers, on national values, on necessity and safety for the Union, and on northern and partisan self-interest. These varied justifications revealed the spectrum of views among northerners as well as the unresolved opinions of some of the speakers. Editors supporting Lincoln's hope for Black suffrage copied and printed these speeches throughout the North.

New Hampshire inaugurated Republican Frederick Smyth as its governor early in June, and he used his inaugural address to take principled ground for Black suffrage. "The great purpose of this war" would not be achieved, Smyth declared, "until free schools, free churches, and a free ballot, are established wherever the federal authority extends." Northerners must make "universal freedom a synonym for universal suffrage," and no state should be readmitted to the Union before "the loyal citizen, of whatever color" enjoyed his rights. To have an enduring peace, northerners must "concede nothing to the prejudices of slavery, and give the freedman the right to assert that manhood peacefully at the ballot-box, which he has so nobly proved on the battle-field." Opposition to Black suffrage was one of slavery's tools to "entrench itself" and regain power.[10]

Ohio's Senator John Sherman had been viewed by many as conservative on "the great and absorbing question of negro suffrage." But on June 10 he demonstrated that, although he was more conservative than some Republicans, his complex views were far from the racist attitudes of his famous brother, General William Tecumseh Sherman. To a meeting of Union men in Circleville, Ohio, the senator insisted that "the Union must be preserved" and "traitors must be punished." Reconstruction would determine "our future national safety," a priority that was as important to him as principle. John Sherman believed that "the spirit of rebellion still lives," and therefore both the national interest and justice demanded suffrage for southern slaves who bore "our flag in battle" and were "slaughtered for our cause." Then Sherman dismantled Andrew Johnson's belief that only states could determine who voted. Rebellion, he argued, had changed "the powers of the rebel states. . . . Can [a rebel] state renounce all its duties, and yet insist upon its rights? If the entire voting population have openly revolted against their allegiance, it is absurd to say that we have power to kill them, and yet have no power to prevent their voting."[11]

It was a "sad fact," Senator Sherman continued, that the number of loyal voters in the South afforded "a very narrow foundation for a republican government." Johnson "intends to try the experiment," but he will find "the spirit of rebellion too deep rooted in those who have taken the oath to make them good citizens." A military government could be established, "but it is expensive and contrary to the spirit of our institutions." Black voters, however, could provide the solution. "If we can put negro regiments there and give them bayonets, why can't we give them votes? . . . Votes are cheaper and better. Both are part of the military necessity put upon us by the rebellion." Loyal states enjoyed the constitutional right to determine the qualifications for voting, Sherman felt, but for "revolted States it is a question of policy and military government."[12]

In closing he addressed "our natural prejudices of caste" and assumptions that freedmen were "ignorant, docile, easily led, and not safely trusted with political power." In fact, "they have been true and faithful among the faithless." To give them freedom but leave them subject to laws dictated "by rebel masters" would be "an act of injustice against which humanity revolted." And without the freedmen's votes, a South of increased political power would be able to "subvert" the government. "All the evils that I perceive may arise from a mixed voting population, are insignificant compared with the only two alternatives—the restoring to rebels vast political power, and the danger and vast expense of military governments."[13]

Ben Butler, the general who had gained recognition for his designation of escaped slaves as contraband of war, spoke at the dedication of a monument in Lowell, Massachusetts, on June 18. His words focused more on justice than on national security. After praising the citizen-soldiers of the North who used their intelligence and political rights to uphold the nation's honor, he posed a series of questions to his audience. "Shall we say," he asked, of Black soldiers who "had no instruction, no political rights, had no joy in the past and little hope in the future . . . that they are not equally as deserving?" Would their loyalty and patriotism, given to "a country which heretofore has been unjust" to them, be ignored or forgotten? Butler pledged that he would "never be guilty of such ingratitude" and would "never cease to urge the government to do justice to the negro." Massachusetts should declare "whether the man who is fit to fight is not fit to vote. [Cheers] Whether a man who can carry a cartridge box is not fit to walk up to the ballot box." Butler admitted "a want of intelligence and cultivation in the negro," but "he knew enough to be right in this contest—to be loyal—and that is a great deal more than his master did. [Cheers and laughter]." Butler concluded by saying that among Confederate prisoners whom he supervised, "only one in eight was able to sign his name." Loyalty was more important than intellectual achievement. The Black man had established a claim by his loyalty and service. "Now, do him justice."[14]

On the next day Massachusetts' Governor John Andrew declined an invitation to speak in a letter that made his views public. Andrew insisted that the North must *"hold on to the power"* that it had over the rebellious South. Loyalty had not returned among rebels, and in the future there must be "suffrage for all men of competent capacity, irrespective of color or national origin." Andrew declared himself "a radical believer in the suffrage" for Black men and deplored the fact that "the last vestige of heresy on that question" still needed to be eradicated from New England. He thought Andrew Johnson shared a determination to "make the country 'permanently free'" and was convinced that the freedmen's *"votes* will be wanted just as their *arms* were wanted."[15]

Vermont's Representative Justin Morrill addressed the Republican Convention of his state at the beginning of July. His speech combined support for Black suffrage in the South with a continued confidence in Andrew Johnson and Congress. It also accepted the existence of discrimination in the North that the Union should regard as unacceptable in a reconstructed South. "Here in Vermont," Morrill said, "we believe in universal suffrage, in true fraternity and equality of human rights for all before the law." But even in Vermont "equality of rights" did not mean that everyone could vote, for the state denied the ballot to women, minors, and unnaturalized foreigners. Morrill then noted that other free states either restricted or prohibited voting by African Americans, and he agreed that "this is a question which properly belongs to the *States* to settle." He also believed that "President Johnson is trying to do right in this matter," and "if the measures he has tried do not succeed, he will try others. But the final determination of this great question rests with Congress." That body could insist on *"free government"* as a requirement for readmission, and to Morrill that meant suffrage must not be denied on the grounds of color. "If [southerners] insist on making a white skin the test, I, for one, would exclude their representatives from Congress till doomsday." He did not trust southern whites, who hoped to exploit the freedmen and gain power in Congress, and therefore he believed that some punishments for treason would be necessary, along with "firmness and sagacity."[16]

Fourth of July celebrations furnished additional opportunities to support Black suffrage. Senator Henry Wilson of Massachusetts addressed the Colored National Monuments Association in Washington, D.C., on the Fourth and welcomed a new era in national life. Thanks to Union victory, slavery was destroyed, and Wilson declared that the *Dred Scott* decision had been thrown on the rubbish heap. Wilson promised that "the freedmen of the United States shall be protected in all their rights" and announced that he was preparing a bill to guarantee "the personal liberty of every freedman of the Republic." He believed that 95 percent of those who voted for Lincoln in 1864 stood for "humane and equal laws. [Cheers] They believe with Andrew Johnson, that *all men should have a fair start and an equal chance in the race of life, and that merit should be rewarded without regard to color.*" Wilson asserted that if the government had told the defeated South it must adopt equal laws and grant the suffrage without regard to color, "every rebel State, South Carolina included, would have within a hundred days accepted these conditions." He regretted that Andrew Johnson had not seized that "golden moment," yet he still had faith in the government and in the motives of a president who had told Blacks in Tennessee "that he would be their Moses." Wilson declared that Congress must insist on Black suffrage before rebels returned to office, and he predicted that if former slaveholders passed oppressive laws, "we will annul them in the Congress of the United States." He urged his audience to aid the cause by petitioning Congress for the right to vote in the District of Columbia.[17]

Henry Winter Davis, the Radical Republican from Maryland, also spoke on July 4 in Chicago. With considerable oratorical skill, he wove together arguments of principle, justice, and national interest and reconciled his goals to President Johnson's current policy. Democratic governments, he declared, cannot ostracize any "great mass" of the population, and "when negroes become free they become a part of the people." Therefore, to ostracize them would be "to sanction a principle fatal to American free Government." Governing the defeated South by military "proconsuls" was unacceptable as a threat to democracy, Davis said. But Reconstruction must not create governments run by "oligarchies of pretended Union men" who had never been loyal before. The South did not have a loyal white population and yet was going to gain representation due to the abolition of slavery. The large population of Black men, however, could "break the terrible unity of the Southern vote that plunged us into the rebellion." It was not true, he said, that former slaves would vote with their masters or that they lacked sufficient intelligence. "They have proven themselves to be men and not beasts," and "they know a Yankee from their masters. [Applause]."[18]

Davis admitted that "I have as much prejudice toward them as any of you; but to talk of this after we have had to call them to our aid in putting down this rebellion is either driveling folly or infinite madness. [Applause]

If you did not wish to have the negro hereafter to enjoy the rights of a man, why did you bury him on the battle field? You white men of Illinois, why did you not have the quota of your State increased so that the negro should not be needed?" Davis added that "I, like you, am no worshipper of the negro" or a believer in "his intellectual superiority," but "it is numbers, not intellidence [sic], it is right intentions, not philosophic judgment, that casts the vote at the ballot-box." In regard to President Johnson's policy, Davis argued that Johnson gave the white South the opportunity to "incorporate universal suffrage as the basis of their constitution" and might have hoped that they would do "what justice and humanity require." But in any case, "there is nothing" in the proclamations "to conclude the judgment of the present Congress of the United States or the recognition of State governments in the rebel States." The president "may have more confidence" in southern whites "than I have," Davis added, but "he knows that the only authority that can recognize State governments at the South is the Congress which admits their Representatives and Senators."[19]

In San Francisco a lawyer prominent in state and local politics used July 4 to declaim against prejudice. Americans had "violate[d] our moral instincts," he said, by allowing slavery to continue, grow great, and "wield all the powers of the Government." Now that African Americans were free, there was no reason to be afraid of them. The war showed that they would fight; Lincoln's assassination proved that they were "capable of discipline" and civilized sorrow. Men like Frederick Douglass and the governor of Liberia demonstrated the potential of their intellects. They deserved freedom and opportunity, he concluded. Whites may prove superior, but "if the liberated slave is our equal, then in God's name let him enjoy the equality; if he is our superior, we will give to him the precedence."[20]

Ohio's Representative James Garfield added his voice to the Fourth of July declarations in favor of Black suffrage, and he chose to emphasize principles of justice and equality. The end of slavery was a great consummation in which

> God brought us face to face with the mighty truth that we must lose
> our own freedom, or grant it to the slaves. In the extremity of our
> distress we called upon the Black man to help us save the Republic,
> and amid the very thunder of battle, we made a covenant with him,
> sealed both with his blood and ours, and witnessed by Jehovah, that
> when the nation was redeemed he should be free, and share with us

its glories and its blessings. [Applause] The Omniscient witness will appear in judgment against us if we do not fulfill that covenant.

Freedom for the slave, Garfield asserted, meant "the realization of those imperishable truths of the Declaration, 'that all men are created equal.'" Therefore, Black men must have the "right to be heard" through their votes, and "there ought to be no pariahs in a full grown and civilized nation, no persons disqualified except through their own defaults." He challenged his fellow Ohioans to reject "the absurd and senseless dogma, that the color of the skin shall be the basis of suffrage, the talisman of liberty."[21]

There was considerable anti-Black prejudice in Ohio, but despite that fact another Republican officeholder, Representative Columbus Delano, spoke out for Black suffrage later that month. Delano praised the "heroism" of Black troops and stated that "without the negro's aid our armies would not have succeeded." Then he forthrightly declared that the African American "deserves his reward. He has a right to sit on juries, to hold office, and to vote as a freeman at the ballot box." Appealing to northern patriotism, Delano asked his audience, "Who is there here who would not rather vote for a negro than to vote for a Democrat?"[22]

The energetic Ben Butler further publicized his views in July through a letter that became public and reached some newspapers. This former Democrat turned Radical Republican was uncompromisingly in favor of a hard policy toward the defeated South. Looking back to the American Revolution, he pointed out that Massachusetts had confiscated the property of Tories, whereas South Carolina had not done so. "The result," Butler declared, was "two States with dissimilar institutions. . . . Which do you prefer as a pattern for the regenerate South? Without confiscation, South Carolina? With confiscation, Massachusetts?" He also reiterated his stand in favor of Black suffrage, saying that he preferred to rebuild the South's "edifice of straight black walnut, rather than cross-grained white oak, especially if the sticks of the latter are so crooked that they will not lie still." Like other Radicals, Butler professed not to be worried about President Johnson's policy. It was "as yet . . . only experimental," and Butler believed Johnson "will do in this matter what is right and best." In the end "earnest and true men" would "agree with him or he with them."[23]

A few weeks later Pennsylvania Republican William D. Kelley took to the newspapers to warn loyal men that the victory won "at such cost of life and treasure" was in peril. "Southern leaders mean to avenge their supposed wrongs," he charged, by "degrad[ing] labor over the whole South" and repudiating the national debt or paying the Confederate debt. To prove his point Kelley quoted a public statement by former Confederate colonel A. DeBlanc as a specimen of southern feeling, even in "free Louisiana," which had been occupied since spring 1862. Colonel DeBlanc called peace "a farce" and the Confederacy "a just and sacred cause." Emancipation, he claimed, was neither "*just*" nor constitutional and would "convert our laborers into hordes of vagrants." Slaves, whom DeBlanc called the "pretended victims of our tyranny," were being given "privileges . . . denied to the white laborer" or soldier. Jefferson Davis was a "pure and noble patriot," and the South's crime was simply to have lost. DeBlanc vowed that he would repudiate "nothing of the past" and urged his compatriots to re-enter the Union only "as the equals of our victors," with "legitimate pride" and without degradation. Kelley therefore sounded the alarm against any "precipitate reconstruction."[24]

Kelley also delivered an address in Philadelphia's Concert Hall in which he pointed out that his state had given the vote "to every freedman without regard to color" in 1780. It was a mistake, he argued, that the state later bowed to "injustice and inequality" in "the vain hope of securing peace" with the South. Prejudice was a "melancholy truth" that exposed Philadelphia's hypocrisy, for "*pride of race*" was an "*unchristian and anti-republican prejudice.*" He challenged her citizens to live "the truths of the Declaration of Independence" and rejected the racist feelings that were "enthroned in our Northern hearts." Although he feared that Johnson had "made a mistake," Kelley hoped it would be corrected, and he closed by urging his audience to "take the poor blacks into our political family." They showed a zeal to learn and had "been ready to lay down their lives for you [enthusiastic cheers]." The choice was to ally with such friends or with "the brothers and friends and associates of John C. Breckinridge and Jefferson Davis."[25]

Congressman George Boutwell had an opportunity at the end of July to address some of his constituents in Boston. After noting that the South would in the future gain representation in Congress due to emancipation, he asked if southern whites—"the enemies of this country," racially prejudiced and "contaminated by the vilest crime, the crime of slavery"—would have the sole right of suffrage. The "path of justice" and of safety for the Union required that northerners "secure to the negro the right of suffrage in this country." For southern Blacks, "their security is in the ballot,"

which would enable them to defend their "natural, essential and unalien-
able rights." Black suffrage would ensure the South against future "intestine
commotion" and guarantee that white men had the same voting power in
both North and South. "You must be just to the negro," Boutwell added, for
the North "put the musket into his hand," and slaves sacrificed their lives
"in defense of the country." Without "the right of suffrage," the freedman
would be "bound hand and foot . . . into the custody of his enemies." About
a month later Wisconsin's attorney general agreed in a public address that
the ballot was necessary to defend freedom. Blacks had earned "equality"
through their faithful service. "The black man ought to vote in the Southern
States, for his sake, for our sake, for eternal justice's sake."[26]

Republican editors also publicized the advice of prominent foreign
voices such as John Stuart Mill. By mid-June Republican newspapers had
seen the text of a letter that Mill, the renowned British philosopher and
political economist, had written to an American friend. Although Mill
shunned "savage revenge," he was convinced that a brace of stern measures
was required in Reconstruction. The "power of the slaveholding caste" had
to be broken, and to outnumber southern aristocrats at the polls Black men
must have "full equality of political rights." He also hoped to see "a large
immigration of settlers from the North" in order to make freedom safe and
to realize the ideals of the Declaration of Independence. With Black suffrage, northern immigration, and grants of land, "the Declaration of Independence will cease to be a reproach to the nation."[27]

Robert Dale Owen, the Scottish-born reformer who had served in the
House from Indiana, used his fame and status as a naturalized citizen to
write a long letter to President Johnson. Recalling the time when they had
been in Congress together, Owen set forth a detailed statistical argument
about population by race that was quoted by newspapers in Ohio and
Maryland. Owen concluded by arguing "with great force" for Black suffrage. He declared that "if the negro is admitted to vote, the Constitutional
rule will operate justly." Otherwise, "all the political power which is withheld from the emancipated slave is gained by the Southern white." Owen
also took his arguments to the lecture dais.[28]

New information about Lincoln's support for Black suffrage likewise
appeared, lending the martyred leader's backing to arguments that living
politicians made that summer. By the end of June a private letter Lincoln
had written in March 1864 to the governor of occupied Louisiana became

public. In that letter Lincoln "favored the extension of the elective franchise to the intelligent blacks and those who have fought bravely for the country." Thus, Republican editors could argue, Lincoln's support for Black suffrage had taken shape in his mind well before his assassination. Papers in Cincinnati and Vermont also carried reports that "on the evening before the assassination Mr. Lincoln exhibited to several members of the Cabinet the letters received by him from Chief-Justice Chase in favor of negro suffrage, and expressed his strongest possible indorsement of the views set forth in them."[29]

All these speeches, letters, and arguments were ammunition for Republican newspapers. They reported on or reprinted many of them, and they developed their own arguments to defend Black suffrage. In the summer of 1865 many of these journals were fully engaged and outspoken for the rights of African Americans, especially the right to vote. Their motives and rationales were not all the same, however, and they often used a mixture of arguments springing from different sources. Very few Republican papers embraced Lincoln's dual emphasis on generous conciliation and Black suffrage. Although some took a stand for principle and morality, it was more typical for editors to rely on a variety of practical, political justifications. The future security of the Union, a determination to keep victory from being degraded into a species of defeat, was a common motive. Dissatisfaction with Andrew Johnson's policy was growing, but most Republican journals still found a way to reconcile their views on the future with the worrisome implications of his method of Reconstruction. Before the fall, most editors avoided making an outright break with the president.

The *New York Tribune* was virtually alone in its embrace of *both* parts of Lincoln's final vision for Reconstruction, a vision that included Black suffrage and clemency for repentant, amnestied southerners. Its pages appealed to the South's "educated, intelligent property-holders" to take charge of their local affairs and then deal justly with the freed people: "There is no civilized country on earth—not even slaveholding Brazil—whose constitution excludes Blacks, as such, from office or denies them the Right of Suffrage. . . . Four Millions of Americans . . . shall not be doomed to hopeless, perpetual impotence and pupilage in the land of their nativity and the home of their affections," especially when white "blacklegs" are allowed to vote. The *Tribune* could accept some rules of qualified suffrage, as long as they applied to both races, and noted that many freedmen "*are* qualified, while others will make haste to be like them if properly encouraged."[30]

At one point Horace Greeley's paper presented a litany of reasons why Black men should be enfranchised. Black suffrage was right:

> 1. Because they are human; 2. Because they are rational, accountable beings; 3. Because they are required to pay taxes and fight to uphold the Union, the same as other men; 4. Because they are required to obey the laws, and punished, at least equaly with the whites, whenever they break them; 5. Because it is proved that they can never be shielded from crying injustice and abuse unless they are enfranchised; 6. Because it is not right to tax away their money to educate white children, yet not let them send their own children to neighboring schools sustained in part by their money.

The paper also rejected arguments that white officials could represent the interests of Blacks just as men represented the interests of their wives. Such virtual representation was invalid for a people "shunned, despised, detested." Given rebel "hate" and "persecution," it was essential to recognize "Equal Rights of All" and make "the enfranchisement of the loyal black . . . the corner-stone of successful Reconstruction!"[31]

The New York Tribune remained firm in this rather lonely position. It denied that it had succumbed to "Negromania" or "negro-worship," and challenged northerners to "unlearn" the "wicked fright" that caused some "to manufacture a bugaboo out of the Blacks." It rejoiced that northern Baptists, New School Presbyterians, and United Brethren had "declared in favor of negro suffrage." The Tribune urged "fidelity" to the Declaration of Independence, "the political creed of the nation." By August it worried that slavery's spirit still survived—an "illiberal, inhuman un-Christian" spirit, so it repeated its call for justice for all. There should be "no outpouring of vengeance or wrath on the defeated," but "freedom" should be "guarded by the votes of those most interested in its preservation." The paper desired "a peace based on the broadest mutual recognition of each man's rights as under the protection of every man's interest."[32]

Along with these idealistic counsels, the Tribune could be politically realistic as well. Reconstruction had to result in readmitted states that were loyal. "To enfranchise the Southern Blacks," it wrote, "is to make their several States preponderantly loyal. To leave them disfranchised is to leave all their political power in the hands of a caste preponderantly DIS loyal." The paper also faced the fact of prejudice, granting it some ground but trying to disarm common fears among whites. It insisted that fear of "social equality" was invalid because social relations are "entirely matters of choice," but the *Tribune* also judged amalgamation to be not "desirable. . . . There seems to us a natural repulsion between Whites and Blacks . . . which must have been implanted for some good end." Still, there should be "no legal obstacle" to intermarriage or to Black suffrage because "*legal* equality between the highest and the lowest in the social scale" was the correct principle.[33]

The *Boston Traveller* argued against permitting any limitation on Black men's right to vote. Although some people, like Lincoln, favored "restricting the power to vote to men who shall be able to read and write," that idea was impractical because Blacks "would be kept in ignorance hereafter, and therefore they never could vote." It was folly to suppose that "the Southern States would permit schools to be held for the teaching of blacks, which would exist as manufactories of colored voters." President Johnson's "theory" was that "the government has no right to say what shall or what shall not be done in the States." That theory would "abandon" the freed people to their former masters. In fact there was "never a greater mistake" than to treat the rebel states "as anything but a conquered country. . . . We derived our right and power to abolish slavery only from the sword." Likewise, "the suffrage question" should be "settled by the sword," by the right of conquest.[34]

The *Boston Journal* saluted Vermont Republicans for favoring "universal suffrage" and asserted that "the patriotic masses of the North" would "ultimately" take the same ground. This paper was pleased that Vermont's Republicans had "call[ed] upon Congress to use all its constitutional powers to secure" Black suffrage. "This is right," the editor declared, and "a matter of indispensable justice" as well as "safety to the nation at large." The New York *Independent* also took principled grounds, saying that if the freed people "are to be enumerated as citizens, and be represented as such, then they must have conferred upon them the rights of citizens. . . . If they cannot vote, they cannot be represented." The *New York Evening Post* similarly backed Black suffrage and believed that it was possible, "with proper and judicious efforts," to "set the majority of the Southern people right upon this important question in a very short time." One reason for "the loyal whites" in the South to "favor general suffrage" supposedly was "to save themselves from falling under the control of their old and bitter enemies, the rebel leaders."[35]

The *Chicago Tribune* supported Black suffrage despite a prediction by the *New York News* that freed slaves would vote for the ex-rebels and the Democratic ticket. Voting was the "natural, logical" consequence of emancipation, citizenship, and military service. In addition, the *Chicago Tribune* advanced political arguments that were convincing to many Republicans and northerners. Its editors actually preferred a qualified suffrage, such as Lincoln had proposed, with universal male suffrage waiting on "the gradual education and development of the black man." This important Republican paper even said that it "trembled" at the idea of enfranchising "a mass of ignorance" before Blacks earned the ballot through "patient industry." But Andrew Johnson's policy would not lead to suffrage. Instead, it would turn the freed slave over "to the guardianship of those who hate him with greater intensity than they coveted him as a slave." Therefore, if "premature admission" of rebel states occurred, well-qualified Blacks should be "allowed their rights at the polls," and "if that is denied" and a color-based exclusion applied, then "the lesser evil is to agitate for the right of franchise for all the negro race."[36]

Within a few weeks the *Tribune* laid greater stress on the defects of President Johnson's policy. After publishing a letter insisting that Congress should decide which southerners could vote, it advocated continued "Military Government." As things stood, "the old slave-oligarchy" would come back with its power "unimpaired," with poor whites "uninstructed in their rights," and with the former slaves again oppressed. "If only the whites in the South shall vote," it asked, "will not that whole section speedily fall under the control of the rebel leaders?" Already before the end of the summer, such men were committing "Daily and Increasing Outrages upon the Freedmen" and inventing supposed uprisings in order to adopt "severe restrictions on the negroes."[37]

A mixture of motives made Black suffrage a priority for many Republican papers. Michigan's *Hillsdale Standard* hailed resolutions by Iowa Republicans that "the elective franchise should be based upon loyalty to the Constitution and Union, recognizing and affirming the equality of all men." But it also took note of reports to the *New York Times* that southern whites were "exceedingly bitter" and "as mean and proud as ever." These were the men responsible, said the Michigan editor, for 12,884 deaths of Union soldiers at Andersonville out of 17,524 prisoners. He also quoted the *Boston Journal* on the alarming "increase of political power" that emancipation was going to give the South in Congress. "It seems peculiarly hard, therefore, that the colored population can have no share in the exercise of this power," which will make "the late leaders of the rebellion . . . only the stronger." The Michigan paper publicized calculations by the *Toledo Commercial* showing that if rebel states gained representation without Black suffrage, white southerners would enjoy one representative in Congress for every 82,874 white inhabitants, whereas northerners would have only one for every 127,871 white inhabitants. Republican journals, like one in Delaware, shared the fear that "the South will take political power in the lower branch of Congress," and that that power would be exercised by men who have "committed almost every crime in the catalogue."[38]

Discussion of southern crimes escalated dramatically when the *Chicago Tribune* ran a story on "Barbarous Treatment of Union Prisoners." The centerpiece of this story was a letter, written by Henry S. Foote, that was likewise carried in other Republican journals. Foote, formerly a governor of Mississippi and a Confederate congressman, asserted that the Davis administration had purposely chosen to abuse Union prisoners. He claimed that he had demanded an investigation of Confederate policy and had obtained documents proving that the South's secretary of war, James Seddon, had decided that "the time ha[d] arrived for retaliation upon the prisoners of war of the enemy." A U.S. Senate committee, according to a Michigan editor, had evidence that "clearly shows that tens of thousands of our soldiers" had been shown no mercy and had suffered "acts so horrible that the nations of the earth stand aghast as they are told what has been done." Such charges were emotionally explosive. Obviously, anger and distrust of the former enemy would encourage stern measures. For if defeated Confederates were not erring and repentant brothers but vicious, inveterate foes, all measures to control them—including Black suffrage—should be used.[39]

In a similar manner the *Vermont Watchman and State Journal* reminded its readers of "How the Rebs. Starved Our Soldiers" and "The Horrors of Andersonville." It printed a letter from New Orleans in which the author said, "It is impossible for Northern men . . . to realize the intensity of [white southerners'] hatred." For that reason it was essential to take "a great political stride" and give "all the rights and privileges of freemen" to Blacks, who "have been true as steel." This paper called Black suffrage "a matter of indispensable justice" and "of safety to the nation at large." Congress would need to secure that right, if necessary. As the summer went on, this Vermont paper paired the defense of Black suffrage with warnings that "the wholesale display of clemency to rebel leaders" had encouraged them to organize "a war against Union men and negroes." A Dartmouth College professor made an "exceedingly able argument" that southern leaders wanted to keep "as much as possible of slavery," whereas the Black man had shown "an intelligence not to be deceived" and "a valor not to be daunted." Therefore, Congress must legislate for the states "as for territories."[40]

Most Republican newspapers in the North thus were arguing that Black men in the South must have the right to vote. They joined the informational campaign of abolitionists and the speeches of prominent Republican officeholders in putting forward varied and substantial arguments for Black suffrage. Some advocates took a stand on principle with the abolitionists, while others demanded security for the Union victory, for the national debt, and for the vulnerable freed people. They called for justice for U.S. soldiers, for sectional equality in representation, and for the defense of northern and partisan interests. The range of these arguments could appeal both to idealistic voters and to those who might be indifferent or hostile to Black Americans but who wanted to guard and secure the Union's victory. Considerations of principle and the belief that all men are created equal were important motivators, but so too was the sense that Andrew Johnson's too lenient policy imperiled all that had been gained through four years of bloodshed and sacrifice. The fruits of so costly a victory should not be lost.

Alone among major Republican papers, the *New York Times* gave to the president the solid support that it withheld from Black suffrage. The *Times* often credited reports that "now the whole South accepts emancipation," and it felt that southern "interest" disposed former rebels to be honest in their "loyal professions." They were "our countrymen," and "to represent them as utterly unworthy of trust is virtually to affirm that they are unfit to be Americans." Andrew Johnson was right to have "due regard for the doctrine of State Rights"; he had no power to make "any radical change in the existing fundamental law of the States in this matter" of suffrage. Showing little respect for the capabilities of the freed slaves, the *Times* also argued that Congress and the president were not going to award them the ballot when most northern states refused to do that "for the better trained and more experienced colored men in their section." In these arguments the *Times* anticipated views that would be advanced much more forcefully by Democrats.[41]

But the *Times* was out of step with most Republican newspapers in the North. Its assessment of the freed people also failed to reflect continuing efforts by abolitionists and the widespread, independent initiatives of African Americans throughout the South and North. Their meetings in manifold cities and states generated a large number of petitions and declarations that reflected their readiness for citizenship and their determination to have their rights.

6

Black and White Abolitionists Advocate

M aking the case for Black suffrage was essential in 1865 if Lincoln's last hopes were to be realized and if victory were to bring full freedom and citizenship. That advocacy became even more important after Andrew Johnson initiated a process of reunion that entrusted decision-making to white southerners alone. Republican officeholders and newspaper editors did not have to make the case on their own. They had allies in the abolitionists who had been fighting through the years for Black rights. African Americans themselves also sprang into action to claim the right to vote. Unfortunately, large sections of the northern public were accustomed to dismiss abolitionists as fanatical extremists and to pillory Black people as hopelessly inferior but dangerous. Nevertheless, these two groups added important elements to the argument over Black suffrage, for they were unlikely to accept compromise positions or demand less than equal rights. They raised high the standard that should be pursued. They made the case frequently and in an uncompromised fashion. Thus their voices, though scorned by some and ignored by others, had the potential to push the debate forward and discourage regression. Their arguments, through repetition, could erode the resistance to recognizing Black rights as a logical consequence of slavery's destruction.

Abolitionists made the case strongly during late spring and summer, despite disagreements over whether their antislavery societies should continue to exist in the same form beyond the end of slavery. Fortunately for the cause of Black suffrage, the abolitionists' arguments, and even their disagreements, were publicized in northern newspapers—including in hostile

Democratic journals that wanted to sound the alarm about what they viewed as a pernicious campaign for equal rights and social equality. Such coverage increased awareness of the issue in the general public, including among Republican voters.

When the New England Anti-Slavery Society met on May 31, it received considerable coverage from hostile Democratic newspapers in Ohio and Indiana. The society's Business Committee promptly introduced a resolution declaring that "any reconstruction of a rebel State, without negro suffrage, is a practical surrender to the Confederacy," a surrender that would vitiate the Emancipation Proclamation and even the proposed Thirteenth Amendment. Samuel May argued that the ballot could not wait on education or "instruction" for freed slaves, and another speaker declared that that nation's "real conflict" was now on the political agenda. Wendell Phillips continued to be in the vanguard of advocates for complete equality, arguing that "immediate suffrage" was essential to avert the "disaster" that President Johnson's policy would bring. Phillips warned northerners that Reconstruction based on white suffrage alone would lead to "assumption by the nation of the Confederate debt," but he also stressed that the position of the former slaves was extremely tenuous and vulnerable. States like Tennessee were already enacting laws that would keep the freed people "bound to the soil" and bereft of protection or basic rights. Others agreed that the right of suffrage "is the one question of paramount importance," and that any policy of Reconstruction should ensure that "not a fibre of the slave system" or of anti-Black prejudice was "left in it." Theodore Tilton and Lucretia Mott called for an energetic, moral campaign and for "immediate" ratification of the Thirteenth Amendment and adoption of Black suffrage.[1]

Wendell Phillips also insisted that progress must come immediately and even that "there was no time to agitate" because discussion might delay Black suffrage "for twenty-five years." He argued that "the condition of every black man was to day no better than in 1833" and that even the "technical abolition of slavery" through ratification of the Thirteenth Amendment would consume another year. Others argued that "no State" should be admitted "which does not give every man his rights." Black abolitionists spoke out even more strongly, contradicting the optimism of some of their white colleagues and stressing that southern racists would find substantial support in the northern states. Before the New England Anti-Slavery Society adjourned, it officially called for immediate Black suffrage and the rejection of any plan of Reconstruction that fell short of equal rights. It enlisted the "pulpits of New England" in efforts to convert the public and reach these goals.[2]

The *National Anti-Slavery Standard* trumpeted that it had "hoisted the banner of No Reconstruction without Negro Suffrage," and it vowed to "keep it flying, and nail it to the masthead. It shall never come down till the nation has woven it into the Stars and Stripes, and till it becomes . . . the accomplished policy of the Republic." On June 3 this abolitionist journal labeled Andrew Johnson's Reconstruction policy "The Fatal Step," a strategy that would enshrine "a merciless aristocracy" and render freedom "a mockery and a sham." Citing the hatred toward Blacks among rebels, whether former slaveholders or poor whites, the *Anti-Slavery Standard* declared that Johnson's approach would doom ex-slaves "to a century of serfdom."[3]

Reports on the meeting early in June of the Emancipation League in Boston publicized Charles Sumner's assertion that "the colored suffrage is now a necessity." The Constitution, he declared, "stipulated" that each state must have a republican form of government, and the Declaration of Independence supplied its meaning—"the equality of all men before the law, and the consent of the governed." Congressman George Boutwell swore that he would never support the readmission of any southern state "unless under a Constitution which gave the right of suffrage to black as well as to white." In fact, said Boutwell, "The black man must vote, at all events, whether the whites did or not." He also favored organizing a territory in South Carolina and Florida where Black settlers could "build up States of their own" so that they would be able "in a few years" to "send black Representatives to Congress." Wendell Phillips used the meeting to condemn President Johnson's policy as "an absolute surrender of the helm of the Union into the hands of Alex. H. Stephens and his co-workers." Anyone who did not support "absolute equality" for Black men "with the white man" was a "sycophant" of Jefferson Davis.[4]

Wendell Phillips again attracted the attention of various newspapers when he joined other abolitionist speakers at a Fourth of July celebration in Framingham, Massachusetts. "If the President yields to the influences from the South," he warned, the struggle for Black rights would have to continue "for twenty years to come." Rebel states should be kept out of Congress until the victory was certain. Citing the "principles of the Declaration of

Independence," Phillips said that advocates of equality must not be like General George McClellan, who hesitated to attack until the enemy had "completed his fortifications." Instead, abolitionists and Radical Republicans should emulate General Grant, who told his foe, "We shall move immediately on your works."[5]

Other speakers at that celebration also gained some attention. William Wells Brown, the Black abolitionist, playwright, and author, charged that President Johnson was giving power in the South to "the very men who were prominent in the rebellion." His policy was leaving "the negro, who has been fighting, 'out in the cold.'" As a result the ex-slaves would "be ground into powder." Without rights and with low wages, "we have been fighting for almost nothing. A new form of slavery is being inaugurated." When another speaker urged patience on the grounds that Johnson came from a "poor white" background and would oppose the aristocrats, Wendell Phillips retorted that as a southern man the president "knows slavery, root and branch. . . . If he gives up the black man to the control of the white in these reconstructed States, it is because he wishes to do so." Other speakers pointed out that ex-slaves, though without formal education, knew enough to be loyal and warned that "any compromise" would render the Union victory in vain.[6]

At this same time George Stearns was expanding his efforts to influence public opinion in favor of Black suffrage. The Emancipation League and Republicans in his home state of Massachusetts backed Stearns's initiatives and added financial support to his own substantial contributions. He enrolled twenty thousand people in a new "Universal and Equal Suffrage Association." Reproducing speeches by "Phillips, Douglass, William D. Kelley, Sumner, Henry Ward Beecher, Benjamin Butler, and Richard Henry Dana," Stearns hired clerks and with their help mailed "10,000 newspapers and 3,000 pamphlets per week." His actions trebled the circulation of the *Boston Commonwealth*, and he continued increasing his mailings throughout the summer, aiming to generate the public support needed for Black suffrage. These efforts greatly magnified the influence of the abolitionist press, which was a small, though outspoken, element of northern journalism.[7]

On August 1 communities along the northeastern seaboard gathered for the annual celebration of West Indian Emancipation in 1834. The meeting in Massachusetts drew attention because Massachusetts was either admired for its idealism or reviled by some Democratic journals that denounced it for Puritanical condescension. Samuel May drew from the West Indian experience the lesson that freedom must be complete, not fettered by a "wretched *apprenticeship* system." The West Indian record also proved that the former slaveholder "CANNOT BE TRUSTED" to educate or elevate his former slaves. The United States, May judged, had made a better start than the West Indies with schools, savings banks, and a Freedmen's Bureau, but it must carry the work to completion. Other speakers argued that "the ballot was now needed to complete the work that the bullet had begun," that pressure must be put on Congress, that the Republican Party must be challenged to move forward, and that justice was the right of every "child of the living God." Charles Lenox Remond declared that no rebel state should enter the Union except "upon the basis of free suffrage, a free religion, and free social and civil rights." Jefferson Davis's former coachman testified from his knowledge of white southerners that "if the black man was ever to get the rights of citizenship, they must be given to him by somebody else than by the Southern rebels."[8]

Abolitionists in the North had fought tenaciously for years and were not about to give up. It was certain they would continue to argue for equality once the summer was over. In a logical sense, however, they were not the group that most deserved to be heard. The future of African Americans was being discussed, and for that reason the views of Black people should claim a central relevance. But the realities of American society meant that both free Blacks in the North and freed slaves in the South had to struggle to gain the public's attention. In the North the Black population was small, Black newspapers were few, and society's widespread racial prejudice might increase in intensity with every escalation of partisan conflict. Progress in racial attitudes was evident among Republicans, but most Democratic officials and newspaper editors continued to denounce the race, insist on its inferiority, and dismiss its aspirations. In the South nearly 4 million African Americans labored under unremitting hostility from whites. They also faced the difficulty of capturing the serious attention or respect of most northerners, who knew little of them and often thought of them in stereotypes. Even among Republicans who had labored for their freedom, there was an underlying assumption that slavery and its sequel were southern matters, realities whose significance had more relevance for rebels than for northern whites.[9] The ex-slaves faced a challenge in trying to reach and convince the northern public.

"The National Colored Convention in Session at Washington, D. C." Beginning in 1830 Black leaders in the North used "colored conventions" to advance their rights, and in 1865 similar conventions and assemblies sprang up throughout the South. (Sketch by Theodore R. Davis, *Harper's Weekly*, February 6, 1869, 85; Library of Congress, Prints and Photographs Division, LC-USZ62-100970)

Nevertheless, Black people worked for equal rights with great energy and determination. In the North, African American activists drew on a foundation of organizational efforts that had accelerated during the war. Local conferences and leagues strengthened the convention movement that had been underway since 1831. Then, in the fall of 1864 the National Convention of Colored Men, which met in Syracuse, New York, launched the National Equal Rights League. Black leaders thereafter continued the convention movement but extended their organizing efforts by founding state branches of the Equal Rights League. Throughout 1865 state conventions and local chapters of the league met, and strong messages came from the educated and accomplished leadership of northern Black communities. Their efforts were marked by a serious, civil, and respectful tone but also by clarion calls for just treatment.

In January 1865, even while the war was still underway, the "Convention of the Colored Men of Ohio" met for three days with the central goal of convincing the state's legislature to repeal "the laws which disfranchise the colored citizens of Ohio." Over sixty delegates from twenty-four counties joined in demands that "colored men shall exercise the elective franchise" not only in the North but in territories and "in the rebel states" as well. Along with the suffrage, they declared, Black men should be "fully clothed with the rights of American citizens." To bolster these aims, the convention's delegates stressed their loyalty to the Union and their hatred of "that hell-born, heaven-defying institution, American slavery." Considering that "men of color" had "rushed" to the defense of the Union and "maintained the honor of their race" in "many bloody fights," they resolved that Black soldiers should enjoy "the path of promotion" in the service. Although pleased by the imminent overthrow of slavery, they recognized that Black people might remain "victims" so long as state or national laws made "distinction on account of color." Therefore, they called for purification of the statute books and for social justice that would accord with "the fundamental truths laid down in the great charter of Republican liberty, the Declaration of Independence." In solidarity with "our newly emancipated brothers and sisters of the South," the convention offered its "fellowship" and advised lives devoted to "education, temperance, frugality and morality."[10]

Ohio's Black leaders also expressed their concern for Black soldiers who had been taken prisoner and worked to ensure that bounties or pensions were paid to their families. They began a petition drive whose purpose was to bring citizen pressure on the Ohio legislature to repeal discriminatory laws. An atmosphere of unity shaped this meeting, but the convention adopted one resolution that was critical of certain Black businessmen. The fact that some barbers or small-business owners had built up an exclusively white clientele posed a dilemma for Black activists in the North. Although the members of Ohio's convention encouraged economic progress and entrepreneurship, they also insisted on the principles of equality and civil rights for all. Blacks who excluded their own race in order to satisfy white prejudices violated that principle. Such businessmen should not shun their own race, the delegates believed, so they resolved that those who would not serve a Black person as they would a white person were "unworthy of our respect and confidence." This issue, grounded in the economic difficulties springing from racial discrimination, would be a topic of concern in other states as well.[11]

Black leaders in Pennsylvania, who organized twenty-two local auxiliaries of the National Equal Rights League, held a convention in February in their state's capital. Their three-day meeting addressed a substantial list of concerns, but the main focus again was on the ballot. Early in its sessions the seventy-one delegates welcomed the supportive white state senator Morrow Lowry, who pledged to help them but also warned that "the Government would do nothing for [Blacks] that it could possibly help; it never had, and never would." Lowry believed, however, that in Reconstruction loyal whites "would be forced to give the colored man his rights" in order to have a loyal Unionist majority. The delegates discussed prejudice, and one delegate voiced an opinion (shared by Frederick Douglass and others) that it was "contempt for the condition of the slave" that caused hostility to free men of color. Another delegate claimed that Black businessmen who served only whites were reinforcing, rather than undermining, a racial prejudice that sometimes was "only skin deep." In his own business, said this delegate, "colored and white men work[ed] harmoniously together."[12]

In their resolutions the delegates looked to Congress and Pennsylvania's legislature for changes that would give Black men "the right to vote," and they urged petition drives for that purpose. They also urged as a "duty" that the state's schools for Black children should have African American teachers, for experience taught them that "colored children make greater advancement under the charge of colored teachers than they do under white teachers." After calling for progress by the race in North and South and commending their Republican allies, the delegates composed an address to the people of Pennsylvania. It reminded whites of the antislavery progress that had distinguished the state's earlier history and branded the current denial of suffrage a "cruel, proscriptive policy." It also condemned the "many, very many acts of barbarity and inhuman aggressions made upon us by the dominant race." Then the address pointed out that twelve thousand of Pennsylvania's sixty thousand Black people had come forward to fight for the Union. It was time "that our rights and interests" were respected and that the state joined in the progress being made against slavery and prejudice.[13]

After the Confederate armies of Generals Lee and Johnston surrendered, northern Black leaders increased their focus on Reconstruction, the ballot, and equality. In June thirty-three "Colored Men of the State of Connecticut" assembled in New Haven. Francis Cardozo, who would become South Carolina's secretary of state in 1868, played a prominent role in the proceedings. The convention organized a Connecticut chapter of the National Equal Rights League and pledged to promote education and virtue among individuals and "a recognition of our rights as American citizens" through "appeals to the minds and consciences of the American people." Then the delegates challenged Connecticut's voters to approve a constitutional amendment to give Black men the ballot. The denial of the right to vote, "one of the most valuable and sacred rights of man," was a "mark of political degradation . . . impious before Heaven, unjust and cruel to those affected by it." Saying that "our beloved State" should "remove this blot from her Constitution," they drew up an appeal to the voting public. Looking beyond Connecticut, they implored their friends in Congress to secure "for ourselves, and our brethren in the South, our full rights, as loyal American citizens, in the reconstruction of the rebellious States." Black soldiers had borne their part in the war. "More than two hundred thousand (200,000) brave men rushed to arms" and displayed "indomitable courage and endurance in the many hardfought battles of Port Hudson, Fort Wagner, Olustee, Petersburg, Fort Fisher, and others." Since they had been "always faithful" to the Union, it was time to complete "the platform of equality."[14]

In mid-July New Jersey's State Convention of Colored Men met in Trenton. To bolster their claims for equal rights, they laid plans to take a census of the state's African American population. The information to be gathered covered such items as the number of soldiers furnished to the Union cause, the amount of property owned, the value of taxes paid, and the number of schoolhouses and churches owned by Blacks. These data would serve to document the contribution of African Americans to the state. Like Black leaders throughout the North, the thirty-two men in attendance were eager to show and encourage achievements of their people "in morals, education, industry, wealth and religion." Those were among the goals of the Equal Rights League, and this convention drew up the constitution for New Jersey's branch of that organization. In an address to the people of New Jersey, the convention "respectfully" appealed for restoration of "*all* the rights of *Loyal Citizens*." They sought this "as our right" and despite the "many wrongs" and "many disadvantages" under which they had labored for years, barriers that had "retarded our progress and elevation." The address went on to declare that they had always been "law-abiding, loyal people" and had "rallied to the rescue" in "the hour of the nation's peril." The Declaration of Independence "declares *all* men to be free and equal born" and to be entitled to inalienable rights of "life, liberty, and the pursuit of happiness." The address concluded, "Without the acknowledgment of our *political* rights, these cannot be enjoyed."[15]

By the beginning of August many of Pennsylvania's Black leaders came together again in the annual meeting of their state's Equal Rights League. The meeting began with a call from its presiding officer for greater unity, and the Business Committee promptly reinforced that message. Discord and "divided counsel . . . hostile cliques, petty associations and personal dislikes" were enervating efforts at progress in Pennsylvania. "Let us turn from this insensate madness," appealed the committee, and build unity through "the formation of leagues in every county, town, village, and hamlet throughout the State."[16]

There was much work to be done. Not only did Pennsylvania's Black population face insults and assaults on the highways and railroads, and in hotels and places of amusement, but national policy had turned in the wrong direction. Despite having been "among the first to tender our services" to the Union, "the government who remembered us in her hour of peril, forgets us in her seeming prosperity." The nation now was offering "enfranchisement, protection, office and power" to the very men in the South "who overthrew the government" and "deluged the land with fratricidal blood." In "the name of *justice, humanity and truth*," these Pennsylvania leaders "demand[ed] . . . the fulfillment of the nation's pledges made to us in her darkest hours of trial." They resolved to fight for "full enjoyment of our liberties, protection to our persons throughout the land, complete enfranchisement, and . . . equal[ity] as American citizens before the law." "Equal political rights without distinction of race or color" was the central object of the state Equal Rights League.[17]

Before adjourning, it petitioned the state legislature to instruct Pennsylvania's senators and representatives in Washington to oppose the "admission of any State into the Union that restricts the franchise to any class on account of race or color." Thus the league recognized that it now was up to Congress to block and amend President Johnson's plan, and the group undertook a petition drive among the public to gain support. In additional steps to influence public opinion, this convention circulated speeches by Republicans, abolitionists, and others such as Robert Dale Owen who were advocating Black suffrage. While denouncing "the insane rage" that led southern whites "to persecute and maltreat the freedmen, in the hope of bringing about a war of races," the delegates predicted that such injustice would compel the "United States Government . . . to place the franchise in the hands of her loyal black sons." Former slaves then "will with the ballot save the South, as they have with the musket saved the Union." Loyalty must be "the test of citizenship" in Reconstruction, but the Pennsylvania league would not object to "a reasonable standard of mental culture" as a "qualification for voters," as long as it was "irrespective of color."[18]

Once the summer was over and as fall elections approached in some states, Black leaders in the North would become more active as they fought for rights in their states and prepared for the reassembling of Congress that would occur in December. By contrast, the freedmen of the South used the summer months of 1865 almost continuously to press for their rights. From June through August one community of Black southerners after another met, planned, and acted to demand legal protection, the rights of citizens, and suffrage. They acted not as an ignorant mass less qualified to vote than their mules, as racist opponents charged, but as engaged, alert, and well-informed citizens.

If an example of determination were necessary, African Americans in Louisiana had furnished it back in January. In occupied areas of that state, wartime policies had declared the end of slavery but had not given Black men the right to vote. Military officials also had imposed controversial restrictions reminiscent of slavery or serfdom. To protest such realities, relatively privileged members of the formerly free Black population united with men who had been slaves when the war began. It was "the first time," said the New Orleans Tribune, that "delegates of the country parishes" met "in community with the delegates of the Crescent City." Joining together, fifty-two delegates overcame differences of wealth, skin tone, and language and wrote a constitution for a state branch of the Equal Rights League. Next they voted to gather information on the condition of Louisiana's Black population and to "register their complaints." A Bureau of Industry was charged with using that data to care for the sick and disabled, to help country people gain the right to move about freely without need of a pass, to aid the families of volunteers, and "other similar purposes." Demanding equal rights, this convention urged the U.S. general in command to admit all Black citizens into New Orleans's city railroad cars. The delegates had little faith in the all-white legislature seated under Lincoln's "ten percent" plan, so they debated whether to demand "the right of suffrage" from the legislature or to petition Congress. After three separate, much debated votes, they decided not to deal with the unfriendly white lawmakers and instead looked for support from Congress, friendly Republicans, and the American people. Other matters that were discussed involved education, establishing greater unity, and raising funds to work for progress.[19]

As soon as President Johnson announced his Reconstruction policy, a stream of protests, addresses, and petitions began to appear from African Americans throughout the South. On May 31 "colored citizens" in Petersburg, Virginia, met to "claim, as an unqualified right, the privilege of setting forth respectfully our grievances, and demanding an equality of rights under the law." They recited the military record of Blacks who had fought for the nation at Valley Forge, New Orleans in 1812, and at "Milligan's [sic] Bend, Port Hudson, Fort Wagner, Olustee," and other places during the Civil War. Their sacrifices and the American principle of no taxation without representation required the right of suffrage. Neither color nor former enslavement nor comparative ignorance—which was overlooked in the case of many immigrants—could justify its denial. They stated a willingness to accept any qualification that applied "with equal force to our white fellow-citizens" and expressed confidence in President Johnson. But they warned that rebels taking the oath of allegiance had not abandoned their "vindictive feelings of hatred against the colored man." Nevertheless, on their part they were ready "to let the past be buried" and "to treat all persons with kindness and respect who shall treat us likewise."[20]

The "Colored men of North Carolina" sought to advance their rights by contacting Senator Charles Sumner. They sent him a petition "asking for the right to vote" that was signed by "upwards of two thousand names," and asked Sumner to present it to the president. Their petition asserted that men who had carried the musket "on the field of danger . . . ought to be permitted to carry [the] ballot." It posed the question why men who had "just returned from four years' fighting against" the Union should regain the franchise while loyal Black soldiers were denied that right, and they reminded Johnson that free Blacks had voted in North Carolina until 1835. A similar document came to Johnson from African Americans in Georgia. They cited their consistent loyalty and said that "in order to make our loyalty most effective in the service of the Government, we humbly petition to be allowed to exercise the right of suffrage."[21]

Freed African Americans in Norfolk, Virginia, assembled on June 5 and soon produced a detailed and impressive address. These Virginians had been meeting and organizing since February to gain their rights. When some loyal whites or military authorities took steps to renew civil government, Blacks called for local government "on a 'loyal and equal basis.'" From the beginning they sought "*universal* suffrage to *all* loyal men, without distinction of color" and sent a memorial to Congress. In clubs, religious bodies, and meetings at Mechanics' Hall, they spoke out for their rights and disseminated information about their "movement in behalf of negro suffrage." In May they had passed resolutions demanding "equality before the law, and equal rights of suffrage at the 'ballot box.'" They pledged to prove their worth, to fight to keep "traitors" from gaining power, and to boycott "those who would deny to us our equal rights." They also insisted on their right to vote in elections of the Pierpont government (elections scheduled before Andrew Johnson's Reconstruction policy went into effect) and endorsed friendly candidates.[22]

Then in June they produced an impressive, nine-page appeal to the American people that foreshadowed the tone, strategy, and arguments that southern Blacks in other states and cities would use. This address urged the "Christian and enlightened people" of the United States to recognize their "undoubted right" to vote, a right that was "indispensable to that elevation and prosperity of our people, which must be the desire of every patriot." Contrary to claims by "our enemies" that "this is a white man's country," they cited history, showing that Blacks had fought in the American Revolution, the War of 1812, and the war to preserve the Union. Ever loyal, they had caused no "outbreaks" during the Civil War but now had to contend with "blasphemous" doctrines justifying slavery, the denial of education, refusal to pay wages, and hostile municipal officials. Some whites still held men and women in slavery, and former rebels were returning to elective office. Paired with the appeal to national ideals and Christian morality was a recognition that northern whites would consult their self-interest. Therefore they declared that they wanted "no expensive aid from military forces. . . . Give us the suffrage, and you may rely upon us to secure justice for ourselves, and all Union men." To answer objections that the freed people were ignorant, they first said that "decency" should prevent the use of that argument by those who had forbidden educational opportunities. Then they declared that "no people ever displayed greater earnestness in the acquisition of knowledge," and that "two and three thousand pupils" were already crowding schools in the city. Before concluding, the address called on "our colored brethren" everywhere to be "up and active," to demand fair wages, and to cooperate to buy land. Its final paragraph featured two affirmations: that "we are Americans, we know no other country, we love the land of our birth and our fathers," and that "every Christian and humane man must feel that our demands are just."[23]

On June 7 leaders of the free-born Black community in Richmond wrote to the *New York Tribune* about the scandalous nature of that city's government. "Daily mounted patrol[s]" with "sabres drawn" were intimidating the Black population, requiring passes to allow travel or movement and even "to attend our daily occupations." Governor Francis Pierpont had reinstated the former mayor, who with "all his former nigger-hunters and whippers" was "going into people's houses and taking them out and confining them to the City Jail." Women and children looked in vain for their husbands or fathers, who were under guard in the "bull-pen." To Richmond's unrepentant rebels "Yankee freedom" meant an opportunity to march Blacks "to the bull pen, then to the corn field." Men arrested without cause were being hired out and sent to work on farms. "All that is needed to restore Slavery in full is the auction-block as it used to be." Meeting with blank refusal from local editors who "rejoice to see us so treated," they contacted Greeley's paper to make this situation known.[24]

In the latter half of June Black Mississippians reacted to Andrew Johnson's appointment of William Sharkey as provisional governor. Although Sharkey had been a Unionist and unpopular among some of his Confederate neighbors, these African Americans did not trust him or the president's Reconstruction policy. They made it clear that they "desire universal suffrage." About the same time Blacks in Savannah who had formed a Committee of the Union League drew up a petition to President Johnson and asked Charles Sumner to "use all your influence" when he delivered it to the executive. Their message to Sumner noted that 350 "loyal citizens" had signed the petition, which asked for "the right of suffrage." Sumner was away from Washington, but he replied that he had forwarded the petition, along with his own "earnest recommendation." He gave his opinion that Congress would not sanction any rebel state governments that allowed "the prejudice of caste" to "prevail against justice and common sense." From South Carolina came a petition to Johnson in July signed by 1,800 "colored loyalists" who sought "universal loyal suffrage." A chapter of the Union League had been established there, and "among the colored people, the only question discussed is that of suffrage. Many of the leaders assert that they dare not live in South Carolina without it."[25]

At the beginning of August more than sixty determined delegates opened the Convention of the Colored People of Virginia in the city of Alexandria. Like African Americans in other parts of the South, they professed "no ill-will or prejudice towards our former oppressors" and offered to "forgive and forget the past." They hoped for support from their white friends but acknowledged that others hated them, despite their record as "a people of docility and obedience." Their appeal was for equal protection and "equal rights without regard to the color of skin; and we believe this can only be done by extending to us the elective franchise, which we believe to be our inalienable right as freemen." The right to vote was essential as a means of protection, as a right of citizens, and because "the time has come" for Black people to have the power and representation that had long been denied them. In addition, they argued that Black voters could restore "the balance of power" among "conflicting elements" in the South and thus maintain loyalty to the United States.[26]

In a statement of "Our Wrongs and Rights" these Virginians denounced slavery's "brute force" and prejudice and did not shrink from describing whippings, sales, and seeing "our daughters ravished, our wives *violated*." They were proud of their military service, called on the American people to honor the nation's ideals, and rejected "any attempt to remove, expatriate, or colonize us in any other land against our will." They claimed the "rights . . . immunities and privileges of all other citizens" and sought the "aid of the entire Christian world." A letter threatening them with violence and death before autumn did not deter the convention from publishing resolutions that repeated the claims to citizenship, civil rights, "perfect equality before the law," and the ballot. The convention then petitioned Congress "not to receive the Senators and Representatives elected from this State" but to maintain "military control until all the rights and immunities accorded to white citizens shall be accorded to us."[27]

Finally, the convention published an *Address to the Loyal Citizens and Congress of the United States.* In addition to strong declarations about their rights and wartime service, this address made practical points that northerners needed to understand. "Four-fifths of our enemies are paroled or amnestied, and the other fifth are being pardoned." As Virginians the members of the convention "*know* these men—know them *well*," and "with the majority of them, loyalty is only 'lip deep.'" Their design after readmittance was to make freedom "more intolerable" than slavery had been. For that reason it was imperative to keep military government "until you have so amended the Federal Constitution that it will prohibit the States from making any distinction between citizens on account of race or color. In one word . . . the *possession of the ballot*. Give us this, and we will protect ourselves." Before closing they referred to discussion about "assigning freedmen and refugees forty acres of land" and made clear their desire for "a chance for pre-emption and purchase when it is confiscated or sold for taxes." In an act of racial and class solidarity, they rejected a proposal to raise money for the founding of a college because the greater need was for education for the masses. After arranging for the printing and distribution of five thousand copies of their proceedings, they knelt in prayer and adjourned. The work of this convention, which included conferring with the Freedmen's Bureau to establish schools throughout the state, gained substantial coverage in newspapers as far north as Vermont.[28]

A few days later Tennessee's State Convention of Colored Men met in Nashville. In the record of their work, delegates to the convention began by referring to white critics who had "burlesque[d]" the planned meeting and "laugh[ed] at [the delegates'] ignorance." In response the attendees charged that such hostility to the "freedom, education and equality before the law of all loyal citizens, irrespective of race or color" ignored "the word of God." The convention then welcomed speeches from a white supporter, who was "one of the very few Southern white men who, outgrowing the prejudices of race and condition, stands for the inalienable rights of man." The 105 delegates subsequently challenged the state legislature to respond to a petition for their rights that Black Tennesseans had presented previously. If Tennessee did not grant the petition before December 1, they declared that no congressional delegation from the state should be allowed to take its seats.[29]

Members of the convention surely were pleased to hear from General Clinton Fisk, who headed the Freedmen's Bureau in Tennessee and Kentucky. Fisk described a "new era" that had opened with the end of slavery, one in which "the Government should do something to aid you . . . for the good of the white race as well as yours." The Freedmen's Bureau's agenda included "fair play" in agricultural labor and education as a priority, and Fisk asked for "your co-operation in the schools." Fisk believed that "suffrage will come round all right" and stated his support for it. The convention pledged its cooperation and published an address to Tennessee's white citizens. Calling on white citizens to support Black suffrage, the address noted that Blacks and whites were all "made in the image of God" and pointed out that many whites as well as Blacks lacked education. As for fears of "social equality . . . you are exercising yourselves needlessly. . . . You have the right to select your company." An address to "Colored Americans" in Tennessee urged virtue, progress, and harmony and ended with the declaration: "We should stand shoulder to shoulder and make one grand effort, undivided, for equal rights."[30]

In September more than one hundred North Carolinians opened the State Convention of Colored People. The delegates heard thoughtfully prepared speeches from experienced leaders such as James W. Hood, James Harris, and Abraham Galloway. Hood, the president of the convention, sounded "their watch-words, 'Equal Rights before the Law.'" He identified critical needs—fair and equal treatment in all aspects of the judicial system and "the ballot." Harris advised his colleagues not to rely on the external support from a prejudiced North but to "work out their destiny side by side with the white man." All were acutely aware that their meeting took place in the shadow of deliberations by the all-white constitutional convention required by President Johnson. Therefore, in addition to discussing internally their goals and strategies, they composed an address for external consumption, one designed to appeal most effectively to the white men who, at that moment in Reconstruction, controlled their destiny.[31]

The tone of this address was respectful and constructive, even humble, in its appeal for acceptance and fair treatment. "Disclaiming" any intent to "dictate" to the white constitutional convention, they professed to trust

James W. Hood, born free in Pennsylvania, was both an abolitionist and a minister in the African Methodist Episcopal Zion Church whose work spread the denomination throughout the South. (From James Walker Hood, *One Hundred Years of the African Methodist Episcopal Church; or, The Centennial of African Methodism* [New York: AME Zion Book Concern, 1895])

in that body "to guard the interests of all classes" and to act with "justice, wisdom and patriotism." "We are fully conscious," the address said, "that we possess no power to control legislation in our behalf." Consequently, they relied on a "moral appeal to the hearts and consciences of the people of our state." Citing "an intimacy of relationship unknown to any other state of society" except domestic slavery, they valued their "attachments for the white race which must be as enduring as life." Saying "we cannot long expect the presence of government agents, or of the troops," they intended to find "protection and sympathy . . . at home and among the people of our own State, and merit them by our industry, sobriety, and respectful demeanor, or suffer long and grievous evils." With thanks to "former slave masters who have promptly conceded our freedom," they noted that mistreatment also was occurring. Their call would be to the whites in power to rectify practices that were neither "just or Christian."[32]

Nevertheless, a careful reading showed that North Carolina's Blacks wanted all their rights and full equality before the law. With subtle phrasing and in a lower key, the address mentioned that Black people had "groaned" under slavery and "pray[ed] for the freedom of our race" during the war, even while remaining "obedient and passive" and serving the Confederacy in camp, in the building of fortifications, and in the raising of subsistence for the army. Although unable to "conceive . . . that our God-bestowed freedom should now sever the kindly ties which have so long united us," the address spoke of those who had been expelled from their plantation homes, denied food or shares of the crops or wages, and left to suffer. Seeking "mutual cooperation," the text pointed out that "our longer degradation cannot . . . make us more obedient as servants, or useful as citizens." Therefore, they asked for "education for our children . . . protection for the sanctity of our family relations," and support for "the reunion of families" broken up by slavery. Moreover, the careful language of the address included these words: "We earnestly desire to have" legal disabilities removed "and to have all the oppressive laws which make unjust discriminations on account of race or color wiped from the statutes of the State." Of all the documents issued by southern Black conventions, this was the most placating in tone, yet it shared the aspiration for suffrage and legal equality as essential elements of freedom.[33]

Former slaves in New Bern, North Carolina, and on St. Helena Island, South Carolina, assembled at about the same time in early September to address their needs and concerns. The multiplication of such local meetings revealed that African Americans in the South were alive to the issues affecting them as Reconstruction proceeded. There appears to be no surviving record of the actions taken at New Bern, but on St. Helena Island the freedmen marshaled essential arguments for their rights. Citing their service to the Union Army during the war as a solid claim for equal rights, they then petitioned the constitutional convention that was to meet in Columbia in nine days. They urged that body "to so alter the present constitution of South Carolina as to give the right of suffrage to every man twenty-one years of age, without other qualification than that required of white citizens." In addition, they voiced "a determination never to cease their efforts to this end." A few weeks later freed people in Wilmington, North Carolina, assembled. They heard from J. P. Sampson, editor of the Cincinnati *Colored Citizen*, who claimed "the immediate, unconditional and universal enfranchisement of every Black man in every State in this Union."[34]

That kind of determination, shared throughout the South, ensured that the issue of Black suffrage would not fade away. The addresses, protests, and petitions from southern freedmen demonstrated to their northern

J. P. Sampson, born free in North Carolina and educated in Massachusetts, launched his newspaper for Black soldiers and later became a lawyer and Methodist minister. (C. M. Bell photographers, Washington, D.C., ca. 1873–90; Library of Congress, Prints and Photographs Division, LC-DIG-bellcm-00026)

allies and to others that many in the South were qualified, by any measure, for Black suffrage. Southern Blacks along with northern Blacks and abolitionists were calling loudly and persistently for suffrage. Its fate in 1865, however, would depend on actions and reactions in the North, among its white electorate. There, opinions about the value and efficacy of Andrew Johnson's policy on Reconstruction would influence the northern Congress when it convened in December. During the summer, while African Americans in the South were seeking their rights, Democrats in the North were intensifying their campaign against Black suffrage.

7

Northern Democrats Attack

Public debate over Black suffrage and Reconstruction policy intensified markedly in the North during the summer. Newspaper editors stepped up their arguments about the issues of Reconstruction. Even as these matters became more prominent, however, they did not monopolize everyone's attention. Many northerners were readjusting to lives in peacetime, Congress was not in session, and the numerous details of what was happening in eleven southern states could be confusing. In addition, politics had to compete with a number of dramatic and newsworthy events.

On an oppressively hot day early in July, four of the individuals charged as conspirators in Lincoln's assassination mounted the steps to the gallows. Hooded and with their legs bound by strips of white cloth, the four stood on the "drop" for about ten seconds. Then, at an army officer's signal, the supports were removed and their bodies shot downward. Mary Surratt and George Atzerodt died quickly, but Lewis Powell and David Herold twisted and struggled for almost five minutes before life left their bodies. Newspapers everywhere carried accounts of the hanging, and many Democratic editors agreed with Lewis Powell's claim that Mrs. Surratt, a Catholic and the first woman to be executed by the federal government, was innocent.[1]

More positive and thrilling stories in newspapers across the North told of the effort to link Europe and North American by means of a telegraph cable laid on the floor of the Atlantic Ocean. This ambitious project had begun in 1857, and in 1858 the engineers and promoters momentarily achieved success before their cable failed and lost its connection. By the summer of 1865, however, 2,300 miles of a stronger cable, able to bear a strain of more than seven tons, had been manufactured, and in July the steamship the *Great Eastern* began to commit it to the deep. "If successful," trumpeted *Harper's Weekly*, the Atlantic telegraph "will be the greatest triumph ever achieved by mechanical art over nature . . . more thrilling than the dénouement of the most exciting romance, more poetic than Shakespeare's happiest thought." Failure at the end of July gave way to renewed hopes, and detailed stories in local newspapers chronicled every advance or reverse. The *New York Tribune* devoted half of its front page early in August to an illustration showing the dimensions and route of the cable.[2]

Nevertheless, the significance of Reconstruction was undeniable. As political conflict intensified, the terrain for future struggles was coming into sharp focus. Northern Democrats had called the war a "failure" in 1864, but now that war had ended in Union victory. The ratification of the Thirteenth Amendment was underway and seemed certain to be accomplished. Democrats thus had to decide whether these changed circumstances required new directions for the party and different political positions. As time passed and Reconstruction went forward in the South, it was not surprising that Democrats' favorable attitude toward Andrew Johnson solidified. Race and the question of Black suffrage loomed larger, and fall elections in several states lay not far over the horizon. This was, in short, a defining period for the northern Democracy, and Democrats chose not to move in new directions. Instead, most doubled down on strategies proven to have considerable appeal—conservative dogmas, white supremacy, and the deployment of racist arguments that escalated from ordinary prejudice to extreme virulence and the fomenting of social fears.

The *New York World* exemplified the growing satisfaction among Democrats with President Andrew Johnson and his policies. "All up and down Democrats," said the *World*, were pleased with the president's "course of conduct in regard to the reconstruction of the Southern States. . . . It is much more in accordance with Democratic doctrine than the fanatical creed" of the Republicans. By rejecting theories of state suicide and leaving "each State free to control its own affairs," he was taking "his stand square upon Democratic ground." Soon, the *World* added, "If he stands by his recognition of State governments, the people will support him till that battle is won." Democrats therefore should rally behind Johnson and fight "under his banner." A Maryland paper that had sided with the War

Democrats answered that call. It now praised Johnson because as president and throughout his career he "has steadily adhered to the doctrine of States' Rights." Early in July he told some South Carolinians "that he was a better States' Rights man than either of them." Quoting a speech Johnson made back in 1850, this paper concluded that he was "a patriotic and honest statesman."[3]

Johnson had "repulsed" a "secret meeting" of abolitionist Republicans, wrote an Ohio Democratic editor, when they tried to "coerce him into the extremest measures." It was reassuring that he had announced "the States must settle who shall be voters." Johnson was not leading a "Reconstruction" of the Union but "the Restoration of States," which is "the true ground." The *Chicago Times* confidently asserted that "it is folly for the Abolitionists to delude themselves with the hope that the President will interfere with the State Governments he has assisted to re-establish. His declarations concerning their rights are too explicit to warrant any expectation of that kind." Another Democratic paper in Illinois praised Johnson's position on the rights of rebel states and concluded that the difference between him and "his party . . . is not one merely of expediency, but of principle." The conservative *New York Herald* anticipated some Democrats in predicting that "the violent, threatening course of the leading Northern abolition radicals" on Black suffrage would cause a split in the Republican Party. Johnson's administration then would lead a new organization of "the moderate men of all parties," and it would "control the next presidency."[4]

Buoyed by these prospects and by Johnson's position on states' rights and suffrage in the rebel states, many Democratic newspapers reaffirmed their wartime ideology. The *Cincinnati Enquirer* proudly stood by its 1863 claim that the war "would fail to restore the Union. . . . We say now that the war has failed to accomplish that object. It has been a dead failure." The *New York Evening Post* expected that Republicans would lose their "distinctive creed" and unity as a result of emancipation, but the Democratic Party remained "the party of the people." Democrats would continue to champion the cause of "the universal rights of man" and the "sacred truth that local self-government, or the rights of the separate States, is the most effective means for the security of that end." A Democratic editor in Ohio emphasized that friendship and mutual respect between North and South were essential in Reconstruction. They had been the watchwords of the Democracy "for many years . . . [and] if the other party had adopted [this principle], we should never have had a war, and the Union would never had been in peril." Pennsylvania Democrats agreed and blamed the breakup of the Union on Republicans by claiming that they, not abolitionists, had "pronounced the Constitution 'a covenant with death, and an agreement with hell.' . . . If the counsels of the Democratic party had prevailed, the Union would have been saved in all its integrity and honor, without the slaughter, debt and disgrace of a civil war." Another Ohio editor repeated the old claim that the Emancipation Proclamation was invalid and "a nullity," one of the "unlawful acts of usurpers."[5]

Fundamental to the Democratic Party's creed was white supremacy. This racist ideology had always been one way the party claimed to defend the interests of the common man, understood as a laboring white man. Now that Black suffrage was on the agenda, white supremacy became even more important. Pennsylvania's *Franklin Valley Spirit* flayed the abolitionists and said, "What we object to is the unnatural attempt to treat as equal in human institutions what God has made unequal." Republicans sought to transform the nation into a "Black Republic," and this editor asked if "white freemen" were "willing to share political power with the miserable, ignorant and degraded African." The choice was between "Democracy and white mans government; Republicanism and negro equality." Black suffrage would "degrade the government formed by Washington, Jefferson, Franklin and other patriots," but the Democratic Party would "restore 'our erring sisters' to equal rights . . . [and maintain] the great WHITE REPUBLIC established by the men of '76."[6]

Another Democratic newspaper claimed that "thousands of honest voters" were deserting the Republican Party, a party whose members were willing to place themselves "upon a level with negroes for the sake of the spoils of office." Inspired to poetry, this editor made a declaration and asked a question: "Worth is estimated / By the form and figure / Won't you feel elated / Equaled to the 'nigger'?" Ideas of racial equality were "the ruin that puritan abolitionism has brought upon the country." The *Philadelphia Age* proclaimed its opposition to any "attempted degradation of any portion of the white people of this country." Black suffrage would bring about the "destruction of the whole fabric of society, political, social and industrial." Ohio's *Ashland Union* agreed with Clement Vallandigham, perhaps the North's most extreme critic of the war, that "the Democratic party . . . has proclaimed that . . . governments here were made by white men to be controlled by the white race," but Republicans threatened that principle. They want "social and political equality" for Blacks, which would "elevate (!) the poor white man to the level of the negro." It was a formula for "the degradation of the white man."[7]

Another Democratic newspaper in Ohio asked, "Which is to become Supreme, the White Race or the Black?" It was a law of nature, this article declared, that "when two races wholly opposed by nature are brought in contact, on terms of equality . . . the superior race, both by moral and physical means, exterminated the inferior one; or else the two become extinct." "Half-breeds," such as those that multiplied in Mexico, cause "complete demoralization and depopulation of that country. . . . If we want to preserve our race, let us take warning in time." The *Philadelphia Inquirer* carried a letter from a Democrat who objected to the word "prejudice." That sentiment, rather than being anything blameworthy, was actually "the instinct that has made the Anglo-Saxon the only successful colonists, and enabled him to carry religion, liberty and civilization around the globe." It was simply a fact that if the superior Anglo-Saxon had mixed his blood with Native women, "the United States would, like Mexico and South America, have been a land of Sambos, mestizos, mulattoes and quadroons, morality impracticable and liberty a dream."[8]

Democrats were the party that would defend white superiority, and even many Republicans, claimed an Ohio editor, "are unwilling to be lowered to the degraded level of an equality with the negro race." Contrary to the Republicans, boasted the *Daily Ohio Statesman*, Democrats pledged "devotion to the Union, the Constitution and the White man's interests." White men had the right to vote, but Black men, along with women and minors, had no legitimate claim on the franchise. Democrats should "call themselves the White Man's Party," wrote another editor, since they believed "that this government was made by white men, for the benefit of white men, and should be controlled by white men." Let Republicans call themselves "the Black Man's Party."[9]

Indiana's *Jasper Weekly Courier* charged that "fanatical fools" in the Republican Party were determined to "force the issue of political and social equality with the negro upon the country." The Union had been saved by "white men," it argued, asking, "Where . . . has the negro struck for his own freedom . . . even where the able bodied negroes were twenty to one of the rebels?" Any service they rendered in the war could not compare with "the white men comprising the Federal armies!" Praise given to Black soldiers was a great "insult" made "at the expense of white men." Even in Vermont, where Black suffrage had long been practiced, Democrats resolved "that the government of this country was organized for, and should be administered by, the white race therein." Suffrage should be restricted to whites for the "good of all. . . . We are unalterably opposed to conferring the right of suffrage upon the ignorant negroes of the country."[10]

Democrats often cited Stephen Douglas, along with Thomas Jefferson and other founding fathers, as authorities on the wisdom of white supremacy. But in the summer of 1865 the party sought additional support in the fame and respect won by a war hero, General William Tecumseh Sherman. A Pennsylvania newspaper trumpeted Sherman's statements in a speech that he gave in Indianapolis late in July. There Sherman bluntly affirmed that "the whites must have the governing power." The general declared not only that he opposed Black suffrage but also that he rejected "indiscriminate intercourse with the 'whites.'" In regard to the nation's racial future, Sherman felt that freed people "might be colonized in Florida," away from whites, and have their interests represented in Congress from that area. Another Democratic newspaper in Ohio noted that Sherman explained that "his experience in Mexico and South America" strengthened his belief in white supremacy. The editor of this paper added with satisfaction, "This is certainly explicit enough!"[11]

The united front by Democratic newspapers against Black suffrage now was a central element of the party's identity and appeal.[12] A Pennsylvania paper urged returning soldiers to vote against Republicans to show their opposition to Black rights, and it highlighted a letter that insisted freedmen were incapable of exercising the right to vote. The nation's democratic system, this letter maintained, could be preserved only by restricting the suffrage to whites. This paper also published an article which declared that returning soldiers "to a man" were "opposed to negro-equality; opposed to negroes voting." Frank Blair, the former congressman and general, signaled his family's defection from the Republican Party by warning voters in Kentucky that Republicans were indeed planning to give "the right of suffrage to the negroes in these Southern States. . . . There has been a plan harbored at the North . . . to enforce that upon the South." Using racist satire, an Ohio editor warned of the results if Black suffrage were permitted. "Politics Ten Years Hence" would see "Mr. J. Caesar Crow," member of Congress, fighting to give white men "the right to marry colored ladies. . . . It am my great desire," Crow would say, "to establish de superiority ob de colored race," but in a generous spirit he would give whites "some measure of de rights" they had lost. An editor in Indiana credited Ohio's Democrats with the realization that efforts "to confer the right of suffrage upon negroes" would only "bring the right to vote into disgrace" since "negroes are not competent." He went on to assert that "the experience of 4,000 years has demonstrated that negroes are not equal to white men."[13]

To strengthen opposition to Black suffrage, Democratic newspapers deployed the full spectrum of racist attacks. Statements that African Americans were not equal to white people and were an "inferior and ignorant race" ranked among the mildest accusations. The *Chicago Times* claimed to be overwhelmed, not just by Republicans' promotion of the "nigger" but also by his "odor" that "stifle[s] us. . . . The country is asphyxiated with unclean odors." Other forms of disparagement included common stereotypes, such as "the filthy, greasy negro" who never could compare with "the noble Caucasian." African Americans were supposedly characterized by "insolence, laziness and dishonest habits." Typically "they won't work." Another common claim about the freedmen was that they were "ignorant vagabonds, convertible at any moment into an army of as many barbarous criminals, and murderous desperadoes . . . miserable paupers." An editor who said he was pleased that African Americans were leaving Virginia called the migrants "black vomit" since "a population of free blacks is a nuisance." Racist poems published in Democratic newspapers defamed the possibility of "Kinky-headed lawyers, / Curley headed employers, . . . Mixed in everything."[14]

The inferiority of African Americans was, according to Democratic newspapers, inherent and irremediable. "Of all human kind," wrote a "Soldier" to a Connecticut paper, "they are the most debased and worst. They are but little above the brute creation—cattle in human form," and had degenerated in freedom. Now they wanted only to live in "idleness . . . to wallow in their own filth—to steal whatever comes within their reach." A letter-writer to a Democratic newspaper asked, "What has the Negro Race ever done. . . . What have they ever done in Africa where they have lived for ages?" History showed that they were "inferior." A Pennsylvania editor credited the *New York Herald* with reporting that former slaves in Panama had degenerated in freedom. Despite having been better off than Jamaican slaves, the effect of emancipation on their "moral condition . . . has been disastrous," with rising illegitimacy rates and falling morality. The Democratic Party in Pennsylvania declared that a white man with "the blood of the Anglo-Saxon, the Celt or the Teuton" flowing in his veins felt "a thrill of just shame when he is pronounced to be only the equal of the negro of Dahomey or of Congo."[15]

Other Democratic editors nurtured the theme that African Americans were violent and dangerous to whites and society. "What the negroes want," wrote the St. Louis Dispatch, "and the only freedom they are willing to accept, is unbridled freedom to steal and kill, as the dispatches which we publish elsewhere, clearly prove." News stories from any part of the nation could be copied and publicized locally to alarm white readers. Thus an Indiana newspaper borrowed from Virginia a report about conflict between white and Black laborers. "The rumor of a negro plot at Aquia Creed to murder the white laborers there, turns out to be true," asserted the editor. Closer to home this paper reported that "two negroes assaulted a white woman near Evansville, last Sunday, while she was on her way to church, and after beating and cutting her till she was senseless, dragged her into a field by the road, and violated her person." This incident supposedly was not isolated but "one of the fruits of letting the much loved 'freedmen' of the South settle in the States, and those localities which permit it may expect more of such occurrences." The Louisville Democrat took note of the Evansville incident and headlined a different "Outrage by Negroes" in Clark County. The Black men were said to be U.S. soldiers in this case, and Democratic newspapers delighted in publicizing any misconduct by Black troops.[16]

Attacks on African Americans sometimes featured racist theories that predicted social disaster from violence or extermination. Republicans were not merely degrading "the white man to the level of the negro," said an Ohio Democratic newspaper. Their project to extend to Blacks "the elective franchise . . . must inevitably end in anarchy and a war of the races, fatal to the African and to the restoration of free government." The Cincinnati Enquirer agreed that "four millions of well-fed and happy" slaves had quickly been reduced to three million sufferers. One million of their number had already "gone starving, freezing, rotting, to their graves." A letter published in the Urbana Union predicted that the "four millions of contented slaves" would become "an extinct race. For I am satisfied that the fate of the Indian will be that of the Negro."[17]

The fate of white men, if Black suffrage were to become a reality, supposedly would be appalling—a polluted life of social equality and race intermixture. "Give the black man equal political rights," warned Pennsylvania Democrats, "and you give him equal social rights." Social equality then would inevitably result in miscegenation and the replacement of "the highest type of humanity" by a "mixed, mongrel race such as now curses ... Mexico and Central America." A Democratic newspaper in that state revived the 1864 *Miscegenation* pamphlet with a claim that the Republicans' "mission" was to achieve "amalgamation or (miscegenation)" and "the mingling of all the races on this continent." If Republicans had their way, "We will take him into our society, into our churches, into our schools, into our social circles, into our families." The Republicans' purpose was revealed, declared the *Cleveland Plain Dealer*, during a parade in that city. On a parade wagon "beautiful little girls" who were white were seated around the bottom of a pyramid. One seat "on the apex" was "vacant. Upon this seat was placed a negress. We say no more. It must have been extremely disgusting to any one of a refined mind." The *Cincinnati Enquirer* warned that Black suffrage was "the mere stepping-stone to the social platform ... amalgamation and miscegenation." Another editor argued that suffrage was fundamentally "a *social* struggle—a struggle to eat, drink, and live with the white man—to herd with him, to intermarry with him—to become his father-in-law, his son-in-law—in short, a struggle for AMALGAMATION and MISCEGENATION."[18]

To these visceral racial arguments, Democrats added a variety of other appeals, perhaps less emotional but more attuned to self-interest. There was a resentment of New England that could be exploited, especially in southern parts of the states below the Great Lakes. An Indiana editor condemned a "disgusting" parade in Salem, Massachusetts, in which "a beautiful white girl and a coalblack negro man" sat together in the same carriage. Their proximity showed that the African American was "the man of the future in Massachusetts' estimation." An Ohio editor objected to the power that the six New England states possessed by virtue of the two senators allotted to each state. Many of those northeastern states had rather small populations yet still benefited from as much representation in the Senate as Ohio. This paper blasted "Negro Voting" as simply the "new Massachusetts dogma," which men in Ohio need not accept, especially considering that Blacks might dominate in three southern states. A Democratic newspaper in Indiana expressed its rejection of the moral tutelage that it felt came from New England. The moral fanatics of that region should not be allowed to dominate. Sarcastically this journal recommended an amendment to the Constitution so "as to purchase New England, and set it apart for 'freedmen,' Abolitionists, spiritualists, infidels and free lovers." The conservative *New York Herald* claimed that "New England Jacobins" were preaching "disunion of the rankest kind." If they interfered with southerners returning to Congress, the "crusade" by these "Jacobins may yet lead to a war with New England." Those northeastern states were selfish in protection of their "manufacturing interests," and Massachusetts had adopted a ridiculous law letting Black people eat in hotel restaurants along with white patrons.[19]

In contrast to their dislike of New Englanders, many Democrats felt affection and respect for white southerners and former slaveholders. The *North American Review* in July wondered about the "striking" persistence of sympathetic attitudes toward the rebels, "the tenacity with which the theories of the erring brother and the prodigal son were clung to, despite all evidence of facts to the contrary." Where Democrats saw manliness and honor, the *North American Review* saw arrogance and attitudes of caste that should require the North to "Americanize" the rebellious states. In contrast, an Indiana editor endorsed and publicized the view of the *St. Louis Dispatch* that southern whites were "still *Americans* of the same race, blood and language with ourselves. '*Nay, they are in fact our near kinsmen,* and may claim the hospitality of kinsmen from their conquerors.'" The *Philadelphia Age* reminded readers that former rebels remained a "portion of the white people of this country" and ought not to be degraded. The *Hartford Times* supported other journals that were urging mercy for Jefferson Davis by denying that his government had committed atrocities against U.S. prisoners. "The Confederates did not starve the prisoners in their hands," it maintained. "Their rations, though coarse, were sufficient to sustain well men, and there were no deaths by starvation."[20]

The *New York World* went further and urged a handsome gesture of charity and kindness toward Confederate soldiers held near New York. Some of these prisoners had been released from prison and were waiting to go home, but they had no money. Meanwhile, "In cleanly hospitals, in spacious and beautiful barracks, our own negroes, sick and spent, are provided for." If the city would aid and "care for" the released but penniless Confederate prisoners, said the *World*, "New York would gain a new hold upon the heart of the South. . . . We have been two peoples, let the conclusion of peace be celebrated by some act of kindness and charity." Only one Republican newspaper, the *New York Tribune* adopted a similar attitude. Stubbornly faithful to Lincoln's desire for both conciliation and Black suffrage, the *Tribune* called for "Charity Twice Blessed." Throughout the South families and whole neighborhoods were suffering from the "ravages of war." To avert "deeper and still deeper want, misery and despair," it called on "our City [to] take the lead" in a movement to finance "the restoration of Southern industry" and agriculture.[21]

When Democratic newspapers reported on developments in the southern states, they usually painted a picture highlighting the wisdom of Andrew Johnson's policies. The *Philadelphia North American* described itself in August as glad to see "so many rebel States" restored with "loyal Governors." Although the paper wished that "one or more . . . were more pronounced in their opinions" of loyalty and less sympathetic to rebels, it judged only one provisional governor to have a "serious" lack of patriotism, and it was optimistic about the future. The *New York World* asserted that southerners were behaving well and that their leaders were "disposed, to a man, to acquiesce in reunion and make the best of the situation." The *New York Journal of Commerce* argued that only a few lower-class southerners, plus politically interested northerners, were showing rebellious sentiments. The *Chicago Times* criticized Republicans for denying southern Unionism and misrepresenting the South's whites. To "the Abolition newspaper press," said the *Times*, the southerner who "says nothing . . . is a muzzled rebel; if he does speak, he is a rampant unsubdued secessionist." Democratic editors also printed from southern newspapers reassuring professions of loyalty and reformed attitudes. From Memphis came the claim that the South was "loyal" and that the "majority . . . have always preferred the Union." The *Richmond Commercial Bulletin* praised the "thoroughly peaceful and quiet condition of the South," and a second Memphis paper wrote that the South was "ready to renew her old-time allegiance, and indisposed to quibble as to terms." "It is impossible to conceive," claimed the report to the *New York Commercial Advertiser*, "of a more docile and tractable people than are the late insurgents now."[22]

The federal government was still too prone to centralize power and crush civil liberties, according to many Democratic newspapers. A Democrat in Ohio protested that "large armies of negro troops are retained under arms" and insisted that the United States was "not a consolidated empire like that of Russia." The case of Emerson Etheridge of Tennessee received considerable publicity in the North during July. Etheridge had been a Unionist, but he was outspokenly and brazenly hostile to the administration of Governor William "Parson" Brownlow, who had been elected after Johnson ascended to the vice presidency. When military authorities arrested Etheridge and claimed that he was inciting bloodshed, Democratic editors in the North protested loudly. The *Daily Ohio Statesman* used two days to print a lengthy letter that Etheridge wrote defending himself. He accused the military of "a despotism as inexcusable as rebellion" and asked, "Why are bands of armed negroes permitted to roam over the country, plundering and insulting the timid and defenseless?"[23]

Democrats found in national finances another issue to make their claim as the party that cared for poor laboring white men. Congress had exempted some wartime bond issues from municipal taxes on the interest they paid. Bondholders, "who are generally of the wealthiest class," said an Indiana editor, should not escape taxation "while the poorer classes are taxed on everything they wear, eat or drink." When New Hampshire and Connecticut passed bills attempting to tax the bonds' income at 25 percent, the issue gained more life. An Indiana editor publicized an article from the *New York Day Book.* "Our Untaxed Nobility" noted that even wealthy slaveholders had paid taxes, but the Republican Congress was loading the "public debt upon the shoulders of the laboring and producing class." The *New York World* joined in the criticism of these bonds, but knowing that Congress's power was supreme over state laws in this matter, and that repudiation would damage the nation's credit, it ended up arguing for a modest 2 percent *federal* tax on the income.[24]

With arguments like these, northern Democrats developed an almost unqualified attack on Republicans and carried forward the battle against Black suffrage. Democratic appeals stressed white supremacy, scurrilous racism, predictions of social equality and social degradation, states' rights, and a renewal of friendship with southern whites. How Republicans would answer and advance their views in the summer was important, as some state elections would take place in the fall, and the reconvening of Congress would occur in December.

8

Republicans Seek a Path Forward

Heated discussion and debate about Reconstruction was not the only absorbing news during the summer of 1865. In Pennsylvania especially there was excitement about new discoveries of oil and the riches the petroleum business might bring. Reports of new drilling companies or of "five producing wells . . . and five more doing down" were typical stories of progress in "the oil business." Some papers reported the depth of new wells and the number of barrels they were pumping every day. Along with "promising reports" and the "prospect of good success," they sometimes heralded "a rare chance for investments." But across the North attention was focusing increasingly on politics.[1]

A democratic society welcomes and benefits from a multitude of perspectives and political viewpoints, at least in theory. But if the spectrum of opinions narrows to only two or three opposed and inflexible outlooks, the society faces a division that is deep and thoroughgoing. By the summer of 1865 precisely that kind of division was solidifying in the United States. Not only was the wartime division between North and South still undeniable but there also was a political chasm between northern Republicans and Democrats. Democrats reaffirmed their traditional party principles of states' rights and limited government, generally stood behind their criticism of a mismanaged and unnecessary war, and renewed their appeals to racism and white supremacy. Republicans on their side were adopting core positions for the party as the summer advanced and information about Reconstruction in the South emerged. In a very real sense, the battles of the war years were continuing, North and South, only now they engaged editors and politicians instead of armies.

There were very few exceptions to this partisan division among news-papers in the North. Of Republican journals, the *New York Times* was alone among major papers in breaking ranks on Black suffrage. Its apostasy might have seemed surprising. The *Times*'s editor, Henry Raymond, had been one of the founders of the Republican Party and was only the second person to become chairman of the Republican National Committee when he assumed that post in 1864. But Raymond published his newspaper in a strongly Democratic city and state, and he was representative of some Republican leaders who were not racial egalitarians. At the end of 1864 the *Times* had declared that "the black masses of the South, of a voting age, are as ignorant upon all public questions as the driven cattle. . . . To put the ballot in their hands would be not simply a mockery, but a cruelty." Then in 1865 Ray-mond continued to oppose suffrage for freed slaves, whom he had called "an enormous mass of animal ignorance."[2]

In July 1865 the *Times* predicted that former slaves would be influenced by their old masters and concluded that the duty of "all good citizens" was simply to "prepare them by education for the rights and responsibilities of citizenship." The granting of suffrage and other rights should occur only when they were "qualified to discharge them wisely and safely, and no faster." The *Times* also insisted that states' rights must be respected and gave full support to President Andrew Johnson. His provisional governors, asserted the *Times*, had proved themselves "singularly well adapted to their positions." Regarding the former rebels as "our countrymen," the paper ad-mired their "high-spirited readiness to meet all the responsibilities of their conduct" and asserted that they could be "trusted and cherished upon their return." Southerners had "recognize[d] the real aspects of their new situation" and "yielded with far better grace than was anticipated." Although the *Times*'s positions made it a distinct outlier among Republican papers, its stance was consistent with the views of conservative Republicans who had once been members of the Democratic Party—men like Gideon Welles and Frank and Montgomery Blair.[3]

On the Democratic side the *New York News* was almost alone when it endorsed Black suffrage for the South. Because the *News* had been known as a vehemently pro-rebel journal, Republican leaders immediately sus-pected a deceptive strategy. The editor of the *Evansville Daily Journal* ac-cused the *News* of using Black suffrage to gain "political power that will enable the Democracy to overthrow the Black Republican party." And indeed the *News* showed its hand when it described African Americans

as "imitative creatures" who would follow the lead of their former masters. "President Johnson," the *News* added, "with true Democratic instincts,
foresees the future agency of negro suffrage as an element of Democratic
supremacy and understands the legitimate way of bringing it into action."[4]

The *New York Sun* was a more surprising convert to Republican views on
Black suffrage. The *Sun* was originally a "penny daily" popular with work-
ingmen, and Republicans would not normally have expected it to be an ally.
But in July this paper spoke out for a suffrage "within the reach of all classes
and complexions" based on "an educational qualification" that would
"guarantee an intelligent exercise of the franchise." The *Sun*'s editors,
though not ready to support voting rights for all African Americans, believed that the war had settled some things. "The time for invidious and
narrow-minded distinctions against race and color has passed," they wrote.
"The country is now taking higher and more enlightened ground."[5]

Republican newspapers were almost fully united in support of Black
suffrage and were as opposed to Democratic supremacy as they were to
seeing the war's hard-fought, costly victory nullified by a resurgent South.
For the latter reason Republican newspapers were far more interested
than their Democratic rivals in news from southern states. Some reports
from the South had arrived through the spring, but now the pace quickened.
Republican editors sought and shared stories in order to gauge the amount
of change that was occurring in the defeated Confederacy, and they were
alert to indications of its fitness for reunion. Republican editors printed
many items about the condition and treatment of the former slaves, the
character of newly elected officials in rebel states, and the attitudes of white
southerners generally. Such reporting forced Democratic journals to address
the subject.

What Republican editors found was not reassuring. In fact, as the evidence accumulated, it signaled to many Republicans that the war's divisions remained deep. The fighting on hundreds of battlefields was over,
but the underlying issues that had fomented the war were still alive and
potent. That fact put the results of four years of sacrifice and bloodshed
very much in doubt. Indeed many Republicans came to feel, in a reversal of
Clausewitz's famous maxim, that peace was becoming the continuation
of war by other means—debate in peacetime over Reconstruction policy
now extended a deep and lasting conflict.

Republicans believed that slavery had caused the war, and although slavery was ending, harsh treatment and widespread violence against Blacks

revealed a purpose to continue racial domination. Moreover, white southerners did not always hide their racial goals—one former officer in the Confederate Army admitted defeat but added, "All we ask is to be allowed to
make an honest living and to manage the negro in our own way." What
that meant in Tennessee was that former slaves could not serve on juries,
faced more severe penalties than whites for the same crimes, and could
be sold for "vagrancy." Such facts often were clear in reports generated by
the Freedmen's Bureau, and the *Chicago Tribune*, one of the larger Republican papers, sometimes publicized that disturbing information. The article
"Daily and Increasing Outrages upon the Freedmen" reported that in Virginia former owners "residing at a distance from our military posts, still
maintain their slave rule." The harshness of that rule was "aggravated by a
determination to make the most of the colored people, before the authorities can successfully interfere." "Outrages Upon the Freedmen in South
Carolina" described whites as "too indolent to work" but energetic enough
to use "the lash and the practice of other cruelties" on Black labor: "The
slightest attempt on the part of the freedman to assert his rights is met by
the master with severe punishment, and in numerous instances death."
Poor whites also "persecute them unmercifully," and "letters state that to all
intents and purposes the negroes are in a worse state of slavery than they
were before the war"[6]

Many Republican editors did not have access to reports of the Freedmen's Bureau, but news about southern violence reached the North from
personal letters, published accounts, speeches by U.S. personnel, and dispatches from newspaper correspondents. Albert Browne, the Massachusetts abolitionist working for the Treasury Department in Georgia and
South Carolina, wrote that former slaves were "at the mercy of their former
masters" and suffering "*extreme* cruelty." Esther Hawks, a northern doc-
tor and missionary working in Florida, wrote that she heard news "every
week of the shooting of negroes by infuriated white men, and no account is
made of it." The *Boston Advertiser* and *Cincinnati Gazette* copied reports to
the *New York Tribune* about "a record of crime and outrage" against African
Americans in Richmond, Virginia. Black men were assaulted, thrown in
jail, and robbed, and police were "gobbling-up the most likely looking negro
women" and putting them in jail, where they were "robbed and ravished at
the will of the guard." In North Carolina, reported a nearby paper, Blacks
"are being hunted down like dogs and dispatched without ceremony." In
the whole South "brutal murders" added up to "several hundred deaths per

day. . . . An Alabama paper says that this business has become so extensive and common that some planters even boast that they could manure their lands with the dead carcasses of negroes." An item copied from the *Raleigh Progress* said that after a slaveholder fled from his coastal plantation, slaves raised a crop, only to be ordered to leave when the war was over. They refused, so the former owner recruited white neighbors and killed six of the former slaves.[7]

A Republican newspaper in Delaware reported that "the chivalry" in a district of South Carolina were "beating the blacks, formerly slaves," and that the commanding U.S. general had had to intervene. In Fayetteville, North Carolina, "a negro was recently strung up by the thumbs, and received forty-nine lashes. The government has found it necessary to garrison the place with negro troops." An Indiana paper reported that across the river in Kentucky, whites were organizing mobs and violence against Blacks to drive them back to their former masters. Another tactic was to jail them and then permit new masters to buy them out of prison by paying a fine. Other Kentuckians a few months later were "abusing negro women and children, driving them from their homes and compelling them to sleep in the wet grass." The *New York Tribune* printed a troubling Associated Press dispatch from New Bern, North Carolina. Whites there "refuse to recognize the freedom of the blacks, who are whipped and tortured in the most fiendish manner for even expressing a desire to be free, and that shooting and killing these creatures appears to be the order of the day."[8]

The *Ottawa Free Trader* informed its readers that 140 Blacks had been killed by whites in Alabama. It quoted a letter from a Freedmen's Bureau officer that "for a black man to be seen with 'greenbacks' in his possession is death. Colored people are hiding in the woods, living on berries, fruits, etc., to escape the fury of their former masters." The homes of freed people were being burned down. A Vermont editor published a detailed letter from Louisiana that recounted a variety of abuses by planters who believed that compulsion of Black laborers was necessary: "On one plantation . . . one hundred field hands died . . . from being fed on condemned commissary stores. On another, over one hundred field hands were docked one month's pay each" because "*Providence*" allowed too much rain to fall, which interfered with labor. Bloodhounds tore at Black men's flesh, and the letter's author concluded, "I might go on enumerating acts of barbarity almost without number,—but enough." A judge who made "an extensive trip through the Southern States" reported "that cruelty to the freedmen and [the] number of homicides among them by the whites are increasing to a fearful extent. . . . The Judge has a copy of the *Southern Sun*, which says if the Yankees are alarmed at the killing of a few hundred negroes a day in States where they have the protection of the Yankee troops . . . what will be their alarm after the departure of the military forces and re-admission into the Union of these states as soverigh [*sic*] powers."[9]

Southern violence was an expression of hatred toward African Americans, the fruit of deep prejudice. Most former slave owners as well as former non-slaveholders lived by cultural assumptions founded on the supposed inferiority of African Americans. When General O. O. Howard, head of the Freedmen's Bureau, gave a speech warning of some hard times ahead but "hold[ing] out the ultimate promise of 'racial advancement and development,' " he met with aggressive rejection. Josiah Nott, an Alabama surgeon and racial theorist, attacked Howard's views "in an article excerpted in more than twenty southern newspapers." Nott claimed that any hope of progress by Blacks was a "phantasmagoria" because the cranial capacity of African Americans was "nine cubic inches less than those of the white man." Therefore, in his supposedly scientific judgment, "to talk about 'improving the race' was 'manifestly absurd.' " Southern whites who were less inclined to write supposedly scientific books and articles assumed the same thing.[10]

But racism and racist violence also was a means to dominate the freed people, control their labor, and replace slavery with a form of serfdom. One of Vermont's congressmen, Justin Morrill, visited the South and reported that former slave owners wanted to put conditions on freedom, and none "believed that slavery was actually gone." The *Philadelphia Press* warned in June that the slaves' former masters would attempt "to restore the horrors of an accursed system." By August it had received a detailed letter from an observer asserting that the goal was a form of peonage worse than slavery. Former owners wanted to be free of obligations to their laborers yet likewise free to drive off the old or infirm. Peonage would "keep the old slave material still in ignorance and degradation, as timber for the new system." With helpful laws, even "a small debt would, of necessity, consign the poor debtor to a long slavery." Such a system "has long been under Southern discussion," warned this writer, and "would be vastly more profitable to the planter, and a thousand times more dreadful to the negro than slavery ever has been."[11]

Such violence and oppression were all the more unjustified because African Americans were adjusting well to a free labor system. Free Black workers did not want to work if they were not paid, but with reasonable and dependable wages they were proving to be productive laborers. A Freedmen's Bureau report on agriculture in Arkansas appeared in the *New York Herald*. This report testified that the freed people "are generally working industriously and appear to appreciate freedom, without being disposed to abuse it." A Vermont Republican newspaper confirmed that in Louisiana opposition to the free labor system came from the white planters, not the Blacks. The assistant commissioner of the Freedmen's Bureau in Huntsville, Alabama, provided evidence that Black workers were sustaining themselves in freedom. He reported that between Nashville and Louisville, "there were 67 whites to one black man drawing rations from the government."[12]

From General Rufus Saxton's district in the Southeast came news that the more than 100,000 former slaves there were "absolutely self-sustaining, save those swept in the wake of Sherman's march." Even the *New York World* sometimes printed news that Black labor was doing well. On one day in Raleigh, North Carolina, it reported, thirty thousand rations were distributed, mainly to whites. "*There are few people at work besides the negroes,*" declared the report. Confederate officers and soldiers were merely "loafing about the streets." A correspondent of the *World* visited the Sea Islands. There, he reported, "over two hundred thousand acres of land [are] under cultivation by free labor." Some former slaves worked on contracts, others "on their own account." Blacks were profiting to the amount of $500 to $5,000 per year and had bank accounts totaling $140,000. These facts should "induce the whites to take hold of the free labor system" as the former slaves had done. The *Memphis Commercial* admitted that forty freedmen on an island below the city had raised 75 acres of cotton and 60 acres of corn and cut 1,200 cords of wood, a good showing.[13]

Southern whites ignored these examples because they were reacting with anger to emancipation, the loss of their human property, and the overthrow of their racial system. The spirit of caste, said a Pennsylvania editor, encouraged their "old barbarities and wrongs upon the race." The "conquered rebels acknowledge slavery to be dead, yet they are racking their brains to invent some mode by which they can avail themselves of the labor of their old slaves without compensation," and it would take time for such attitudes to change. *Harper's Weekly* wrote that southerners who "have themselves never lifted a finger to work, now complain that the negro is a dreadfully lazy fellow, and will work only upon compulsion." Holding on to the mentality bred of slavery, former slave owners want to return to "obsolete, inhuman, and dangerous prejudices and passions." A Republican paper in Kansas sought to explain why "in some places at the South the rebels kill the negroes if they refuse to be slaves." It concluded that southern whites remained "bitter in spirit" due to slavery's indoctrination in "prejudice and caste." The *New York Tribune* agreed that "slavery is dead, but its spirit survives."[14]

In Ohio a Republican paper shared with its readers an insightful, penetrating analysis of the prejudice of southern whites by copying an article from the Nashville *Colored Tennesseean*. That Black newspaper explained why whites reacted with such hostility to the slaves' new status: "It is hatred of the negro's progress." The change in his status provoked "hatred of his freedom, of his manhood, of the rights which belong to that condition, and the consequent curtailing of the bestial privileges" still claimed "by the vicious and the ruffianly." The more Blacks progressed, said the *Colored Tennesseean*, the angrier whites became. The *Cleveland Leader* warned northerners that "upon one thing we may rely—all the whites of the South *can do* to thwart us in our work of restoring the Nation they *will* do." Given their attitudes, disloyal southerners could regain power and "force [us] back into the position we occupied before the war," a position in which slavery's interests were dominant.[15]

Evidence from the South indicated that rancorous and unrepentant white leaders were regaining power. Local elections in Richmond, Virginia, said a Pennsylvania editor, should teach northerners an important lesson: "The whole ticket chosen were lately Rebels, and are probably Rebels still." Victorious candidates boasted of "los[ing] a leg in the Confederate service" or of having a "number of his sons who had died in the cause of the Rebellion." The contest was over who could "prove the greatest complicity with treason," and no candidates were staunch advocates of the Union. A Maryland paper agreed that in Virginia's elections "the regular Secession candidates have been uniformly successful. The vilest and most blatant Rebels" want to guide the state back into the Union. In another report from Mississippi, this paper concluded that former Confederates "are more violently rebellious than ever." A Republican paper in Michigan noticed that citizens in a Georgia county had resolved they would submit to the Constitution *"for the present"* only and were eager to put down crime, "especially among the black population." It also reprinted an article from a nearby journal saying that southerners coming to Washington for pardons "are open in their avowals of adherence to the principles for which they have fought, and of their disregard of . . . oaths of allegiance."[16]

A Republican newspaper in Kansas alerted readers that the provisional governor of South Carolina, Benjamin Perry, had "bewail[ed] the failure of the Confederacy" and incited anger toward "Northern Vandals." An Ohio editor noted that Perry had ranked Robert E. Lee on a par with George Washington and lamented "the humiliation and degradation of going back into the Union." Similarly, the *Boston Advertiser* commented that Perry's speech was a "mixture of disloyalty and submission, of unrepentant reason and of sober counsel." It included the prediction that freedom would be a curse to African Americans. In Louisiana, reported the *Chicago Tribune*, Governor James Madison Wells was registering the disloyal "generally" and causing loyal men to despair even of staying in the state. A more loyal governor in Arkansas had become so troubled by "the ingratitude and rebellious spirit evinced by the leading returned rebels" that he had decided he would not and could not recommend any more pardons.[17]

Andrew Johnson's pardons were a major part of the problem, declared many Republican newspapers. The *Independent* in Oskaloosa, Kansas, protested that "President Johnson is sending all the rebels back to the South, to vote and control affairs in their respective States. . . . This may be wise policy, but we 'can't see it.'" Another Kansas editor worried that the Democrats were "win[ning] President Johnson's Administration over to their purposes," despite the fact that "The First Essential" in Reconstruction was to civilize the rebels—something that might take twenty-five years. An Ohio paper agreed that the president's appointments "may well fill the country with lively apprehension" and was concerned about the number of pardon applications. "Won't Do to Pardon" was the headline in an Indiana journal that warned against "too free use of the pardoning power" for rebels whose "defiant and insolent conduct" showed they "have not yet dropped a tear of repentance." A Delaware paper was certain that the founders never assumed "that hundreds and thousands of red-handed, unrepentant traitors and criminals, would be amnestied or pardoned by the President, without the form of trial." This paper also quoted General John A. Logan, formerly a Democratic congressman from Illinois, as saying "he did not like this wholesale system of pardoning rebels." Johnson was restoring their rights before they "had brought forth fruits meet for repentance."[18]

As evidence accumulated during the summer, many northern Republicans began to conclude that the president's policy was not working. A correspondent to a Vermont newspaper declared that it "will prove a failure." Pardons to wealthy whites might be economically necessary, but Congress would have to insist on Black suffrage "as a condition of general amnesty to the rich whites." A Kansas editor agreed in August that "the President's pet plan of reconstruction, by appointing as Governors of the seceded States, bogus or half-hearted Union men, who are acceptable to the rebels, will prove a failure." Instead of a weak policy, "Radical Military governors, plenty of troops, and iron rule, are the things needed down South."[19]

Newspapers carried reports that General Judson Kilpatrick had concluded from his travels in the South that most former rebels were not to be trusted. As soon as they managed to reenter the Union, he believed, they would persecute Union men and African Americans and attempt to reenslave the Blacks as well as repudiate the national debt. Kilpatrick declared that Reconstruction "has been commenced at least four years too soon." A Maryland editor agreed because "the same malignant and destroying spirit" of the previous thirty years was "manifesting" itself again. When a Republican newspaper in Indiana learned that Carl Schurz had been appointed to make an inspection trip through the South, it saw "little doubt that he will vote the President's experiment a failure." Nowhere had this paper "seen indications that the rebels repent of their rebellion. . . . They are the most arrogant submissionists we ever heard of. . . . They boast of their deeds of arms, including we presume, the starvation of helpless prisoners."[20]

The treatment of Union Army prisoners, especially at Andersonville, remained a sore point for Republican activists as well as prisoners' families. One editor came across a letter written by Confederate general P. G. T. Beauregard in 1862. Beauregard had asked about possible legislation to execute abolitionist prisoners of war and, according to this newspaper, had advocated the "black flag." The paper was glad that a U.S. officer had recently been sent to Andersonville to make a special investigation of "the brutal treatment of Union prisoners there." An editorial column in the *Cleveland Leader* demanded justice against the "fiends in human form" who had "practice[d] horrible cruelties" on Union prisoners. The worst of those fiends, according to a Vermont editor, was Henry Wirz, who presided over

"The Horrors of Andersonville." The revelations of his trial were "likely to fasten upon the rebels a degree of infamy eclipsing" even the "guilt of their treason and rebellion." *Harper's Weekly* denied that men who "gloried in the torture of our soldiers" should be considered "our political brethren." A writer in *Harper's New Monthly Magazine* also wondered if Jefferson Davis in his prison cell ever thought of "the hapless victims of Andersonville and Belle Isle." He was "a Moral Criminal" who had been aware of "the starving, the freezing, the slow reduction of human beings to idiocy by exposure, by hunger, by contact with filth and disease."[21]

For all these reasons Republican newspapers argued that a different policy on Reconstruction was needed, both to protect the Union victory and to produce the right results. They also agreed, almost unanimously, that an essential, vital element of a different policy was Black suffrage. The *Syracuse Journal* listed all the reasons freedmen should vote: they were loyal, they had fought as and aided U.S. soldiers and prisoners, they would support Republican policies, they paid taxes, they were as literate as "thousands upon thousands of white citizens throughout the South," and they deserved to vote and needed the ballot for self-protection. A Kansas editor agreed that suffrage was "necessary" as a "means of protecting their freedom." Without the ballot and "without any civil rights," freed people would be "at the mercy of their former oppessors [*sic*]" and "worse off free, than they were as slaves."[22]

Vermont's Republicans urged the former slave states to take notice of the fact that the Green Mountain State had a "happy experience" with a suffrage exercised by "native or naturalized citizens of quiet and peaceable behavior, irrespective of color or race." The Vermonters predicted "inestimable blessings" would flow from this policy, but if "any reorganized State" failed to allow Black suffrage, "we insist that Congress" must act "to secure a republican government, both in form and essence, to the people of such State." An Indiana paper quoted two army officers in favor of Black suffrage, both on the same day. General James Brishbin, a native Pennsylvanian, spoke out in Louisville, Kentucky, in favor of the right to vote for all men of at least twenty-one years. The paper also quoted a letter to the *Indianapolis Journal* from another veteran officer who defended manhood suffrage and called it "an indisputable and humiliating fact" that Negroes had shown "more intelligence and more patriotism . . . than a large class of [illegible] white men in the North."[23]

The *New York Tribune* continued its campaign for Black suffrage plus a generous reconciliation with southern whites. But it demanded to know "why those who have done their best to destroy our country" should be allowed to vote when "those who have done their best to preserve it" are denied the ballot. The *Tribune* hoped that the "latent force in the Right," in morality and justice, would prevail. The *Chicago Tribune* published a letter arguing that Johnson had "no right to clothe the rebels and traitors with the elective franchise" but "deprive the loyal blacks of the greatest of their newly acquired and well earned rights of citizenship." Later it argued that Black suffrage was necessary because if only whites could vote in the South, "will not that whole section speedily fall under the control of the rebel leaders?" By September the paper asserted that "the Northern people," if permitted to vote on the question, clearly "would give as large a majority to-day for extending the ballot to the negro race in some form, (say to the colored soldiers, to those who could read and write, and to the tax-paying), as they gave last fall to elect Abraham Lincoln." Republicans "cannot as a party repudiate the principle of universal suffrage. The whole world knows we believe in it."[24]

An "intimate friend" of Andrew Johnson who was elected to Congress from the Knoxville area foresaw that the North would require Black suffrage. During the Civil War, he pointed out to southerners, "the nation was not eager to resort to emancipation, but you forced a resort to that measure by obstinate rebellion." The same was true of the decision to enlist Blacks as soldiers: "If the nation finds that all its magnanimous offers to you are in vain . . . it will be very apt to give suffrage to the negro population." Rightly perceiving the thoughts of many Republicans, he predicted that "the nation will be compelled to resort to negro suffrage for self-preservation, especially for the preservation of the white loyalists of the South."[25]

The *Atlantic Monthly* denied that "victory has smitten us with impotence." What the North "must" do is "the prescribing of the qualifications of voters." Democrats and Andrew Johnson, by claiming the North could not dictate who voted, were using states' rights to "shield" rebellion "from Federal regulation in defeat." "Loyal citizens" were needed in the reconstructed South, and former slaves needed "the power of political self-protection" provided in the ballot. "Unless we are destitute of the commonest practical reason," said the *Atlantic Monthly*, "negro suffrage is . . . the logical sequence of negro emancipation." If it were denied and the South gained representation from the end of slavery, rebels would try to repudiate the national debt. The federal government, it concluded, must require "a republican form of government" in southern states or "hold them in the grasp of the military power of the nation."[26]

Northern Republicans did not want a still rebellious South to gain more power than it had before the war, and support was growing for the idea that the South must be kept out of Congress until loyalty was assured. The views of many were summed up by a Dartmouth College professor in an address to that college's Phi Beta Kappa Society. "Instead of working our brains this week on the great question of the day," wrote the *Vermont Watchman and State Journal*, it made sense to publish much of the address. Professor Alpheus Crosby began by arguing that the southern states were "*out of*" the Union "as a governing partnership, but in it as a governed community." That is, their situation after rebellion was "simply that of territories." In states like South Carolina, he declared, hardly "a baker's dozen" of truly loyal voters could be found. To regain their rights, white southerners were taking the amnesty oath "with a mental reservation," and southern newspapers were even excusing perjury. "The determination of the influential classes at the South is manifestly to keep just as much as possible of slavery, aristocracy, State sovereignty, and disloyalty," in order to make the North's victory "barren" and to "conquer by political action and party intrigue." Black southerners, however, had shown "an intelligence not to be deceived . . . a valor not to be daunted." These were "the appropriate attributes of a citizen and a voter." Therefore, Crosby favored Black suffrage, in his view "with the requisition of an ability to read and write." Congress had a "duty . . . to keep all candidates for admission on probation" until loyalty was assured and it was impossible "to revive slavery, or to establish serfdom in its place." Professor Crosby also favored seizing and subdividing the estates of "great land-holding barons" so that the numbers of landowners could be "greatly increased." The war "has abundantly authorized" confiscation, which would benefit "poor whites" as well.[27]

Confiscation was the centerpiece of the address that Thaddeus Stevens, the leading Radical Republican in the House, delivered in Lancaster, Pennsylvania, on September 6. He proposed to confiscate almost 400 million acres by taking land from individuals who owned over 200 acres. By giving 40 acres to every Black head of household, 40 million acres would provide opportunity to the freed people, and the sale of the remaining nine-tenths of the land would defray most of the Union's large and looming debt. "The whole fabric of Southern society must be changed," argued Stevens, and "never can it be done if this opportunity is lost." Without these measures, he insisted, "this government can never be, as it never has been, a true republic."[28]

Stevens's views were in the vanguard of Radical opinion; most members of his party were not so determined. But most northern Republicans were convinced that President Johnson's plan was not succeeding and that stronger measures were necessary. That fact received confirmation when a committee of leading businessmen in Boston published an address "to the President." Speaking as citizens after being given their assignment at a meeting of the Board of Trade, they understood Johnson's desire to complete the process of reunion. But they argued strongly for the necessity of "delay, and even, should it be necessary, a protracted delay." Emancipation had ended slavery, under whose system only three-fifths of the slave population had been counted for purposes of representation. It was not "either just or prudent to restore to" the rebellious southerners their previous power in Congress and "at the same time make them a present of the other two-fifths." If white southerners gained additional representation while Blacks were not allowed to vote, whites in South Carolina, for example, would command with their suffrage two and a half times the power of patriotic voters in Iowa. The country's safety and the Union's "great debt" would be endangered. African Americans in the South were "enthusiastically loyal," and their "assistance" as soldiers helped to win the war. There was no danger that their votes would be controlled by their former owners. The "determined opposition to freedman suffrage" by white southerners revealed their awareness of that fact. The freedmen deserved protection, yet "already we see," while military control continued, that southern legislatures were taking away "all power of self-protection and self-defence." Few northerners, declared these merchants and business leaders, accepted the idea that "the colored race . . . should be permanently disfranchised." Some wanted to wait "until they are better prepared," but "what preparation, what improvement, can be hoped for" when the freed people's enemies hold all the power over them? "The nation cannot do so great a wrong," asserted this address, nor permit "disfranchisement . . . to do the work of slavery." Delay in readmission was essential. It would protect the nation and allow a "rapidly ripening" public opinion to mature and settle on universal suffrage or some type of qualified suffrage.[29]

The nation remained in the grip of bitter sectional conflict and was not ready to experience a true reunion. Not only did events in the South demonstrate that fact, but in addition social contacts revealed that wartime's bitter feelings remained strong. The *Philadelphia Inquirer* described the atmosphere at a "famous summer resort in the Virginia mountains." Two respectable Yankee ladies were treated "with contumely and marked incivility" by "the *effete* and detestable aristocracy of Virginia." Not only did Virginians refuse to associate with Yankees, but a Georgia clergyman "intruded himself on one of the Yankee ladies, and entertained her with a long discourse as to how much better in every respect a southern lady was than a northern one." According to this man, southern ladies were "more beautiful, more stately, more accomplished, and more virtuous." The "Disposition of the South," concluded a Kansas editor, was almost "as bitter in spirit now as . . . in the hight of the secession fever."[30]

As Republican newspapers made the case for Black suffrage and against any speedy readmission of the southern states, they did not neglect to answer the Democratic opposition. Early in the summer many editors recognized that the Democrats were going to oppose Black suffrage and do so with virulent racism. A meeting of Democratic leaders at the beginning of July reached agreement on treating African Americans as a race "greatly inferior to the whites," and Republicans knew that strong racist rhetoric would follow. Therefore, in addition to arguments for the rightness and necessity of Black suffrage, Republicans undertook efforts to contradict Democratic attacks. One important strategy was to defuse, even ridicule, fears that Black suffrage would lead to social equality.[31]

A Republican newspaper in Ohio used history and the reasoning of a Kentucky editor to prove that the right to vote did not lead to equality, mixed public schools, visits "in gentlemen's parlors," or the much-feared amalgamation. Where, after all, was hostile prejudice obviously very acute? In the slave states, was the answer, and yet "in every Southern State, except South Carolina, the right of suffrage was originally exercised by all 'freemen,'" some of whom were Black. Free African Americans voted in Tennessee, Maryland, North Carolina, and Pennsylvania into the 1830s. "Was amalgamation any more common in those days than it is now?" The opposition was "offensively talking" about social equality, but its warnings insulted "common sense."[32]

Yet humor could be more effective than facts and historical data, and Republican newspapers made good use of the amusing, satirical writings of

Petroleum Nasby. The Nasby pieces were the creation of David Ross Locke, who owned and edited one Republican newspaper in Findley, Ohio, and wrote for and edited another in Toledo. His fictional creation, Petroleum Nasby, was a poorly educated Copperhead, champion of the Democratic Party, supporter of the Confederacy, defender of slavery, and inveterate racist. Newspapers across the North, from the Atlantic Coast westward to Michigan and Kansas, made use of Nasby's penetrating commentary on Black suffrage and the issues of Reconstruction.

In June, for example, papers like the *Cincinnati Commercial* and the *Hillsdale Standard* of Michigan published Nasby's prescription for the Democracy's campaign themes. Worried that "the surrender ov our armies to Grant and Sherman, hez hurt us" and that "we hev no way uv keepin our voters together," Nasby came to the party's rescue: "Ther will alluz be a Democrisy, so long ez there's a nigger." Spanish bull fighters "inflame the bull to extra cavortin" by waving a red flag, and "ween yoo desire a democrat to froth at the mouth, you will find a black fase will anser that purpus. There4 the niggir is, to-day, our best and only holt. Let us use him." Nasby proceeded to

> lay down a few plain rools to be observed, in order to make the most uv the cappytle we hev: 1. Alluz assert that the nigger will never be able to take care uv hisslef, but will always be a public burden. He may possibly give us the lie by goin to work. In sich a emergency the dooty ov every Dimecrat is plane. He must not be allowed to work. . . .
> 2. Likewise assert that the nigger will come North and take all the good places, thorwic all uv our skild mekaniks out ov work by under bidden ov em.

Nasby admitted that rule no. 2 thereby "crosses slitely Rool the 1" but the contradiction did not worry him. "Nigger equality" could always be used to advantage, because "all men, without distinction uv secks, air fond ov flatrin theirselves that sumbody's lower down in the skale uv humanity than they is. Ef twan'fer niggers what wood the Dimocrisy do fer sumbody 2 look down upon?" Columns in this vein took some of the vitriol out of Democrats' racist attacks.[33]

On the subject of Reconstruction, Petroleum Nasby had a dream in July. During his nightly slumber, time jumped nine months ahead and, dreaming, he saw the glorious results of a South "consillyated and recontructid." Prominent secessionists and Confederate generals now were representing the readmitted states. Moreover, "the ginooine Dimocrisy uv the North hed enuffh members to give the South controle uv Congris." From the House gallery he saw a New York representative propose a monument "to the memry uv the Union soljers who fell at Gettysburg." Fortunately, two former Confederate generals and one "kernel . . . walked over to his seet, and with their canes beat him over the hed, twenty or fifteen minits. He wuz carried out fer ded." Southerners then boasted of their generosity in drawing their pay "in greenbax . . . notwithstanding every wun uv em bears the portrait uv that fiendish ape, that thirster after gore, that destroyer of habis corpusis and constooshnel rites, our late lamented President." Northern Democrats stood up for additional measures of reconciliation, such as a rule that "the word 'war' shall never be yoosed in the halls," that "no book be publisht givin any akount uv prison life or sich," and that any future "hallooshuns to our military fame [come] soley from the Mexikin war." At that point Nasby "awoke from this refreshin sleep" and reflected that "so long ez we hev a Suthern Dimocrisy to demand, and a Northern Dimekrat to give, all will be well. Bless the lord."[34]

Thus Republicans were developing a strengthened conviction that Black suffrage was necessary and that formerly rebellious states were in no condition to rejoin the Union and reclaim their seats in Congress. Some support for Black suffrage came from principle, but evidence of various kinds showed that Johnson's policy was not working, and therefore Black suffrage was needed to safeguard loyalty, northern interests, and the progress of the Union. With these ideas and arguments Republican editors and their readers prepared for fall elections in several of the northern states. How closely would Republican candidates follow their lead? The campaigns of the fall would be hard-fought and end in many victories. But there also would be complications and defections that placed limits on what could be accomplished for Black suffrage in 1865.

9

Toward Elections

The Atlantic cable excited a great deal of interest during the late summer and early fall of 1865, even surpassing the approaching execution of Henry Wirz, commander of Andersonville prison. Many publications monitored the progress of this ambitious project, and as one popular magazine put it, the hearts of "the public . . . throb[bed] with alternate hope and fear." An illustration in *Harper's Weekly* showed King Neptune ordering a bevy of beautiful mermaids to stop playing on the cable, for "that's the way t'other one was wrecked!" But success was not certain, and the public's emotions rose and fell as news proved to be favorable or discouraging. More than once the cable's prospects grew brighter or slipped into shadow, because real progress was made but undeniable setbacks also occurred.[1]

After various positive dispatches, on August 23 the *New York Tribune* headlined page one, "The Atlantic Cable a Failure." The *Great Eastern*, the steamship that was playing out the cable, had lost its signal a week earlier, and the breaking of the cable "may now be considered certain. No commercial misadventure of modern times has ever excited more wide-spread interest and deep regret than this almost national disaster." It was feared that "the 1,250 miles paid out is lost—is severed from the ship, and now lying useless at the bottom of the Atlantic."[2]

Five days later the front page of the *Tribune* featured a map of the Atlantic, with "Further Particulars of the Loss" of the cable. Papers throughout the North competed for details, and in Vermont one journal quoted various London newspapers as well as opinions from expert engineers on whether the "effort to haul the Cable and repair it" might succeed. The *New York Herald* told its readers that a buoy marked the spot where the cable parted, only "600 miles distant from the coast of New Foundland." Ships had not "abandoned all hopes" of recovering and "eventually laying the cable." Then in mid-September *Harper's Weekly* devoted two full pages, including a large illustration, to celebrate how the ships were able to grapple a lost cable, even at "2000 fathoms" deep. The article further described how crews worked to splice the broken cable and repair the damage. Nevertheless, hopes of completing the project in 1865 faded, and readers looked toward 1866 when efforts would, in fact, be successful.[3]

The drama of the Atlantic cable mirrored the fortunes of Black suffrage, which made important progress but also suffered telling reverses in 1865. During the late summer and fall the right to vote for African Americans gained stronger support in some states and among many elements of the Republican Party. But it also met with reverses—racist Democratic opposition, defections by some Republicans, and then voters' rejection in certain states. These reverses effectively doomed its prospects for that calendar year. Before December it was becoming clear that conclusive support for Black suffrage would not materialize in 1865, either in the North or within all parts of the Republican Party. This chapter covers the first part of those developments.

During the late summer and fall the discussion of voting rights took on a more exclusively political tone, for elections to many statewide offices were approaching in the North. Arguments for Black suffrage still were based, in part, on principle, with emphasis on the nation's ideals or the moral duty of paying a debt to African American soldiers. But considerations of safeguarding the hard-won victory, ensuring the Union's future, or thwarting the disloyal became more significant. To Republican campaigners, the Democratic Party remained the sanctuary of Copperheads, states'-rights ideologues, and enemies of the Union. Commitment to the war's goals had to continue, argued Republicans, to the point of victory in politics. Democrats held onto their principles, often to a reactionary extent. They stressed that the wartime emergency was over and that sound party principles of limited government, low taxes, and local autonomy should prevail. Many continued to condemn all aspects of Republican policies during the war or before, in the sectional crisis. Most significantly, racism and white supremacy were essential and emotive parts of the Democrats' appeals. With emancipation, the party's devotion to white supremacy was increasing. Democrats faced growing acceptance of the need for Black suffrage among many Republicans, but by mobilizing racist and white supremacist emotions, they aimed to blunt its progress.

Belief in equal rights had gained ground in the North through four years of war and the first months of Reconstruction, but public sentiment was not uniform, and racism remained potent. Ideals of racial equality or equal treatment under the law were vibrant among some Republican editors and officeholders everywhere, but they were most firmly established in New England. There Republican leaders took their stand in favor of Blacks' right to vote. Vermont Republicans held their convention early, in July, and quickly showed that they were "in favor of universal suffrage." They were so convinced, wrote one editor, that Black suffrage was "a matter of indispensable justice" and a benefit for both southern states and the nation, that they demanded it be adopted voluntarily or required. While maintaining confidence in the patriotism of President Johnson, they declared that "all native and naturalized citizens" must have a "constitutional guaranty" of "equality of civil and political rights." If any southern state failed to provide that guaranty, then "Congress shall use all its constitutional powers" to secure a true republican government.[4]

Early in August Maine's Republicans set a similar example by declaring the necessity for a thoroughgoing Reconstruction with Black suffrage. After a standard statement of support for President Johnson, the state's Union convention declared that the government had a "duty . . . to hold the States under provisional government" until the character and behavior of the former rebels was satisfactory. Not only must the Thirteenth Amendment be ratified but there also must be "the removal of all disability on account of color" and the securing "to all" of "perfect equality." The enlistment "of over 100,000 colored troops" and "the good faith of the colored race amidst treason" meant that "the national honor" was pledged to ensure "all the rights of freedom." The vote on these positions was unanimous.[5]

Massachusetts's Republicans opened their convention with an "eloquent speech" by Charles Sumner, who warned that "neither the Rebellion or Slavery is yet ended. . . . The Whole Black Code . . . must give place" to "equality before the law," and the former slaves must have "the full panoply of citizenship." An impartial suffrage was needed, said Sumner, along with education for all southerners. The convention then adopted resolutions that pledged goodwill toward Andrew Johnson while promising vigilance over the South, demanded that no southern state be readmitted until its constitution secured to all "the inalienable right to liberty and the pursuit of happiness," called for "condign punishment" of those "especially guilty" of the rebellion, and warned against a seizure of power by southern rebels and their northern sympathizers. The convention did not commit to any particular theory of suffrage, such as universal manhood suffrage or impartial suffrage, but it stood firm on the idea that it was unacceptable to "admit to the elective franchise Rebel soldiers and traitorous politicians, and at the same time exclude the loyal men who have borne arms and shed their blood in the nation's defense, and whose votes may be indispensable hereafter."[6]

In Connecticut, where the Thirteenth Amendment gained ratification without a single negative vote, Republicans succeeded in putting on the ballot an amendment to the state constitution. The amendment would broaden suffrage by deleting the word "white" from the existing provision, which required voters to be able to read and write. Fewer than 2 percent of the state's population was African American, and Republicans urged this change to remove "an unreasonable and unjust discrimination, which exists in no other New England State." The Union State Central Committee called on voters to approve the measure, saying, "Old prejudices have melted away in the fires of the great contest. Loyalty everywhere welcomes and honors true loyalty." A group named Connecticut for Impartial Suffrage published a pamphlet presenting the favorable arguments made by various officials, and Republican newspapers joined the effort. The *Hartford Daily Courant*, for example, urged a vote "with right, and reason on our side. . . . This simple act of justice," it said, would recognize that "all men are born free and equal." The *Norwich Weekly Courier* contended that "aristocracy" was the only system based on "superiority of birth or race." The *New York Tribune* tried to cheer Connecticut's Republicans on, urging "our friends" to "advance with the times" and to stress "the sense of justice, and the fundamental principles of Democracy."[7]

Outside New England many Republican activists also campaigned for Black suffrage. Minnesota's Union Convention declared for the measure, in a state where there were fewer than 500 African Americans in a population of 172,000. Republican editors in Mankato and Faribault used the pages of their newspapers to argue for principle and practicality. "The spirit of our institutions," they said, required that "the measure of a man's political rights shall be neither his religion, his birthplace, his race, his color, nor any merely physical characteristic." Black men had fought for the Union and deserved "the perfect equality of all men before the laws," which was "the fundamental principle of true democracy." Denial of the suffrage would bring "peonage and serfdom" and "preserve the causes of the rebellion." Moreover, emancipation meant that the South was going to "gain fifteen representatives in Congress," whether it increased its voting population or not. With that additional support, warned the Minnesota Republicans, prejudiced Copperheads might soon oppose "free suffrage to the foreigner."[8]

In Iowa Black suffrage was the dominant issue between Republicans and Democrats. Edward Russell, a prominent Republican from Davenport, led the effort "to make an emphatic declaration in favor of Negro suffrage," which the state's voters had turned down in 1857. He succeeded, and the party's convention called for the beginning of a constitutional process to remove the word "white" as a requirement to vote. Some Republicans, such as Congressman Hiram Price, sincerely wanted to "wip[e] out the last vestige of the black code that has long been a disgrace to our State," but others feared that Democrats would be able to use anti-Black prejudice against the party. Editors of some Republican papers tried to minimize the issue by noting that the question would be decided by the state's voters and that any change would take two or three years, in accord with legal procedures. But Democrats made Black suffrage the central issue by encouraging what they claimed was a spontaneous movement of returning soldiers. A "Soldiers' State Convention" fiercely opposed Black suffrage, and Democrats promptly endorsed that group's candidates for office. Republicans denounced these actions as a Copperhead trick, but Black suffrage clearly had become the campaign's main issue.[9]

Pennsylvania did not have a gubernatorial election in 1865, and only lesser state offices were to be contested. The Republican state convention said little directly about Black suffrage, probably because some feared that "*Negro Suffrage*" would allow "Copperheadism to *rule* this *State* again." One letter writer warned Thaddeus Stevens that if he ran "upon the footing of Negro Suffrage" he would "be defeated in Lancaster County," where Stevens made his home. But the *Chicago Tribune* reported that Pennsylvania Republicans had already committed to the position that no state should be readmitted until it granted "equal rights to all men, white or black." On other issues Pennsylvania Republicans adopted the kinds of measures for Reconstruction that Thaddeus Stevens advocated. They urged the confiscation of rebel estates "over $10,000 in value, to pay pensions" to Union soldiers and reduce the federal debt. Black suffrage would be the prominent issue, as Democrats in the state vowed to oppose "negro suffrage and negro equality" and declared that "white citizens ought never to be degraded by the admission of the negro to the rights of citizenship."[10]

Notably strong arguments for Black suffrage came from some Republican editors in Kansas. The *Big Blue Union* in Marysville, Kansas, asserted that agitation "will not cease until all men in this Union are indeed free and enjoy political rights." Black suffrage "inevitably follow[ed]" from emancipation and embodied "the democratic principle which is the corner stone of our Republic. . . . There is no virtue in blue eyes; no inherent priveliges in yellow hair." This paper also agreed with Stevens that the rebellious states were now "a conquered enemy, to be dealt with as such." Another Republican journal reminded any prejudiced soldiers that southern slaves had "befriend[ed] them in the enemy's country" and that "freed negroes should have the means of protecting their freedom." After Black citizens in Oskaloosa rallied for the right to vote, the local Republican paper demanded strong measures. Loyal men, it declared, "*are the nation.*" Readmission should not be hasty, a stable government should "protect the rights of all citizens," and the "old masters" should regain no power "until their recent slaves are secured from their domination beyond a peradventure."[11]

Wisconsin, where the Black population was roughly one thousand out of three-quarters of a million people, also put Black suffrage on the fall ballot. Republican advocates there, however, faced opposition within their ranks. Senator James Doolittle, who had advocated colonization persistently during the war, opposed Black suffrage and warned that it would lead to a war of the races. When the party's platform, drafted by Doolittle, did not endorse Black suffrage, supporters organized a second "Union Mass Convention" that demanded equal and impartial suffrage in Wisconsin, the ratification of the Thirteenth Amendment by southern states, and a new amendment to the U.S. Constitution that would make representation depend on "the number of qualified male electors" rather than population. Republicans argued for "justice over treason," praised Black soldiers who "helped conquer treason," and blasted the Democratic Party's "disgraceful peace platform" of 1864. In Milwaukee Black citizens also met to affirm their loyalty and seek recognition of their right to vote.[12]

Like Senator Doolittle, however, not all Republican politicians or editors were ready to share the commitment to Black suffrage, and geographically Republicans had areas of relative weakness. New York and New Jersey for some time had been states where Republicans contended against a strong Democratic opposition. Nominees in those two states often remained cautious on racial issues in order to prevail. The *New York Times* was a prominent example of this caution, supporting both Andrew Johnson's exclusion of Blacks from voting and the state party's resolution that states have "jurisdiction over all their local and domestic affairs." New York's Republican State Convention merely hoped that when southern states regained their authority, it would "be exercised in a spirit of equal and impartial justice, and with a view to the elevation and preparation for the full rights of citizenship of all their people."[13]

In states that bordered the Ohio River, such as Ohio, Indiana, and Illinois, southern counties had always exhibited many anti-Black attitudes, for men of southern backgrounds were numerous there. Across the river in Kentucky anti-Black emotions also were strong. As it happened, some of the earliest political contests developed in that region, and consequently those campaigns revealed the timidity of some Republicans who campaigned

Senator James Doolittle was but one example of the racist element within the Republican Party that did not support Black suffrage. (ca. 1860–75; Brady-Handy Photograph Collection, Library of Congress, Prints and Photographs Division, LC-DIG-cwpbh-00204)

before a more prejudiced electorate than their colleagues in New England. The contests of 1865 further revealed that some men who had joined the Republican Party in the 1850s had been antislavery yet unsupportive or positively hostile on issues of racial equality and Black suffrage.

Divided attitudes about the right to vote were plainly evident in Ohio, where the progress toward equal suffrage had not converted all members of the Republican Party. Communities such as Oberlin, in the northern part of the state, had long been fervently abolitionist, in contrast to some southern counties, where there was a great deal of prejudice. During the war the governor's chair had been occupied by two War Democrats who accepted nomination on the Union ticket: David Tod and John Brough. Tod served only one term because he alienated Republicans by his lack of enthusiasm for abolition. Brough's Unionism was of a stronger kind and more acceptable to Republicans, but after Appomattox the Ohio Republicans planned to choose their own nominee.

Opinion coalesced around General Jacob Cox, a lawyer and politician who had served creditably as a volunteer in the army. Ohio's Republicans planned to hold their nominating convention in August, and before that date pro-suffrage leaders from Oberlin challenged Cox about his views on suffrage. His rather surprising answers showed that not all Ohio Republicans were ready to take a clear and positive stand. Cox's positions were illustrative of gaps in the Republican Party's views on race, and they foreshadowed a fissure that would affect the party elsewhere. A number of conservative Republicans, particularly men who had been Democrats before 1856, began to desert the party. The unfolding of the campaign in Ohio also illustrated the problems that would hamper Black suffrage before the reconvening of Congress.

Cox's views on race and the future of the former slaves were summarized in the *Cincinnati Gazette.* He held "that the white and colored people of the South cannot live together as equals, politically, and he therefore favors a peaceable separation of the two races, on Southern soil, the blacks in their separate condition, to enjoy full political rights." Cox suggested that territory in South Carolina, Georgia, Alabama, and Florida could become a place for freed people to live "in a dependency of the Union analogous to the western territories." There they could gain education, homesteads, and "full and executive political privileges." Then, in an evasive addition, he pledged to support whatever Congress and the president decided about this issue.[14]

When Cox, as nominee, opened the campaign on August 15 he tried to focus attention not on race but on the wartime records of the two parties. Republicans had defended the nation, defeated the Confederacy, and overthrown the doctrine of states' rights. In contrast the Democracy had "in every possible way endeavored to . . . paralyze the efforts of the Government." Democrats had "applauded the rebel leaders," assailed Lincoln, opposed the draft, encouraged desertions, and urged abandoning the noble cause it called "a failure." The lesson for voters in 1865 should be clear—only the Republican Party deserved their loyalty. This emphasis on the wartime record of the two parties seemed a winning strategy to other Ohio leaders, including Congressman John Bingham, whose devotion to Black suffrage was unquestionable. Bingham would emphasize that fall that "by supporting the Union candidates you support your friends, the tried friends of the Union. By supporting the Democratic candidates you support the friends of secession, the advocates of disunion, the tried and firm supporters of that rebellion which has filled the land with sorrow and ridged it all over with graves."[15]

In regard to the position of the former slaves, Cox insisted that the nation had a "duty" to "make their freedom real and complete." But he foresaw great difficulty. It seemed necessary to "weigh the prejudices and the enmities of men; the antipathies and even the wicked hatred which may exist." All classes of white southerners were prejudiced and were "positively refusing to be placed upon an equality with the black man." They would make African Americans "a subject and servile race." In Cox's reasoning, that reality produced two "divergent but . . . progressive" alternatives. Either "all classes and colors" should enjoy "complete enfranchisement" or each race could "tak[e] its own way" and move forward toward "whatever intelligence and prosperity it is capable of." Then he promptly added, "Fortunately for us, the question is not now pressed upon us. Our State Convention very wisely and judiciously declined to interfere with it, preferring to confide its solution to the wisdom and patriotism of those at the head of national affairs."[16]

Cox's idea for a form of internal colonization, as well as his desire to avoid a clear position on Black suffrage, attracted extensive criticism. The *Ashtabula Weekly Telegraph* dismissed his colonization idea as "impracticable" and reasoned that "if the two races cannot live together in their new relation," putting them in "distinct but contiguous locality" would not achieve "harmony." Despite the fact of prejudice against Blacks, this Republican editor declared it was necessary to "acknowledge their manhood, put them in the possession and exercise of the rights and immunities to which they in their partial development and according to the law of nature are entitled." He pointed out that many antislavery Union men dissented from Cox's views. Other Republican papers reacted with "regret and dissent" and argued that the war had been too costly to "allow the claims of party to over-ride those of mankind." Additional criticisms came from the *New York Tribune,* the *Albany Journal,* the *Chicago Tribune,* and "other leading Union journals." Some of these papers quoted General O. O. Howard, head of the Freedmen's Bureau, who said, "I know that I can employ a negro, and he and I can live together." To solve any conflict, Howard recommended that people "get more of the spirit of Christ." Judge William Dickson of Cincinnati, one of the founders of the party, blasted Cox's views as "essentialy those of Calhoun" and urged Republicans to follow "the golden rule of our most holy religion." "The elective franchise," said a Republican candidate for the state senate, "should be based upon loyalty to the constitution and Union, recognizing and affirming the equality of all men before the law." The *Cleveland Leader* published a long letter critical of Cox and agreed on the "necessity of giving the ballot to the freedmen as a measure of protection to the Union against the 'new peril' which threatens it from the rampant disloyalty of Southern whites."[17]

Cox would defend himself by saying that while a student at Oberlin he had "laid aside personal prejudices" and that his idea respected freed people's wishes. Apparently he was aware of General Sherman's interview with Black leaders in Savannah after the March to the Sea, for Cox asserted, "The colored people themselves say that they would rather live apart than with those who had been their oppressors." As the campaign progressed, he added that the policy on Black suffrage should be national, but if the decision were to be made state by state, he would favor it in Ohio. This led Democratic editors to charge that Cox was trying to obscure his support for Black suffrage.[18]

Many pro-suffrage Republicans in northern Ohio were not happy with Cox's views, but other Republican leaders adopted his focus on attacking the Democrats. Senator John Sherman, for example, argued that northern Democrats and Copperheads were eager to gain power by allying "with the public enemy." Although Sherman affirmed his earlier stance that Blacks deserved suffrage on the basis of their military service, he emphasized that the Democrats were unreliable on the public debt or the nation's financial obligations. His colleague Congressman James Garfield warned that the Democrats clung to their "old doctrine as though there had been no war." Republicans also seized an opportunity to quote another well-known general, Ambrose Burnside, against John Sherman's brother, General William Tecumseh Sherman. The family's military hero vehemently opposed Black suffrage, but General Burnside declared that "we ought to grant to every freeman on this continent the right to help rule the land."[19]

Ohio's Democrats agreed completely with General Sherman. Even before Cox's nomination they had begun to speak out about race. Former governor David Tod showed that he was returning to his Democratic roots in July. Speaking at a celebration of Independence Day, he "took distinct and decisive ground against negro suffrage." Tod put himself on record as doubting "the capacity of slaves to exercise the right of voting" and declared that he was "opposed to amending the Constitution of this State to allow Negro suffrage." He feared, according to a newspaper report, that if Ohio recognized Blacks' right to vote, "it may induce many negroes to migrate thither from the South. He would prefer, above all, he says, that the black 'should seek a climate where slavery does not exist—a climate and a country more congenial to his tastes and more profitable to his labor than the Northern States and the Northern climate can be.'"[20]

The state's Democrats met in convention near the end of August. Their candidate was General George Morgan, and they made Clement Vallandigham chair of the committee on resolutions and temporary president. Vallandigham promptly used that post to charge that Republicans wanted Black suffrage and "the unclean thing—miscegenation." Not surprisingly, then, Ohio Democrats declared that the Kentucky and Virginia Resolutions of 1798 were true, that the government had no right to emancipate the slaves, that defeated rebel states remained in the Union with all their rights, and that "the experience of one thousand years has demonstrated that Negroes are not equal to white men." Ohio needed to discourage any immigration of Blacks into the state. Efforts to encourage Black suffrage were "an insidious attempt," said the Democrats, "to overthrow our popular institutions by bringing the right to vote into disgrace." White supremacy remained the lodestar of the Democratic Party, since "this government was made by white men and shall continue for white men."[21]

General Morgan soon objected to the "large armies of negro troops . . . retained under arms" in the South, where they aroused "the anxiety of every citizen." He argued that the United States was not "a consolidated empire like that of Russia," and that southern states had full rights. It was unfair that New England gained more representation per citizen, through the election of U.S. senators, than more populous states like New York and Ohio. Arguing that the South was punished enough, he called for friendly treatment of "the Southern people." Those "people" did not include southern Blacks, however, for they could be inhabitants but not citizens, and they had already "been rewarded with freedom." Morgan accused Cox of seeking "Negro Equality in Ohio." Black suffrage would attract 100,000 African American emigrants and "convert our great State into a negro colony." Was "social and political equality" with Blacks "the reward which our brave soldiers are to receive for all their perils in a hundred battles"—that they would fall "into competition with negroes at half wages?" Countries like Mexico proved that "amalgamation ruined the Europeans" due to "the total incapacity of mongrel races for self-government." He condemned the "monstrous" and "atrocious" idea that "six millions of our own race . . . shall be trampled into the earth, in order that an aristocracy of four million negroes shall be established upon their graves."[22]

Democratic newspapers in Ohio moved swiftly to identify General Cox with Black suffrage and supposedly greater evils. The *Urbana Union* wrote that "Cox is in favor of negro suffrage, and yet is too cowardly to . . . acknowledge it." In fact, the paper soon claimed, Cox was an "Oberlin fanatic" who also wanted to enrich money lenders while making poor men pay heavy taxes. In September editors agreed with General Morgan that a Republican victory would be "the first step . . . toward negro equality. In the northern part of Ohio, . . . the Republicans are united in favor of the negro as against the white soldier and laboring man." Cox's evasions could not hide the fact that his "supporters . . . in their County and Senatorial Conventions, *have* resolved in favor of Negro Suffrage." The *Ohio State Journal* "knows he favors Negro Suffrage." Cox's party was "the Present Abolition Party," and "Abolitionists, Republicans and Unionists are for negro equality." Many of them would allow "intermarriage! What could be more revolting than such ideas?" Cox certainly could not be trusted because he stated that if states made the decision on Black suffrage, he would favor "the *full application of the rights of man*."[23]

Republican editors responded with arguments that the Democratic Party was continuing its support of southern treason. The *Cincinnati Gazette* asserted that secession "was purely Democratic" and that Democrats had "opposed every measure to raise troops" and labeled every "act of defense against rebellion . . . a violation of the Constitution." With victory won, to let white Confederates shape Reconstruction policy was "The Greatest of Absurdities." The victorious North had "succeeded to all the rights of conquerors, the chief of which is the right of dictating the terms of settlement." The *Cleveland Leader* gave prominent coverage to General Cox's appeal "to the loyal men of Ohio to persevere until traitors should have been beaten at the ballot box as well as in the field." It also reminded readers of the "horrible cruelties . . . tales of torture" that came from "The Andersonville Slaughter Pen" and stressed that southern Blacks offered dependable loyalty whereas many white voters were illiterate.[24]

On the question of Black suffrage, Republican editors continued to defend the interests of the freed people, though they often avoided taking an unequivocal position in support of suffrage for freedmen. One paper agreed that "the proofs that the Alabama slave oligarchy intend to reestablish slavery as soon as the Federal troops are withdrawn . . . crowd thickly upon us almost every day." Noting that Blacks were working well in Tennessee and Alabama, this journal regretted that "our four years' struggle has failed to give us the full stature of mental and moral manhood." Another editor defended the Radicals on two important points: the loyal should not be overpowered by the rebels, and the executive had as much power to enfranchise Blacks as to disfranchise rebels. But this Republican journal also yielded some ground before prejudice in the electorate. It made clear that it did not insist "that *all* negroes shall vote, in utter disregard of their ignorance, incapacity, vice, indolence, vagrancy, [or] crime" but did argue that any limitation "shall apply to white and blacks alike." Nevertheless, the editor argued that if some rule based on "worthiness and capability" were not adopted, then "universal suffrage" would be "the only solution of the problem of reconstruction which should find favor with loyal men." This was representative of the ambiguous positions that some Ohio Republicans took to the polls.[25]

The prospects for Black suffrage were even worse in Indiana, where the Republican governor, Oliver P. Morton, was frankly opposed to it. Morton, who had been a Democrat until 1854, supported the policies of President Johnson, describing them as a continuation of Lincoln's views. In a speech in Wayne County Morton claimed that attitudes in the South had changed and said he would "not be surprised even if the State of South Carolina should grant suffrage to her colored population before the State of Indiana does to hers." He favored allowing Black testimony in the courts of his state, but for the present went no farther. "The time will come," he predicted, "when every man in this country will have the right of suffrage," and that right "should not depend upon color." But the former slaves needed "a term of probation," he declared, because they were not ready to govern themselves or their neighbors. "Not one in a thousand," he inaccurately claimed, "can read." Morton affirmed that slavery had been "degrading," and therefore Republicans could not suddenly "stultify ourselves" by claiming that its victims were ready to be voters. Indiana, with its own laws against Black settlement, also had no right to insist on Black suffrage in the South. Moreover, if suffrage were granted, ex-slaves would win public office, control politics in certain states, and possibly hold the "balance of power that might control and govern this nation." He feared this would result "in a war of races." Only after ten or twenty years, with education for the former slaves and immigration into the South from the North and Europe, would Black suffrage seem wise and appropriate to him. Morton insisted that the nation needed the Union Party in power but not Black suffrage.[26]

Governor Morton's views were apostasy to many Republicans, and it was true, as the *Chicago Tribune* argued, that the party was unifying around many demands for a strong Reconstruction. Republicans wanted to see slavery "pulled out by the roots," freed people protected, Confederate leaders punished but the masses forgiven, and change in the South that was serious, not merely cosmetic. They shared a fear that southern Blacks might become "the prey of their late owners" and used "to restore Copperheads to power." Most did not see the need for a hasty readmission of formerly rebellious states. Doubts about the president were growing, but most still agreed that they would "sustain Johnson so far as he does 'equal and exact justice to all men.'" But the *Chicago Tribune* overstated the case when it suggested only a few mistaken politicians opposed Black suffrage. A Kansas editor who strongly advocated Black suffrage estimated that "a majority of the people of every State are opposed to negro suffrage."[27]

That same Kansas editor knew that racism had always found support among some Republicans. Thus it was not surprising that as the suffrage issue became more prominent, some turned against the progressive policies of their party. In August the head of the influential Blair family welcomed to his home Senator Garrett Davis, a virulent racist from Kentucky who soon would join the Democratic Party. "Old Blair," this editor complained, was doing his "best to strangle the party which [he] pretended to belong to." The Blair family had not pretended to be Republicans. In fact, Francis Preston Blair was one of the founders of the party, and his prominent sons, Montgomery and Frank, had played major roles through the 1850s and the war years. Frank was the first Republican elected from a border slave state, and he chaired the Committee on Military Affairs and fought as a general in Sherman's army. Montgomery had represented Dred Scott before the Supreme Court and served Lincoln as postmaster general and a close advisor. But the Blairs also represented a conservative and racist wing of the party, having left the Democracy to become Republicans. For years they had been energetic, tireless advocates of colonization. To audiences across they North they had rejected the idea that Blacks and whites could live together on terms of political equality. By late 1865 they were moving quickly toward the Democrats and the defense of southern interests and white supremacy. Radical Republicans feared their influence on President Johnson.[28]

Late in 1864, as Radical sentiment in the party grew, Montgomery Blair had left the Cabinet to provide some political cover for his chief, Lincoln, but now he was "snapping at the heels of the great and noble of the land—Seward, Chase, Stanton and Holt." He gave a speech in Clarksville, Maryland, in which he blamed William Seward, Edwin Stanton, and President Buchanan's secretary of war, Joseph Holt, for misleading the South over Fort Sumter and thus precipitating the war. His brother, Frank, delivered a "tirade against every Radical man in the land and against negro suffrage," and Montgomery addressed a meeting of New York Democrats in similar terms, endorsing Andrew Johnson's policies. The *Cincinnati Gazette* concluded that Montgomery Blair had joined the Copperheads, and indeed, the Blair family could not abide calls for Black suffrage or equal rights. They rallied to the racial defense of southern whites and left the Republican Party.[29]

The Blairs were not the only conservative Republicans alienated by the suffrage issue and racial questions. In President Johnson's Cabinet Gideon Welles felt he was in close agreement with the views of Francis Preston Blair Sr. Welles rejected efforts by "ingrained Abolitionists to compel the government to impose conditions on the Rebel States" as "wholly unwarranted." He predicted that "equality of the races in the Rebel States" was something "for which the people are not prepared—perhaps they never will be." Nor was racial equality important to him, for he viewed Sumner and the abolitionists as examples of "fanaticism, zeal without discretion." Welles wrote in his diary that "I am no advocate for social equality, nor do I labor for political or civil equality with the negro. I do not want him at my table, nor do I care to have him in the jury-box, or in the legislative hall, or on the bench." Welles felt a duty to remain a Republican, but he dismissed Wendell Phillips as "a useless member of society and deservedly without influence." Over issues of Black suffrage and what to require of southern states, this conservative faction of the Republican Party was distancing itself from the party's more progressive majority.[30]

Thus Republicans would go into the 1865 state elections lacking complete unity, though support for Black people's rights had grown within the party. Northern Democrats would fight relentlessly against Black suffrage, employing the strongest of racist attacks and appeals to white supremacy. Voters in several states would render decisions that had an important impact. The elections of 1865 would, like the Atlantic cable, reveal progress but bring reverses and postpone the outcome for which African Americans struggled.

❖ 10 ❖

Elections Settle Two Questions

Republicans approached the fall elections in a strong position but without complete unity, especially on the question of Black suffrage. The party enjoyed the great prestige of victory in the war, and candidates in the various states promised to secure that victory. Republican editors sharpened their messages to northern voters. A large majority of Republican papers publicized evidence that southern whites were already oppressing the freed people. Most editors showed that former slaves were making laudable progress but warned that stubbornly hostile southern whites were intent on regaining power and nullifying the Union's victory. Many editors feared that, once back in power, a resurgent, rebellious South would ally with Democrats to dominate Congress and repudiate the national debt. These were strong arguments for a Republican approach to Reconstruction. But, as we have seen, some Republicans evaded a commitment to Black suffrage, while others who favored it did not agree on whether all the freedmen deserved the ballot or only some portion of them—those who qualified according to a nonracial, impartial formula. Thus, while voters knew that Republicans in general were favorable toward Black suffrage, the party asked for their votes primarily in order to safeguard the North's victory in the Civil War.[1]

Democrats were far more united around their program, which was traditional, even backward-looking, and emphatically committed to white supremacy and racism. The *New York Herald* was a conservative newspaper but not a committed servant of the Democratic Party, and it had some pointed criticisms of the Democracy. As the fall began, the *Herald* questioned the strategy of most northern Democrats, especially those in Ohio and Pennsylvania. Under the banner of "time honored principles of the party," they were resurrecting old "copperhead leaders," the Kentucky and Virginia Resolutions of 1798, and the party's 1864 platform that had called the war a "failure." Such "mischievous" declarations, said the *Herald*, ignored the changes brought by the "vast and sanguinary four years' civil war" and "carry with them only the prestige of defeat and disgrace." Like the Bourbons of France, the Democratic Party's leaders "never forgot anything and never learned anything."[2]

But Democrats appeared to share few of the *Herald's* doubts. Belief in their traditional ideology and criticism of the war seemed to be unshaken. The *Franklin Valley Spirit* in Pennsylvania, for example, warned of a "centralized government" hostile to "reserved rights" of the states. It claimed that Federalist-style Republicans had encouraged rebellion and then turned the war into "a crusade for the abolition of African slavery, and the subjugation" of the southern states. The state party declared that if Democratic overtures to the South had been adopted, "the Union would have been saved in all its integrity and honor, without the slaughter, debt, and disgrace of a civil war." In New Jersey the state convention of Democrats condemned the war as "a needless and murderous Abolition crusade for the nigger." It was caused by "fanaticism," and its result was "a mountain of debt" as well as injustice to "rebels [who] were bravely struggling for their dearest rights." The *New York World* likewise declared that the "war was provoked by the success of the sectional and passionate Republican party."[3]

In Ohio one Democratic editor confronted the question "Is the War a Failure?" and unhesitatingly answered "yes." In addition to creating an oppressive mountain of debt, it had degraded the currency with "shinplasters [issued] without authority of law" and "invented" a "War Power for the double object of destroying slavery, and of subjugating the States." Another editor agreed with the state party that "consolidation of all power in hands of the Federal Government" would produce "the most despotic, corrupt and oppressive" government "in the world." Therefore, the Kentucky and Virginia Resolutions of 1798 must be the nation's guide, for they were "applicable to the present condition of the country." Massachusetts Democrats demanded "the return of State power everywhere."[4]

A Democratic editor in Indiana agreed with Democrats elsewhere that Republicans had "plotted against the Union" and perverted "the whole

Government from its original purpose." He conflated Republicans with William Lloyd Garrison, saying that they had "pronounced the Constitution 'a covenant with death and an agreement with hell.'" Democrats would have avoided a civil war that brought "untold calamities upon the country." The Republicans were "fanatical traitors," charged another Democratic editor in Indiana, and their aim was to persecute southern whites. They had already used the war to corrupt elections, make military arrests, and issue worthless greenbacks. Loyal Democrats must follow the party's principles and reject "abolition nominees."[5]

Just as Democrats, on the eve of war, had defended slavery and southern rights and urged conciliation of southerners, now in the fall of 1865 they again spoke out as the friends of southern whites. Although Democratic editors had become supportive of Andrew Johnson and his policies, Democrats in Massachusetts were more extreme, demanding an end to the exclusion of any white southerner from voting "by any subterfuge whatever." Johnson must not disable or exclude any of the leaders of the South. The *Cincinnati Enquirer* emphatically agreed, declaring that "the South comes back to the Union with the principles on which she went out, and having no other men and no other ideas, the same men must be at the helm of the State, and must regulate their conduct by the same ideas."[6]

Loyalty to traditional party principles and old ideas paled, however, in comparison to the virulent racism that Democrats invoked in the fall. Democrats agreed that Black people must be denied their rights and that society had to preserve and defend the principle of white supremacy. There were few alarms in 1865 about a massive influx of former slaves into the North, probably because the fevered predictions of the war years had not proved accurate. But insistence on white supremacy and a staunch rejection of racial equality remained central to the Democratic message.

The *New York World* was part of a swelling chorus when it complained that "the South is being Africanized." Democratic newspapers used racial themes to alarm and mobilize white voters and to identify their party as the party of white supremacy. Power-hungry Republicans did not care that Black suffrage would "degrade the government formed by Washington, Jefferson, Franklin and other patriots into a black republic." Democrats, on the other hand, could be relied upon "to restore 'our erring sisters' to equal rights" and maintain "the great WHITE REPUBLIC." Democrats were "in the field to overthrow the negro supremacy." An Indiana editor was proud that his state's constitution refused "the right of suffrage to the negro," prohibited any Black emigration into Indiana, and barred African Americans' testimony in court. Hoosier Democrats vowed to defend every one of these provisions, and the editor praised the action of his colleagues in Pennsylvania.[7]

A Democrat in the Keystone State warned his colleagues at their state convention that "a large majority" of the Republican Party believed in Black equality. Democrats, however, "believe in the superiority of our race, and we are unwilling to degrade ourselves either socially or politically." The convention's resolves condemned the "wicked attempt to put the States of this Union (all of them more or less, and some of them entirely), under the domination of negroes, to Africanize a large portion of the country, and degrade the white race, morally and socially, as well as politically, to the low level of the black." A Democratic newspaper in Pennsylvania put it more crudely: "agitators" loved "the filthy, greasy negro, in preference to the noble Caucasian," who would be "degraded by the admission of the negro to the rights of citizenship." Giving African Americans the right to "the 'ballot-box' and the right to the 'jury-box'" would also mean "to give him 'social equality.'" To keep Republicans from "confiscating Southern lands for the use of the negroes," this journal trumpeted, "Soldiers! Stand By Your Race."[8]

Other Democratic papers in Pennsylvania asked veterans whether they had fought and suffered "not for the Union, not in defense of the Constitution, but to make the negro our equal." "Practical Republicanism," charged the *Philadelphia Age*, "means negro equality," which would prohibit the return of "peace, union, and prosperity." As bad as continued strife would be, it was "barren and innocent when compared with negro equality." Citizens must defend the southern states and oppose the "attempted degradation of any portion of the white people of this country." A letter from a soldier to the *Age* denounced the "fanatical scheme" of "putting the destinies of our Government in the hands of negroes." When Senator Henry Wilson of Massachusetts drafted a bill for Black suffrage in the District of Columbia, this paper ridiculed giving "control" to "a lot of negroes who 'don't know B from bull's foot.'"[9]

In Ohio the *Urbana Union* warned that the "new Massachusetts dogma" of Black suffrage was a "means of controlling the white people of the South" and achieving Salmon Chase's goal of making Black people "the dominant race." The chief justice supposedly wanted to enfranchise Blacks and "take away" the votes of white southerners, who would suffer from "negro troops—negro patrols—negro witnesses— . . . Spies, Dectectives [sic], Military Commissions, and 'Desolation, thank God!'" To prove that African Americans were inferior, this paper carried an Englishman's denunciation of the society in Sierra Leone and a reader's description of "Savage Africa." Although Democrats warned of higher taxes and unfair privileges for wealthy holders of U.S. bonds, "the main issues before the people," one newspaper emphasized, were "Negro Suffrage and Negro Equality."[10]

The Cincinnati Enquirer featured a letter from sixteen Union soldiers who announced, "The boys are still proud of being white, and they won't march under the black flag." Radicals, they objected, "want to put the nigger on an equality with us, and give the votes to balance ours." These soldiers recognized southern rebels as whites, and therefore "when the fight was over we could always shake hands and be friends." Clement Vallandigham warned Ohioans of high taxes "to support four millions of negroes" and called on all to vote for "the entire WHITE MAN'S TICKET." The Daily Ohio Statesman declared that voters must "see to it that the priceless boon of suffrage is exercised by WHITE men" only. Another editor warned that election day would "decide whether we are . . . to be governed by the Negro Equality party and their negro allies or by White men." He urged readers to remember Stephen Douglas's principle that "this government was made by white men."[11]

The Daily Ohio Statesman also wrote about "fiendish attrocities of barbarous negroes" and deplored Black suffrage that would "degrade and rob the South." Ohio itself needed to be saved "from the hands of the Abolitionists" and "the monstrous scheme of the radicals to place negroes upon a footing of perfect political and social equality with the whites, and to govern this country in all time to come by means of negro votes." Republicans upheld the "repulsive doctrine" of "Miscegenation and negro equality," charged the Dayton Empire, and would "allo[w] intermarriage!" Another editor claimed that Republicans favored "throwing open the public schools to the negroes, who were to be mixed indiscriminately with the white children upon the same seats." Looking to the future, this paper asked voters, "Is the negro of more importance, . . . than the future of their own children? . . . Do they wish to put their sons and daughters on an equality with the blacks?" Republican candidates were unacceptable because they were "exceedingly Negrofied."[12]

The *Chicago Times* similarly warned of racially mixed schools and suffrage meetings where "the whites and blacks participated promiscuously." In contrast, the *Indiana State Sentinel* listed among the principles of the Democracy "the supremacy of the white race." A county meeting of Democrats supported Indiana's constitutional provisions, which "refus[e] the right of suffrage to the negro and prohibit emigration into the State." Democrats in that state encouraged a "Soldiers' and Union Men Convention" that protested against Black suffrage and any attempt at "placing upon [Blacks or mixed-race individuals] a great social or political equality with ourselves." These soldiers pledged "to protect . . . our fearful Democratic citizens from Negro equality." Another Democratic paper in Indiana claimed that a Black soldier in Memphis had killed a white man and that the "abolition press" was inciting Blacks and using Haiti as an example to advocate "miscegenation, bluntly, and unequivocally." The goal of Republican papers like the *Chicago Tribune* supposedly was to persecute southern whites and make them "swear that they will ever hold the negro as their superior."[13]

In the South freed Blacks supposedly were proving their inferiority. "The Negroes at the South," claimed a Maryland newspaper, were "stealing" everything and "insulting the white owners, if remonstrated with." Their idleness would result in "downright starvation at the South, this winter." Without Andrew Johnson's support of the whites, "negro barbarians" would make "the South a desolate waste." A Pennsylvania Democratic editor borrowed from a journal in Georgia to claim that Blacks would not seek employment, ignored their children, cared "but little for each other," and were "rapidly dying." The federal government, said the *Cadiz Sentinel*, was supporting southern Blacks at a cost of "$80,000 a day, $560,000 a week and $26,120,000 a year," while whites in "Virginia, North Carolina, and Mississippi" had to live in fear of "an insurrection by freedmen in those States." Meanwhile, the Freedmen's Bureau arrested a judge in Louisiana who dared to "try a negro for horse stealing." Such events placed the inferior freedmen on top.[14]

When a report surfaced that President Johnson had told the governor of Missouri, "This is a white man's country, and by God, while I am president it shall be a white man's government," the *Chicago Times* stoutly defended Johnson from criticism. "It cannot be considered profanity to affirm so laudable a purpose in this most solemn and emphatic manner." To end the rebellion completely, it was necessary to "'wip[e] out' the last vestige of abolitionism." Another Illinois journal listed several states where Republicans favored Black suffrage and then affirmed that the Democratic Party would maintain "this as a government in which the white man shall be dominant." The key issues, argued a Michigan editor, were "Negro Suffrage" and "the equality of the races—should they be Amalgamated!" The folly of all such radical ideas, according to the *Louisville Democrat,* was revealed in the work of a "negro poet" who wrote, "I'se cold and hungry—naked too; / I'se got no home to go to / . . . De white man's made de matter wuss."[15]

How did Republicans and advocates of equal rights respond to these Democratic attacks? The *Chicago Tribune,* as one of the North's major Republican journals, advanced a comprehensive set of arguments for Black suffrage and against the direction of Andrew Johnson's program. Two hundred thousand Black men had fought for the Union, it noted, and Abraham Lincoln had endorsed the right of suffrage for those patriots and some others. The *Tribune* also argued that loyal citizens understood the liberty of Blacks and whites to be "inseparable." Without Black suffrage, "Emancipation is not complete, nor the liberty of the colored race secure . . . nor the voters of the Northern States placed on an equal footing with those of the Southern." Johnson's leniency with pardons was making it easy for rebels to lie, take the amnesty oath, and then regain their suffrage rights, and this policy would end in Reconstruction by "the disloyal to the exclusion of the loyal." Relying on the Declaration of Independence, the *Tribune* affirmed that "this country belongs to the great democracy of the people, and no race, complexion, or nativity have exclusive right or privileges."[16]

The *Chicago Tribune* also boasted that the Republican Party had endorsed some form of Black suffrage in Vermont, Maine, Massachusetts, Connecticut, Iowa, Minnesota, and Wisconsin, and only the *New York Times* "actually opposes impartial suffrage." Other northern states were considering removing the word "white" from their requirements on voting. The *Tribune* then listed more than thirty prominent Republicans who were "well known" to be in favor of Black suffrage. That list included senators such as William Fessenden, Charles Sumner, Henry Wilson, Benjamin Wade, Zachariah Chandler, Lyman Trumbull, and John Sherman; representatives such as Thaddeus Stevens, Bingham, Justin Morrill, Schuyler Colfax, Elihu Washburne, and George Julian; as well as governors, judges, and other influential figures. Evidently the *Tribune* hoped that such a long list would convince others to join the movement.[17]

Many Republican papers also carried news of the "Wadsworth letter" at the end of September. Its words, directed to the family of General James Wadsworth, who died at the Battle of the Wilderness, were politically potent because they highlighted the martyred president's support for the cause of Black suffrage. Although modern historians have developed evidence that at least some of this document was invented or spurious, a central part of it repeated the position Abraham Lincoln had enunciated in the last days of his life. After speaking of a general amnesty, Lincoln's supposedly went on to write that "if universal amnesty is granted," he could not avoid "exacting in return universal suffrage, or at least suffrage on a basis of intelligence and military service." Even the *New York Times*, which opposed Black suffrage, acknowledged that the letter "shows that Mr. Lincoln . . . desired the bestowal of the elective franchise upon the blacks." Other editors who favored Black suffrage then reprinted the *Times* article and added accounts of hostility from southern whites showing that suffrage was necessary. For example, the *Chicago Tribune* reported that southeastern landowners were planning to dispense with Black labor in 1866. Rebel states were not abandoning slavery, were excluding Blacks from testimony or lawsuits against whites, and were "decreeing that all blacks, who are not in regular employment, shall be considered vagrants and sold to labor by the States."[18]

The *New York Tribune* agreed with the *Chicago Tribune*. The "soul" of slavery was still alive, drawing strength from "the pride of caste, the contempt for Black Humanity, the hate, the scorn, the denial of inalienable rights, born of generations of slaveholding." By a lopsided vote, Alabama's constitutional convention "practically" abolished the right of Black testimony. In the face of such facts, a suffrage not distorted by any kind of racial test was essential. "We ask no exemption for Blacks," wrote the *Tribune*, "from any merely intellectual or literary test of fitness and capacity that bears equally upon all classes." This paper denied that freedmen were "exceptionally ignorant or stolid. . . . We hold them fairly intelligent, while eagerly acquiring knowledge." Admitting that prejudice raised barriers to Black suffrage, the editors declared, "We shall have to struggle for it, to meet prejudices, to oppose narrow and hostile organizations and educate the people to it." The *Tribune* regretted that this issue had to be discussed, for the war logically "did give" manhood suffrage, but "fence men and the mossy politicians threw it away."[19]

Meanwhile, in the South the freedom of African Americans was actually in danger. Alabama, reported a Republican paper in Maryland, had adopted "the chain gang system for the punishment of negroes" and was dragging its feet on ratification of the Thirteenth Amendment. Even worse, according to a Kansas editor, was the "reign of terror" that involved whites' "murdering the negroes in Alabama in the most shocking manner." An article in the *Cincinnati Gazette* reviewed actions by the Mississippi Constitutional Convention and sparked this bleak commentary in Boston: Mississippi's freed people "now have no rights but such as the United States have conferred upon them." Their situation would not improve "until the United States shall enfranchise with the ballot the 270,000 free dark people." The fact that Mississippi's convention called for clemency for Jefferson Davis demonstrated that its members believed "he was right, and that they were right in following him." The *Cincinnati Gazette* also quoted a U.S. officer sent to investigate "reported outrages against freedmen in western Alabama." For each man who "seemed inclined to appreciate the new order of things," this officer "met fifty who expressed perfect faithlessness in any other system than compulsory labor." He met "many who hardly knew the war was over—certainly many who were not half conquered."[20]

From a Republican newspaper in Delaware came a discouraging report on Johnson's policy, as shown by elections in Virginia and North Carolina. The results in Virginia demonstrated that "the great mass of their citizens are as bitterly opposed to the Union as ever, and are unreserved in expressions of hostility to the government." The situation in North Carolina was no better, since local newspapers were backing "the most treasonable magnates in the Old North State." Georgia's constitutional convention only grudgingly repudiated that state's Confederate war debt by a vote of 133 to 117. These facts were especially troubling in light of the additional representation that the South would gain due to emancipation. Should we give power, this editor asked, to "men who have given birth to conspiracies and committed almost every crime in the catalogue?" The *Vermont Watchman and State Journal* reported that Louisiana's whites were neither "humbled, nor penitent" and rejected the free labor system in favor of compulsion of Black laborers. The inclination of southern whites was "to enslave the black, not to enfranchise him."[21]

Given such facts, Republican newspapers increasingly argued that a strong, unyielding policy was necessary. Few editors denounced Andrew Johnson, for he was the party's head, and the belief prevailed that his policy naturally would be reviewed and revised by Congress. But a growing number of newspapers demanded stronger measures. "Until the Southern leaders become *loyal at heart,*" counseled the *Ebensburg Alleghanian,* "they should be disfranchised." Without that stiff approach, the rebels would achieve "the same wicked purposes through the agency of the ballot box that they attempted by force of arms." A week later another Pennsylvania newspaper emphasized that "The President's Policy" was an experiment and that "a little patient waiting now may save years of future strife and even future wars." The "position of the Union Party" was to restore southern states when that was "compatible with the security of the peace and prosperity of the country," not before. A Kansas editor agreed that haste should be avoided, since thirty years of errors by the South could not easily be forgotten. One of his neighboring editors agreed with John W. Forney, an influential Republican who was secretary of the U.S. Senate and editor of newspapers in Philadelphia and Washington. The freedmen "must be elevated and protected," the national debt must be paid, and no leaders of the rebellion "should ever be admitted to places of trust or honor under the General Government. . . . That's our platform!" His partisan colleague in Vermont agreed, saying, "We do not expect a satisfactory settlement until the resistless power of the nation is brought to bear upon reluctant states."[22]

Articles and arguments such as these could attract some voters and solidify support among those who shared the overall Republican outlook toward the war and its meaning, and Republican editors were as energetic as their Democratic counterparts in working to get out the vote. But the use of humor was helpful as well because it subjected rival Democrats to ridicule and reinforced a sense of belonging to the intelligent and progressive party. For these reasons the columns of Petroleum Nasby appeared rather frequently in the weeks leading up the fall elections in northern states.

A Republican newspaper in Kansas carried a selection from Nasby's wisdom on the front page as election day neared. The Copperhead preacher, in this account, was advising his Democratic friends on the best strategy to defeat Republicans. Nominating soldiers for office, to prove how patriotic Democrats were, was totally unnecessary and ill-considered, said Nasby, since Democrats had called them Lincoln's "shoulder straped hirelings" and had "meant it" and "can't take it back." Far better was the tried-and-true plan: "We have cappytle enouff in the Nigger. Let us plant ourselves boldly on shoor ground. Let us Resolve that Goddlemity wuz rite in makin the Nigger our slave, tho he made a mistake in plantin in his heeving buzum a chronic desire to run away." The Democracy's banner should read, "'No marryin Niggers!' 'No payin a debt inkurd in a Nigger war!' 'Protect us from Nigger equality!'" These slogans were reliable and effective, said Nasby. Why? Because they "cum within range of the Dimekratic intellek." Therefore they were the way to win.[23]

Another Kansas editor reprinted a letter from Nasby in which the former divine sympathized with his southern brethren. Since the prospects of the Democracy were poor and declining, Nasby offered a psalm "of agony, approprit fur the occashun." If God "is ever goin to help us, now's hiz time." In Nasby's psalm, a defeated slaveholder sees "a nigger" on the street. Not only was this man wearing "a coat uv bloo" and "caryeth a muskit," but he arrested "my tender daughter" when she "spit on him." Then the speaker's soul became an "artesian well iv wo" and "gusheth with greef," for "that nigger wuz my nigger!—I bought him with a price." Instead of being a source of profit, he had become "a nitemare." When the slaveholder "wuz rich," he "owned him, sole, body, muscles, sinooz, blud, boots and brichis. . . . likewise his labor and froots thereof. / His wife wuz mine, and she wuz my conkebine." The children she bore helped the planter drink "mint goolips" and ride "in gorjus chariots. . . . Wuz this misceginashun or nigger equality? Not any. For she wuz mine, even as my ox, or my horse, or my sheep." Instead of elevating Blacks as "abolishin misceginashun" recommended, the planter proudly explained, "I did it fur gain, wich degraded her muchly." When the "wife uv my buzzm" complained about these sexual violations of the marriage vow, the slaveholder had a sure solution: "half the price uv the infant chattel wood buy a dimund pin with wich to stop her yawp." But now "my dream is busted," and "Dark is my fucher." For all these reasons Nasby's psalm was highly "approprit" for a "day uv fastin and prayer."[24]

When Petroleum Nasby commented "On the Political Situation," he shed light on northern Democrats and on the attitudes of former rebels. Like other northern Democrats, Nasby wanted to revive "a perfeck union with our wunst luved brethren uv the South" and thereby gain "Nashunal" power. To that end he traveled to Washington and spoke with "general Marion Fitzhoo Gusher, of Mississippy," a "troo gentleman of the raal Southern skool." This true southern gentleman wore shirt pins and rings on his fingers made from "the bones of miserable Yanky sogers who fell at Bull Run." Now that the war was over, General Gusher brimmed with devotion to "my beloved country" and was "reddy to take an oath, and resoom the citizenship I lade orf, and agin run the government." He had "no apologys

John Mercer Langston, first president of the National Equal Rights League, was an abolitionist, a recruiter for the U.S. Army, and later the founding dean of Howard University's Law School. (ca. 1868–75; Brady-Handy Photograph Collection, Library of Congress, Prints and Photographs Division, LC-DIG-cwpbh-00690)

to offur" for killing "the niggers at Fort Piller," and southern Democrats must run the national party. His idea that "Linkin's war debt must never be pade, onless ourn is" showed his true desire to conciliate.[25]

Republican leaders had another set of allies in the debates of the fall. Without humor but with energy, resolve, and hope, African Americans renewed their calls for Black suffrage and justice. The National Equal Rights League, which had been founded the previous year, held its first annual meeting in Cleveland in the fall. Outstanding leaders such as John Mercer Langston, James H. Harris, William D. Forten, George B. Vashon, Moses Brown, and James Rapier played leading roles. The League promptly called for "equality before American law" and resolved that "in the reconstruction of the Southern States, justice demands that the Elective franchise be extended to men of color," since they had fought to defend the Union. The Constitution's guarantee of a republican form of government, the resolves continued, also meant that there should be "no legislation . . . against any civilized portion of the inhabitants, native-born, or naturalized, on account of race or color." Any existing law of that type "is anti-republican in character, and therefore void." Just as significant as such statements were the organizing efforts to raise money and build chapters throughout the Union, so that agitation could continue and grow. Nashville, Tennessee, was chosen as the site for the next annual meeting.[26]

Speakers at the Cleveland meeting addressed themselves to African Americans as well as to whites. John Mercer Langston denounced discrimination against Black people by "colored barbers, restauranteurs, and waiters" as behavior that "further degrade[s] us in the eyes of a discerning public." Others appealed for unity among northern Blacks. Various resolutions hailed the freedmen and urged them to acquire property and education and to merit fair treatment by good behavior. William Forten did not hesitate to blister Republican allies who were not standing firm for equal rights. With men like Ohio's Jacob Cox in mind, Forten said, "We have been deserted by those whom we faithfully supported, and *insolently informed that this is a white man's country, though it required the strong arms of over 200,000 black men to save it,* and that the elective franchise is not now a practical question, and we must find homes in some Territory separate to ourselves, as white and Black men cannot live together upon terms of equality." Republicans, he said, had "bound themselves before God and the world, to emancipate, enfranchise, and crown us with all the rights of citizenship," and their backsliding revealed a "murderous intent of the meanest people God ever deigned to tolerate." Colonization anywhere was unacceptable, and equal rights were essential.[27]

Black leaders in Indiana, where Governor Oliver Morton opposed Black suffrage, struggled against the same failure of Republican leadership. To press their claims for fair treatment as American citizens, they held a state convention in Indianapolis in October. One hundred and fifty delegates from across the state assembled in the African Methodist Church and called on whites to honor the founders' goals as stated in the Declaration of Independence. The rights of Black people, the convention resolved, has been "flagrantly, wickedly, and most inhumanly violated," and federal and state governments should repeal "tyrannical laws" depriving them of rights that should be guaranteed to "all men alike, regardless of color." They pledged themselves "to secure that intellectual and moral worth necessary to sustain a republican form of government, and for the encouragement of our race."

After enlisting in the Union Army at age thirty-six and winning the Medal of Honor, James H. Harris continued to fight for Black suffrage and equal rights. (ca. 1900; Daniel Murray Collection, Library of Congress, Prints and Photographs Division, LC-USZ62–118561)

Finally they petitioned the Indiana legislature for access to public school funds, for the right to testify in all cases before the courts, and for the equal rights they deserved "with other men before the laws."[28]

In far-off California Black leaders were likewise engaged and active. They met in a state convention in October and focused their attention on winning the right to vote. An agent of the Freedmen's Bureau urged them not to be discouraged, though "we must expect opposition, even from Union men." The more than three dozen delegates demanded access to public schools, citizenship rights, "'Equality before the Law' . . . [and the] political franchise." Speakers recalled "the damning prejudice against the negro" that was evident at Fort Pillow and judged that "the country is only half saved . . . the war but half ended, until all of the disabling laws which were the natural fruits of slavery are repealed, and universal suffrage exist in every State in the Union." The convention published statistics on the churches, schools, business pursuits, professions, and wealth of Black Californians and urged unity, morality, and progress to distinguish the race. To continue their work, delegates named a State Executive Committee and provided for the election of county executive committees.[29]

In the southern states Black leaders also were organizing and alert, but the slower pace of constitutional conventions there meant that protests did not materialize until after the North had held its fall elections. Across the northern states voters went to the polls at different times in the fall to choose a variety of officials. Some races were for congressional representatives or for state posts as high as governor, but in other states only lower-ranking state positions were contested. Citizens and observers viewed the elections as judgment on the past conduct of the Republican administration and its newly begun program of Reconstruction. The results would show whether voters believed that the Republicans were on the right track, or that a change to Democratic leadership—virulently racist and far more sympathetic to the South—was needed.

Across the board Republicans or Unionists won clear victories, even capturing some offices that Democrats had held previously. In September Vermont Republicans won the governorship and amassed majorities in both branches of the legislature. By mid-October results were coming in from some of the most populous states, and Republican editors began to shout "VICTORY!!" The Union candidates carried Pennsylvania, where even Democratic editors admitted that their foes had gained a nearly two-to-one majority in the state legislature. "The Union party has gained in fifty-four" counties and lost ground "only in eight." In Ohio Republicans prevailed and Jacob Cox easily won the governorship. Most voters held to the conviction that a "planter conspiracy" had caused secession and the war, and therefore Republicans needed to control Reconstruction and secure basic rights for former slaves. One Democratic editor sighed that his party's major candidates were "again defeated," although the *Cincinnati Enquirer* claimed that Cox won only because Republicans "dodged the issue of negro suffrage" while Cox took "an equivocal position on it—had they openly avowed their real sentiments they would, despite their previous majority, have been badly beaten." To that charge the Republican *Cleveland Leader* replied—with more cleverness than honesty—that Democrats "fought the campaign out, almost solely on this one issue," insisting that Republicans were "committed in favor of negro suffrage." Therefore, "will they [Democrats] admit the principle is endorsed by the people?"[30]

These results encouraged John Forney's *Philadelphia Press* to expect victory for Republicans all across the northern states. Since the Republican Party represented "the undying loyalty and patriotism of the nation," Forney's paper predicted that nothing could "throw the great Union train from the track, at least for a generation of time." Although the *Press* was looking far into the future, immediate results in 1865 justified such optimism. News came in of Republican victories in the state of Iowa, which chose a Republican governor against the candidate backed by a racially inspired "soldiers" movement. By early November the *New York Tribune* could headline "Union Majorities Everywhere Increased . . . Good News from All the States." The *Chicago Tribune* boasted of "Victory the Backbone of the Copperheads Broken Splendid Union Triumphs." Other Republican editors celebrated victories in New York, Illinois, Massachusetts, New Hampshire, Connecticut, Minnesota, Wisconsin, Missouri, Maryland, and even New Jersey. Democrats were reduced to arguing that Republican majorities had shrunk in certain areas.[31]

But all was not brilliant for the Republicans or for the principles that most state parties had adopted. The Republican triumph was a general one, endorsing the party's record and its future direction over policies favored by the Democrats, but the cause of Black suffrage suffered a sharp reverse in more than one state. The voters in Connecticut, Minnesota, and Wisconsin all considered measures to extend the right of suffrage to African Americans in the fall of 1865. These three states—one old, two new—all had extremely small Black populations, and in all of them the Republican Party proved dominant in most contests for offices. But when voters in these states considered Black suffrage, the ingrained racial prejudice of northern society blocked equality before the law.

The defeat in Connecticut was the most devastating, because Connecticut was part of New England, the region most supportive of equal rights. The state also was proud of its patriotic role in the Revolution, when it had supplied much of the food for George Washington's army. Republicans there argued that voters should remove the stigma of being the only state in New England to bar Black voters. But Black suffrage received only 45 percent of the ballots cast. Some Republican newspapers tried to explain the embarrassing outcome as the result of apathy among some who simply neglected to vote, and indeed fewer people cast ballots on this issue than for the major offices. Others argued that "many good Republicans" had been misled into thinking that a favorable vote "would be in opposition to the policy of President Johnson." Still, some editors admitted that white citizens who would not support a Copperhead "were not yet rid of that prejudice which belongs properly to a less enlightened age."[32]

Democratic newspapers were jubilant and more certain about the outcome's wide significance. The *Albany Argus and Patriot* proclaimed that Union veterans rejected "negro equality" because "they have seen enough of the colored cuss from Africa." To the *New York Journal of Commerce* the vote meant that Connecticut's "government is a government of white men." The *Journal of Commerce* continued, "It will not do to rail at this decision. The people of that State are notoriously the most intelligent people in all the United States." They lead in "education, intellect, wealth, or civilization." The *New York Sun* happily proclaimed, "Every County but One against Negro Suffrage," and predicted "an 'irrepressible conflict'" between rank-and-file Republicans and the Radicals, who now should have great difficulty in imposing their goals.[33]

The Springfield *Republican* feared that the result in Connecticut "renders it impossible at present to make equal suffrage a doctrine of the republican party." The public "must be educated up to it." The *New York Tribune* deplored the "gross injustice" of the vote, which had disgraced Connecticut. More importantly, the *Tribune* soberly admitted that the defeat had "deeply injured the cause of the country." Its bad effects were many. The vote would add "moral strength to the Copperhead party" and hearten states like Alabama to believe that their "struggle for lost dominion is not without hope." The principle "that 'this is a white man's government'" was reinforced, and "southern white men" had reason to believe that they could regain power. Connecticut's decision, concluded the *Tribune*, "will be quoted all over the country as a Puritan endorsement of a Pagan prejudice. 'How,' every Copperhead will exultingly exclaim, 'can you expect negro suffrage in the South, when it will not be tolerated in New England?'"[34]

In Wisconsin Republicans were not united behind Black suffrage. Senator James Doolittle had begun his political career as a Democrat, and during the war he opposed Black suffrage, stated that no northern state wanted Black residents, and zealously promoted colonization. Now he declared that the president could not require Black suffrage and warned that imposing it on the South would lead to a war of the races. Lucius Fairchild, the party's candidate for governor, was another former Democrat, and his support for Black suffrage was uncertain. Republican newspapers in the state also were divided, although some editors and Republican activists whom Doolittle could not control made a strong case for suffrage. African Americans in Milwaukee organized and spoke out about their record of loyalty and sacrifice, which merited the right to vote. Pro-suffrage Republicans emphasized the basic argument that 4 million people should not "be excluded from all participation in the choice of their own rulers." They also praised the conduct and progress of the freed people and warned of the added representation that the South would gain because slavery had ended. Even if Black suffrage were approved, Republicans pointed out, there probably would be no more than two hundred African American voters in Wisconsin. In response to Democratic scare tactics the Republicans declared that suffrage did not entail any "peculiar marital privileges."[35]

But Wisconsin's Democrats did their best to flood the state with racist propaganda. They described the freed people and African Americans in general as worthless, "ignorant and degenerated," and "inferior to the Indian." Republicans, in their telling, were encouraging "negro emigration, amalgamation and miscegenation." After the police in Memphis, Tennessee, clashed with Black residents, the *La Crosse Democrat* not only blamed Blacks for the violence but warned that suffrage would inspire "these Memphis niggers to flock to our cities." White supremacy was a core argument for the Democrats, who said that national greatness had developed "because the white man was elevated to his true position in the scale of being." As had been the case in Connecticut, Republicans won the governorship and other races, but Black suffrage went down to defeat as many Republican voters either opposed the measure or failed to vote for it. The majority against Black suffrage was nearly six thousand votes, although Lucius

Fairchild claimed the governor's chair with a majority of almost nine thousand votes.[36]

Minnesota was another severe disappointment. A state with fewer than five hundred Black residents—only about three-tenths of 1 percent of the total population—rejected Black suffrage while electing the Republican candidate for governor. Despite that overall Republican majority, many who supported the party did not vote on the suffrage issue, which went down to defeat by a margin of 55 percent to 45 percent. Minnesota Democrats had publicized the criticisms of the Blair family and contrasted Andrew Johnson's "mild, sensible, statesmanlike and patriotic" policies with the "oppressive" and "despotic" goals of "fanatics" in the Republican Party. They spared no epithet against Black Americans, calling them "worthless," "thieving," "dangerous," "insolent," "enervated and ignorant," "unqualified by education," and "greatly inferior to the whites." To give the ballot in Minnesota to Blacks would introduce "danger and corruption" in the political system and put the state's "social organization" in peril, because immigration would make the state "a place of refuge for the scum of Southern slavery."[37]

The Democrats also exploited racial fears about a loss of white supremacy. The *St. Paul Pioneer* warned that "if negro voting is allowed," the Republicans' "next step will be in favor of 'miscegenation.'" Why should white men want "to humiliate and degrade" their own race? They should instead preserve "the government founded by white men for the use of white men." Black suffrage would inevitably lead to immigration, which would turn the state into "a paradise of darkies," and then Blacks would "jostle white men out of the way" for many jobs, hurting "especially the Irish and Germans." Releasing all its bile, this newspaper howled, "If you wish to have niggers in your schools, niggers at the polls, niggers in the jury box, niggers in your fields, niggers on your public works, niggers gallanting your white girls, niggers corrupted by demagogues, niggers voting, niggers holding office, niggers miscegenating, and NIGGERS TILL YOU CAN'T REST," then vote for Wendell Phillips and the Republicans.[38]

Republicans sometimes countered with statements of principle and warnings that holding the freed people "in a condition of peonage and serfdom" would "preserve the causes of the rebellion." Moreover, to deny Black suffrage in the South would give rebellious states "fifteen representatives in Congress . . . without increasing their voting population." In a bid for support from the state's naturalized citizens, Republicans called the Democrats "Copperheads" and warned that their prejudice against Blacks would lead to measures against voting rights for "the foreigner." But leaders of the party in Minnesota also revealed their own racism. General William R. Marshall, the Republican candidate for governor, said he was willing to see Blacks make the most of their "capacities and opportunities," but he himself had been "born in a slave State and had a prejudice against the negro." He was not in favor of "mingling socially with the negro," but he could believe that "the superior race ought to elevate the inferior" because he had no "fear for his self-respect, and his superiority." A Republican editor assured readers that "we don't know of any Republican that is desirous of sending a negro to Congress, or making them Justices of the people, or fear their rivalry in the social circle." With such attitudes at the head of the ticket, it was not surprising that Black suffrage failed.[39] The voters could trust Republicans to put Reconstruction on the right track, but they were not yet ready to concede equal rights in the North.

Farther west, in the territory of Colorado, Black suffrage similarly went before the voters and met a remarkably fierce rejection. Colorado had gained territorial status in 1861, and residents there, eager to become a state, were prepared to adopt a constitution. They went to the polls and narrowly approved the constitution's text by 155 votes out of 5,895. But the proposal to allow black suffrage went down to crushing defeat, 4,192 votes to a mere 476. Later that year Andrew Johnson would veto the statehood bill for Colorado, an act that disappointed residents of the territory. But their vote on suffrage already had deepened the dark shadow that shrouded prospects for Black suffrage.[40]

A few prominent individuals contributed to the drift away from Black suffrage. Henry Ward Beecher, the North's most prominent minister, had taken a strong stand in favor of Black people's right to vote early in 1865. Yet now in October he defected from the cause, reversed himself entirely, and gave full support to the policy of Andrew Johnson and the interests of white southerners. In a Sunday night sermon Beecher announced that he would refrain from lecturing the South since, in the prejudiced North, Black people still could not "ride in the cars . . . appear in court . . . own property . . . [or] attain to the full stature of citizenship here." Then he praised Johnson's character and asserted that the nation supported the president with "extraordinary unanimity." Northerners, Beecher asserted, "cannot aid" southern Blacks, and it would not be "wise for the central government to attempt to regulate" the affairs of southerners. "The laws and interests of the government and of our ourselves will prove of no avail if they are hostile and unpleasant to the white men of the South." Pleasing southern whites had become more important for Beecher than the rights of African Americans. He concluded, "I thank God the President is a Southern man; he's just the man we want, if we are going to reconstruct. You can't manage hearts as you can bricks and mortar. No New England man could do as well as Mr. Johnson." Beecher, the Christian minister, had given up on educating hearts to a higher morality.[41]

A member of the Cabinet, Treasury Secretary Hugh McCulloch, also made news with anti-Black sentiments in the fall. Although McCulloch was born in Maine and had attended Bowdoin College, he had moved to Indiana, where he practiced law and evidently imbibed some of the racial prejudice that was notable there. McCulloch staunchly supported Johnson's policies and demonstrated that he was not one of those New England "fanatics" denounced by Democratic newspapers. In a conversation with an ex-judge from New Orleans, McCulloch voiced the emphatic, stereotypical arguments of white supremacy. "The history of fifteen centuries," he was reported as saying, "had proven that the Anglo-Saxon race must dominate or exterminate." He rejected and had no sympathy for "the pretended equality of races. . . . No sane man, no American, could dream for a moment of making this country, where God had showered so many blessings to the race made after His own image, the inheritance of any but those He had endowed with an intelligence almost divine." McCulloch's words must have been as reassuring to many southern politicians as they were disconcerting to advocates of equal rights.[42]

Thus events in the fall had strengthened the Republican Party in the North but weakened and retarded the momentum toward Black suffrage. The party surged forward, but many Republican voters, when asked directly, held back, while Democratic voters despised Black suffrage. The gap between emancipation and equal rights had never been small. Racism threw a chasm between them, and advocates for Black suffrage realized that bridging that distance would not be easy. Certainly real progress had been made, particularly among many activists and voters in the Republican Party, but it was clear that the necessary level of support was still lacking in northern society and in the party. The cause of Black suffrage often benefited from the support enfranchisement could give to other interests. Such alliances would have to continue, and suffrage surely would be enmeshed in the many issues of Reconstruction policy.

As December approached, the future of Reconstruction and of Andrew Johnson's policy was nearing an important decision point. Congress was due to reconvene, and northern lawmakers prepared to give their judgments on the course of events in the South. By this point they had an abundance of information, not only about the provisional government but also about Andrew Johnson himself. The ambiguous or confusing attitudes of the chief executive were becoming more clear over time.

11

An Ambiguous and Deceptive Executive

Andrew Johnson was the nation's most important public figure throughout the last eight and a half months of 1865. After the assassination of Lincoln, a shocked northern public and an anxious and uncertain southern population looked to Johnson for guidance. In the first weeks of his presidency, he successfully projected stability and reassurance for the North, while for white southerners he probably did little more than heighten hopes or anxieties in a situation that remained uncertain. Thereafter, as historian Eric L. McKitrick has shown, Johnson failed to give white southerners an accurate sense of what would be expected of them by the victorious Union. This failure encouraged the evasion, resistance, and intransigence that damaged any possibilities of an outcome which might have been more positive—or more consonant with the nation's founding values—than what ensued. For months Johnson's course misled white southerners and was unclear and inconsistent for northern whites.[1]

It is, of course, impossible to know what Abraham Lincoln might have done had he lived. But based on the record of his first term in office, it seems likely that Lincoln would have devised a policy that was carefully considered, more consistent, and probably more satisfactory in results than Johnson's. Lincoln's past performance showed that he advanced slowly, but he also was proud that he did not retreat. Therefore, it is likely he would have adhered to the position he staked out in his last address. He would have attempted to be generous to rebels while also obtaining some rights of suffrage for former slaves. That task would not have been easy, and Lincoln surely would have encountered resistance. He would have had to enlist allies, North and South, and find a way to make compliance with his program the most practical path for southern leaders. As he had done during the war, he might have used a more demanding Congress to nudge southern whites toward his policies. But Lincoln probably would have moved patiently and firmly toward his goal, offering incentives and establishing penalties in order to steer the former Confederate states toward a reunion acceptable to both northern public opinion and his own sense of what was right.

Assassination, however, left the nation with a chief executive who was more emotional, more impulsive, and less far-sighted about his goals. Andrew Johnson was always more outspoken, blunt, and strident than Lincoln in expressing his views, but he also was less clear and consistent. His statements suggested different directions for policy without specifying an overall, defining framework of values and goals, and thus they invited different readings or interpretations from the various elements of an interested public. It is possible Johnson did not foresee in April what kind of results he would insist upon or accept by December. The members of the party that he officially led had reason to disagree about what his policy was and whether his intent was desirable or unacceptable.[2]

Charting the twists and turns of Johnson's public statements and the statements that were widely reported as coming from him is the agenda of this chapter. A careful reconstruction of Johnson's course reveals the evolution of his policy, makes possible a clearer identification of his political purpose, and explains the complicated but changing relationship of Republicans toward his leadership. Over time northern Republicans gradually lost confidence in him, but for many months Johnson gave them reasons to allay their misgivings or believe that anticipated disagreements would be manageable. As December and the reconvening of Congress approached, however, the certainty grew that the president and the majority of northern lawmakers would be pursuing different, conflicting paths.

As a lifelong Democrat, Andrew Johnson was an unlikely leader for the Republican, or Union, Party. Rising from an impoverished background in North Carolina and taught to read by his wife, the young Johnson worked as a tailor before entering politics as a Jacksonian Democrat in Tennessee. After serving as mayor of Greenville, Tennessee, he became a congressman from 1843 to 1853, then governor for four years, and finally U.S. senator. Although he had frequently criticized slaveholding aristocrats and championed small farmers, he owed his nomination as vice president to his stubborn Unionism and the party's need to attract pro-war Democrats. In the first weeks after Lincoln's assassination, many newspaper editors went to the historical record to get a better sense of the new president's views and values. What the record showed could not have been reassuring to Radical Republicans or advocates of Black suffrage. They surely would have wondered how much the war had transformed a staunch defender of slavery and southern interests. The prewar attitudes of Andrew Johnson were those of a racist southerner rather than a northern critic of slavery and the slave power.

Democrats did not trust the new president, so they led the way in searching his political history, hoping to find a less dangerous political enemy than Lincoln had been. One of the newspapers that did a thorough job was Ohio's *Ashland Union*. It uncovered a record of firm, unqualified defense of slavery. Going back to 1850, the paper found that during Johnson's time as a congressman, he had declared that "negroes are not included in the Declaration of Independence"—a standard and essential pro-slavery argument. When the Kansas-Nebraska Act was debated, Johnson was governor of Tennessee and had less reason to speak out about national controversies, but later, as secession neared, he made himself heard often in the Senate. In 1860 he voted in favor of propositions declaring that the states are "free and independent sovereignties," that "interference with slavery in the States [is] a breach of faith," and that "the Union . . . rests on the equality of the States." He also affirmed that "Congress has no power over slavery in the territories," and that "new States shall be admitted with or without slavery, as the people may decide." In addition, "the provisions of the Constitution in relation to the rendition of slaves, must be carried out." These positions tied Johnson firmly to Mississippi's Jefferson Davis, for the Ohio newspaper was very slightly misquoting (but not misrepresenting) Davis's Resolutions on the Relations of States, for which Johnson voted. Numerous other statements reinforced this pro-slavery, pro-southern record. For example, in February 1861 Senator Johnson asserted that he was "opposed to war upon the south—that the General Government has no right to coerce a State—that the Abolitionists are disunionists—Secessionists are nullifiers."[3]

A Democratic editor in Illinois also felt some confidence after reviewing Johnson's long-held Democratic principles. For example, in the Senate in 1859 Johnson had challenged Republicans for their misplaced devotion to the Declaration of Independence. When they spoke about human equality, Johnson charged, they thought they were "embracing the doctrines laid down by Mr. Jefferson, and showing that he really meant to include persons of color in the declaration." But anyone who believed that was "an idiot or a knave," he insisted, and white southerners were completely united. If any effort were made "to abolish slavery, and turn them loose upon the country," he predicted that "the non-slaveholders of the South will be the first men to unite with the slaveholder to reduce them to subjugation again." In fact, the non-slaveholders would be even "more ready to do so" than the slave masters, "and if resistance be made," more ready "in extirpating the negro race." That same year Johnson excoriated John Brown and followed the Democratic strategy of tying Brown to the Republican Party. He "boldly charged home upon [Republican] Senator [James] Doolittle" of Wisconsin, falsely insisting that Brown was the acknowledged head of the Abolition or Republican Party. In 1860 Johnson also joined Democrats like Stephen Douglas and Horatio Seymour in denying that there was any irrepressible conflict between the slave system and the economy of the free states; in fact, Johnson claimed, they were complementary and aided each other.[4]

In the first days after Lincoln's assassination, the new Union or Republican Party president expressed emotions that fit the mood of the shocked northern public. Northerners had been deprived of their leader in the very moment that the costly war was giving way to peace and a brighter future. There was intense anger and resentment but also an underlying hope that reunion would be accomplished. Johnson's natural reactions spoke to both emotional states. In fulsome and belligerent terms he threatened dire punishment for traitors, using words that blamed southern leaders for the war's suffering and destruction and promised harsh justice for those who had assassinated Lincoln. At the same time, however, he promised leniency to many who were less responsible, thus indicating that the Union could be restored and fraternal bonds reestablished.

Newspapers recalled that just a few weeks before, when he was vice president, Johnson had spoken to a "vast crowd" celebrating the fall of Richmond. On that occasion he had said that he had "been in camp" and "in the field," and had seen the "infamous . . . diabolical . . . savage mode of warfare" that traitors had practiced. He believed that "evil doers should be punished. Treason is the highest crime known in the catalogue of crimes; and for him that is guilty of it—for him that is willing to lift his impious hand against the authority of the nation—I would say, death is too easy a punishment. [Loud cheers]." But at the same time he was "in favor of leniency" for "the honest boy and the deluded man who have been deceived into the rebel ranks." The "halter" was for "intelligent, influential traitors." This was the message that Johnson frequently repeated in his first weeks in office. When a Massachusetts delegation called on the new president, its members reported, "*He declared with great emphasis that traitors should be punished by death,* but that discrimination should be made between their ignorant tools and the intellectual leaders." This address "was most warmly applauded." Editors across the North carried news of Johnson's denunciation of the chief rebels but his leniency toward ordinary southern whites, and these sentiments were congruent with the public mood.[5]

Over the next several weeks Johnson began a pattern of voicing views on Reconstruction policy and the future of African Americans that pointed in different directions, alternating between progressive promise and rigid Democratic ideology. His words were pleasing to first one group and then the other. The uncertain, alternating pattern of the president's pronouncements made it difficult to discern where he truly stood.

Republicans and supporters of Black rights looked for and found some reasons for cheer. Many newspapers noted that during Johnson's appointment as military governor of Tennessee from 1862 to 1865, he had spoken to an audience of Blacks in October 1864. In words that seemed "almost prophetic," he had denounced the lust of slaveholders, promised to free Black women from "a concubinage compared to which polygamy is a virtue," and affirmed his "desire to see justice done." Then he voiced the hope that, "as in the days of old, a Moses might arise" to lead the freed people to the "promised land of freedom and happiness." He was sure that God had "prepared somewhere an instrument" for that great work, and the crowd spontaneously replied, "You are our Moses. . . . We want no Moses but you!" Johnson answered their shouts by saying, "Humble and unworthy as I am . . . I will indeed be your Moses, and lead you through the Red sea of war and bondage to a fairer future of liberty and peace." He added that he regarded as his friends "all who love equal rights." To some observers the "noble height of feeling" in this address indicated that Johnson would bring justice to Blacks.[6]

The public also learned that a delegation of freedmen from Richmond, Virginia, had met with Johnson to complain of their continuing mistreatment, especially by the municipal police force. They presented abundant evidence and made a strong case, and the *New York Tribune* reported that this "fine-looking body of men . . . ma[de] a profound impression upon the mind of the Executive." He assured them that "he should do all he could to have justice done them in their new condition," and that "he would do all in his power to protect them and their rights." Johnson declared that he was glad that Francis Pierpont, still serving as governor of the war's "restored" state of Virginia, had deposed Richmond's mayor, and he referred their case to General O. O. Howard for an investigation and report. Even before that report arrived, "the odious pass system" was abolished and "the colored schools" were again opened.[7]

On the other hand Johnson dealt differently with "a delegation of colored parties from the National Theological Institute for Colored Ministers." Speaking "plainly," he instructed them that Blacks had "friends" in the South, even former masters who "feel as deep an interest in and regard for them . . . as those who live anywhere else." Then he complained that too many freed people were "fall[ing] back upon the Government for support . . . inclined to become loafers." Freedom, he insisted, "simply means liberty to work," and sternly he told these ministers that Blacks must amend their behavior and end their "open and notorious concubinage." Although he claimed that he would "do all that I can for the elevation and amelioration of your condition," he remained unsure if "the two races" could "get along together." If they could not, he "trust[ed] in God [that] the time may soon come when you shall be gathered together, in a clime and country suited to you."[8]

At the same time Johnson marked out the distance between himself and the Radicals on policy toward the rebel states. He said he would have no part of "this idea of destroying States," for he rejected the Radicals' view "that States are to be lost in territorial and other divisions—are to lose their character as States." Despite secession, "their life breath has been only suspended." A state, Johnson held, could lose "a peculiar institution . . . by the operation of rebellion," but "it was a state when it went into rebellion, and when it comes out without the institution it is still a State." Then he declared that as much as he opposed breaking up the Union, "I am equally opposed to consolidation or the centralization of power in the hands of a few." These principles were traditional, sound Democratic doctrine, and newspaper editors of that party welcomed his attitudes. *Harper's Weekly* worried that those who had been sympathetic to the rebellion now gave Johnson's view their "unqualified commendation."[9]

As weeks passed Johnson treated the public to a steady alternation of viewpoints, attitudes encouraging or discouraging to Radical Republicans and defenders of Black rights. A committee of Black leaders from the District of Columbia called on the president, and he advised them to petition Congress for the right to vote. Although he had determined to allow southern states—and the whites forming their governments—to decide who should be able vote there, he claimed that he would "give his whole moral influence to the extension of the right of franchise to colored persons." Active presidential influence certainly could be important, and this statement might have encouraged supporters of Black suffrage. But about a week later a Cleveland paper reported that Johnson had met with nine white men from South Carolina who undoubtedly were pleased by his words. He told them that no state could leave the Union, and that he was a better states'-rights man than some of them. The elevation of the former slaves would be "a work of time," he predicted, and not a "labor of . . . fanaticism." He judged freedmen to be "ignorant," with minds "much inflamed with liberty," so that they were "apt to confound liberty with license" and view freedom as "exemption from work." Further insight into his opposition to Black suffrage appeared when Johnson said that he "did not want the late slaveholders to control negro votes against white men." Improving the lot of ordinary whites was much on his mind, for "he loved the great mass of the Southern people." Also, he said that "the question as to whether the black man shall be engrafted in the Constitution will be settled as we go along."[10]

Reports about Johnson's relationship with those who advocated Black suffrage were sharply contradictory. The *Cincinnati Enquirer* reported in July that he had had a highly contentious meeting with Massachusetts's Senator Charles Sumner. As the two men discussed Reconstruction issues, Johnson defended loyal southerners, saying that they had made many sacrifices for their Unionism during the war, whereas Massachusetts had made money from the conflict. When Sumner objected to this reflection on his state, Johnson said, "You and I might as well understand each other now as any other time. You are awere, sir, I have no respect for secessionists; but as I despise them, I still have a greater detestation and contempt for a fanatic." In another account, according to the *Ashland Union,* the issue of Black suffrage had directly provoked this exchange. Johnson made clear that he was not going to require Black suffrage, and Sumner accused the president of ignoring the people who had elected him. Johnson then condemned fanatics and terminated the meeting.[11]

Some Republican newspapers occasionally carried quite different accounts. According to the *Cincinnati Gazette*, when Johnson and Sumner discussed Black suffrage the president told Sumner, "I quite agree with you." He also "cordially assented" to Sumner's plan to write to Black leaders in North Carolina and tell them that "their right to the ballot is recognized by the Administration." The radical abolitionist Wendell Phillips understood that Johnson had agreed with Sumner and the Radicals on an important issue. In an address on July 4 Phillips reported (although he doubted Johnson's sincerity) that the president had "agreed with Charles Sumner" that the formerly rebellious states "should be kept left out [of the Union] for the present." Another account at this time indicated that Johnson had instructed "a distinguished gentleman" to tell southern Unionists that "if they would immediately organize on the basis of universal loyal suffrage, he would personally be very glad of it, and would officially give them all the aid in his power." In this version Johnson supported Black suffrage and simply believed he did not have the power to require it and wished to avoid the use of "executive force."[12]

Such contradictions surely arose in part from the contrasting hopes of Republicans and Democrats, or from the human tendency—often present in conversations between two people—to "hear" what one wishes to hear. There is a similar, understandable tendency for those in authority to present their views in a manner that would be most acceptable or welcome to the hearer. Even "honest Abe" Lincoln was sometimes understood in very different ways by more than one person. But it is certain too that Johnson saw an advantage in being a bit confusing or unclear, persistently, about the question of Black suffrage. He had adopted a policy that excluded Black voters from the process of Reconstruction that was underway, but he could still claim that he was not hostile to the principle or that he hoped universal suffrage might come about, at some point. Indeed, as intra-party controversy intensified over his policy, he explicitly encouraged this kind of confusion.

The lack of clarity about Johnson's preferences increased from July to August and into September, months when white southerners were winning election to constitutional conventions and beginning to work toward readmission to the Union. First came some additional statements that seemed favorable toward Black suffrage. A Republican newspaper in Michigan, quoting the Washington, D.C., correspondent of the larger *Cincinnati Gazette*, reported that Johnson was in favor of Black suffrage. His proclamations setting Reconstruction in motion in the southern states merely showed that he was against *enforcing* or requiring it. "That he is nevertheless in favor of negro suffrage is a fact, resting on a[s] clear evidence as that other fact, that he believes treason to be the highest of crimes," wrote the correspondent. "I say he '*is* in favor of it,'" for "two months ago I know that his personal preferences were for negro suffrage" and "two months can hardly have wrought a fundamental change in his views." The Michigan editor was confident that this was accurate, because "Mr. Johnson is a believer in the people; he is not a believer in classes," and "to withhold from the freedmen of the South the right of suffrage, so inestimable to all the people of a free country as the badge of citizenship, would be to create a class," something that would contradict liberty and damage "the structure of our institutions."[13]

Within a few days the *New York Herald* and the *Chicago Tribune* reported that there had been a "long and stormy" meeting of the Cabinet at which the "length and breadth" of the president's Reconstruction policy was debated. Given the previous division in the Cabinet, readers could assume that Black suffrage was an important part of the discussion. The outcome of the Cabinet meeting was that Johnson was determined to stick with his policy "and carry it out, regardless of opposition or consequences." Presumably that would mean Johnson was determined to use his influence *against* demands for Black suffrage.[14]

In mid-August events in Mississippi further indicated that the president would throw his support to southern whites instead of to the former slaves. The commanding general in that state, Henry W. Slocum, issued an order putting him in conflict with the provisional governor, William Sharkey. When Sharkey moved to organize militia units in Mississippi, Slocum prohibited their formation because he feared Confederate veterans would dominate the units and oppress the freedmen. President Johnson then countermanded General Slocum's order and let the organization of the militia proceed. This action "aroused the suspicion and distrust of the North," according to historian James M. McPherson, "more than almost anything Johnson had done" to that point.[15]

Soon, however, the *Liberator* reported on a speech by General Robert Schenck of Ohio. Schenck told citizens in his home state that he had enjoyed "a full and free interview" with Johnson on August 6. In that interview Schenck had warned the president that things were moving too rapidly in the South, and that "rebel States" were benefiting from "untried processes" that troubled Ohio voters. In reply Johnson informed Schenck that "the local Governments set up in the rebellious States" were "temporary experiments." They were designed "simply to give the people an opportunity to show whether they will develop the right spirit and policy necessary for a full restoration." Schenck added that Johnson, "while regarding them as experiments . . . intends that the military power of the Government shall hold them in check." Should they "stra[y] back into rebellious ways, the military will be there to prevent them from again making trouble." Johnson pointed to his recent action in Richmond, Virginia, "where the citizens manifested their rebellious spirit by electing to office the very men who had recently been in arms against the Government." Johnson let Schenck know that "it was *with his sanction that the military authorities had set aside that election*," and the same reaction could be expected "in other cases of a similar kind."[16]

Within a few days of the *Liberator's* stories, the *New York Tribune* and a Republican paper in Indiana gave more encouragement to Radical Republicans. Early in September these journals reported on a conversation between Johnson and General Benjamin Butler, who wanted to resign his military commission. Butler had never been a professional soldier, and he explained that he now planned to go to New York and resume the practice of law. Johnson refused to accept Butler's resignation, however, "saying that his present reconstruction policy was an experiment; he did not know how it would succeed; and, if it failed, he would want the General to go into the South and take hold." About two weeks later a paper in Michigan reported a similar exchange between Johnson and "a distinguished New England Senator." In this conversation Johnson assured his visitor that he never had "intended to cut the Radicals" and that "he allowed the largest latitude of opinion on the right of the colored people to vote." Then he reiterated that his Reconstruction program in the South "was an experiment that might be successful and might not, and if unsuccessful . . . no one would be more ready to alter his course than he would be." The Radicals could rest assured that the freedmen "should be fully protected in their freedom and rights."[17]

News about Johnson's possible sympathy for Black suffrage continued to arrive in the first part of September, despite the fact that his white-only Reconstruction policy was well underway. According to a U.S. senator and a northern editor, reported one Ohio newspaper, Johnson had told a group of freedmen from Richmond, Virginia, "You are free, and the vainest Virginian shall yet not only acknowledge your freedom but your *equality, if you are true to yourselves.*" He then added a comment showing that he had a combative attitude toward racist southern elites. "Until those FFVs [first families of Virginia] come to their senses," Johnson declared, "I rather think United States bayonets will be about the only *laws* they will have." One week later he assured a New Orleans journalist that he was not hostile to Black suffrage. "Why cannot you people," he asked the Louisianan, "settle this thing without allowing it to bother me? Why cannot you do as Massachusetts does? If a negro can read the Constitution and write his own name, let him vote. There are 500 in Louisiana who can answer that test; but it will be doing justice all around, and stop this Northern clamor." Such words reinforced his earlier statements that were supportive and sympathetic.[18]

By the middle of the September, however, the tone changed. As southern whites organized governments under Johnson's plan, the president became more wedded to his policy. Meeting with a group of southern whites, Johnson voiced his belief that the South would be true "to her ancient instincts of frankness and manly honor." Such traits of character among southern whites allowed him to trust their oaths of allegiance. Johnson also criticized newspapers for trying "to create the impression that there exists disaffection South." He assured another delegation from Dixie that "they will not be persecuted nor treated harshly." The former rebels and northerners, he said, were members "of the same great family . . . bound to us by ties of affection and to be trusted and cherished upon their return." To a large group of whites from Georgia, Johnson characterized the bloody Civil War as a "feud" that "was a family quarrel." With readmission to the Union "the ties of friendship . . . would be stronger and more enduring than ever." To Provisional Governor William Sharkey of Mississippi, the president wrote that "the people must be trusted with their government" rather than denied participation. Another report of Johnson's comments to southern visitors quoted him affirming Democratic doctrines against monopoly and consolidation or centralization. He also declared, "I am one of the southern people and I love them." The president complimented southern whites and appeared to be aligning himself with them.[19]

Secretary of the Interior James Harlan then tacked in another direction when he wrote to Republicans in Iowa, his home state. Harlan presented an explanation of Johnson's views and policy that could reassure Radicals and advocates of Black suffrage. It had been a mistake, Harlan said, for Iowa's Union State Convention wrongly to assume that the president was "in opposition to negro suffrage. . . . The real question at issue," Harlan explained, "is not whether negroes shall be permitted to vote, but whether they shall derive that authority from the National Government, or from the State Governments respectively." Johnson maintained that the Constitution did not give the federal government the right to interfere with state decisions. But the question of suffrage, noted Harlan, "*may arise and properly be decided by Congress, when Senators and members present themselves for admission to seats in that body,* under the clause . . . which makes each House the exclusive judge of the qualifications and elections of members." Harlan went on to say that if the actions of a southern state showed its government was "other than republican, it would be the duty of Congress to reject applicants for seats, and to adopt whatever legislative remedies would in their judgment be necessary to carry out the guarantees of the constitution." Since congressional Republicans assumed they would play an important role in Reconstruction policy, these comments by a member of the Cabinet suggested the president would be cooperative.[20]

But on September 27 the *National Anti-Slavery Standard* reported that Johnson had declared on the 16th, "This is a white man's country, and by God, while I am president it shall be a white man's government." Other newspapers copied this report, and the Democratic *Chicago Times* quickly defended the president against the *National Anti-Slavery Standard*'s criticism of such "inhuman and atheistic words." The *Times* said that Johnson had been talking with Missouri's governor and probably had reacted to the kind of "fanaticism and impudence" that Missouri radicals had often brought against Abraham Lincoln. Besides, few could object to Johnson's affirmation of "so laudable a purpose."[21]

Early in October Johnson made a long speech to a regiment of Black troops from the District of Columbia. Its language was by turns warmly sympathetic and deeply discouraging. He began by declaring that the African American was a citizen and that the United States was his country: "This country is your country as well as anybody else's country. [Cheers] . . . This country is founded on the principles of equality, and . . . the standard by which persons are to be estimated is according to their merit and their worth." To this point the soldiers had reason to cheer. But then Johnson told them that weakening racial hatreds was "another part of your mission," for they should "give evidence to the world that you are capable and competent to govern yourselves." He lectured the men on "obedience and submission to the law," avoiding "low saloons and other places of disreputable character" and being "industrious . . . virtuous . . . [and] upright." After urging respect for the ties of marriage, Johnson referred to a different kind of experiment he was undertaking. It was unclear, he said, "whether this race can be incorporated and mixed with the people of the United States . . . with all the prejudices of the whites." He wondered if "the digestive powers of the American Government" were "sufficient to receive this element in a new shape . . . and make it work healthfully upon the system." Johnson said he favored making the experiment, though God might show a path to separation of the races in "the far distant future." The *New York Sun* was one of the papers that carried this same speech, and it added Johnson's comment that, with separation, providence might arrange for "the colored man [to be] taken to his land of inheritance and promise." By this point, if not before, abolitionist leaders like Wendell Phillips had concluded that Johnson was "three-quarters rebel."[22]

Several days later some newspapers began to copy the report—somewhat more favorable to Black suffrage—of a conversation between Secretary of the Navy Gideon Welles and the editor of the Hartford *Press*. Welles had asserted that "if Mr. Johnson was at home and a private citizen, he would favor negro suffrage in Tennessee." The *Ebensburg Alleghanian* reported that, according to Senator James Doolittle, the president wanted "each Southern State" to "strike out all constitutional restrictions upon colored suffrage" and empower the legislature "to extend from time to time, the rights of suffrage to certain superior classes of the colored people, such as those who had performed the military service, who had for a long time been heads of families, and supported them by their own industry, and who had demonstrated clearly their intellectual fitness to exercise the right of suffrage." The *Chicago Republican* specified that Doolittle had explained these views as part of a speech he gave in Milwaukee.[23]

A few days later a great many newspapers carried accounts of a conversation on October 18 between Johnson and George L. Stearns of Massachusetts, the abolitionist who took the lead in circulating pro-suffrage articles. Stearns's talk with the president covered most of the major issues of Reconstruction. Stearns then composed a summary of the conversation that Johnson approved as "substantially correct." By making this document available to newspapers, Stearns let Johnson present his ideas in a fashion that the president probably viewed as most attractive, although there could be an important difference between the description of a policy and its execution. Surprisingly, Stearns seemed to be comfortable with the content of the discussion because he asserted that it would promote understanding between the president and "our leading men" and also would "unite the public mind in favor of your plan, so far at least as you would carry it out without modification." Yet Black suffrage clearly was no priority for the president, and now apparently was of diminished importance for Stearns.[24]

Asked if he was moving toward the Democrats, Johnson laughed and claimed they were moving toward him. Speaking to Republicans, the president did not shrink from some of the positions that most put him in conflict with many leaders, especially the Radicals. He began with a declaration that the southern states were "in the Union, which is whole and indivisible." To those who believed these states should be treated as territories or conquered provinces, it was clear that Johnson would not agree. He described his task, now that the rebellion was crushed, as reconstructing state governments that were "prostrated, laid out on the ground." They needed to be "taken up and adapted to the progress of events." Johnson then announced, "We are making very rapid progress, so rapid I sometimes cannot realize it; it appears like a dream." This statement undoubtedly was surprising to many northern Republican officeholders, editors, and voters. Much of the news from the South was clearly troubling and discouraging, yet Johnson seemed elated by what he viewed as progress. Johnson continued, "We must not be in too much of a hurry," but with these words he did not mean that the formerly rebellious states should be kept out of the Union for a substantial period. He meant that "it is better to let them reconstruct themselves than to force them to it. . . . We must be patient with them."[25]

Perhaps Johnson was aware that his words would arouse concern because he immediately claimed that "we can check them" if necessary and "correct their errors." But he justified his conduct on another controversial matter, that of pardons. The chief executive who had begun his term in office speaking loudly and repeatedly about the crime of treason and the necessity of punishing traitors now disclosed that he "did not expect to keep out . . . a large number" of those who had to request amnesty. His idea was that "they should sue for pardon," and he assumed that merely by doing so they would "realize the enormity of the crime they had committed." By this point in 1865 the number of pardons was already very large, and many prominent men who initially had been excluded from Reconstruction's political process were writing constitutions and holding public office throughout the South.[26]

Johnson subsequently turned to the question of "equal suffrage." Again his attitude was sanguine and contented with what he saw as progress. "You could not have broached the subject of equal suffrage," Johnson said, even "at the North, seven years ago, and we must remember that the changes at the South have been more rapid" still. White southerners "have been obliged to accept more unpalatable truth than the North has; we must give them time to digest a part, for we cannot expect such large affairs will be comprehended and digested at once." The former rebels needed "time to understand their new position." Johnson was correct about the pace that change had taken in the revolutionary years of a great civil war, but he had no desire to keep the revolution going. It was becoming clear that this president, a white southerner himself, had more innate sympathy and understanding for white men who had lost their slaves than for Black people who prayed that their emancipation would be thorough.[27]

Johnson went on to argue that the right to vote was not a "natural right, but a political right." He opposed any "great consolidation of power in the Central Government" and declared that if he "interfered with the vote in the Rebel States" and required Black suffrage, he would be able to "do the same thing for my own purposes in Pennsylvania." In fact, "if the general Government controls the right to vote in the States, it might establish" rules that would allow it to "create a central despotism." These views, especially his emphasis on local decision-making and his fear of central power, echoed traditional and fundamental positions of the Democratic Party, his political affiliation throughout most of his career.[28]

Then Johnson endeavored to put his opinions about Black suffrage in a slightly better light for the many Republicans who argued that Black suffrage was not only right but essential for the defense and security of both former slaves and the Union itself. The president told Stearns that his position was identical to "what it would be if I was in Tennessee." Johnson would "try to introduce negro suffrage gradually" if he were in Tennessee, so this meant that his desire was to see it introduced in the rest of the South. He listed the groups that he, and some others, would favor initially—former soldiers, men who could read and write, and men who owned some property, "say $200 or $250." However, to those who would ask why not "let the negroes have universal suffrage now," his reply was blunt and unequivocal: "It would breed a war of races." Such conflict was inevitable, he suggested, because slavery had bred hostility between non-slaveholding whites and Blacks. Former slaves would vote for "the late master," and resentful poorer whites would increase the "outrages" against Black southerners. "Universal suffrage" thus "would create another war, not against us, but a war of races."[29]

Ending the conversation on a note that Republicans and many northerners would welcome, Johnson said that for many years he had favored basing representation in Congress on the number of "qualified voters." Before the South would gain representation in 1872 (following the next census), the nation should change the basis of representation "from population to qualified voters, North and well as South." He continued, "In due course of time, the States, *without regard* to color, might extend the elective franchise to all who possessed certain mental, moral, or such other qualifications, as might be determined by an enlightened public judgment."[30]

Johnson acted on a feeling of confidence in his policies when he laid out his views to Stearns in this manner. He was voicing his own personal beliefs, and he knew that many northerners held attitudes about race that were not very different. Northern Democrats were more stridently racist, yet some Republicans shared Johnson's views. Members of the Cabinet were standing behind him, and Secretary of State William Seward told Gideon Welles that the president cherished warm feelings toward those members of his administration. Johnson had previously developed a relationship with General Grant, the commander of the army, that was "quite friendly," and one of Grant's closest aides praised the president's actions. Adam Badeau had heard nothing but "warm commendation of Mr. Johnson's policy; in New York as well as St. Louis, in Washington just as in Galena." Badeau told Elihu Washburne that "everywhere . . . all the sober substantial men seem to support him. The attempt of foolish impractical men to foist their notions upon the country has met with no success." Reportedly Johnson said "that the sooner they [the Radicals] force the issue [of Black suffrage in Congress], the sooner 'they will learn that the Administration can get along better without the Radicals than the Radicals can get along without the Administration.'"[31]

Johnson's conversation with Stearns troubled some Republican leaders and editors, who responded with arguments against its faulty logic. The *New*

York Tribune, for example, protested that the nation's chief executive had as much right to require suffrage as to decree emancipation. In similar fashion, others asked why the president could decide which rebellious southern whites could vote yet he could not decide on suffrage for freed Blacks. His own policies did not treat the southern states as if they had never left the Union. Johnson's logic also was not consistent. The priority that he favored for Black military veterans, "because they had served," recognized a claim for their rights that justified immediate enjoyment of the suffrage. In addition, if literacy fitted a man for the elective franchise, then "he is, of course, quite as worthy of it this year as next." The *Tribune* seemed willing to accept a partial suffrage, if "Southern Statesmen" would adopt that policy, but it wanted to see "justice . . . done to the Blacks of the South." The *Cleveland Daily Herald* reported that Johnson was going to urge Congress to adopt "some system of manhood suffrage . . . with intellectual limitation as to the freedmen." The *Chicago Tribune* hoped this was true, because the main argument against Black suffrage seemed to be that the president was against it. "What Republicans Believe!" insisted the *Tribune,* was "that every man admitted to be intelligent and self-supporting shall vote." Moreover, since "ignorant" white paupers were allowed to vote, it was necessary that Blacks in the South be "acknowledged as part of their people, and . . . granted the political rights of citizens as rapidly as may be wholly safe." At least "all the intelligent, self-sustaining, tax-paying" southern Blacks should vote.[32]

A few Republican newspapers remained confident that Johnson would "act with Congress in requiring that the Southern States" let all men vote. Others either concentrated on state elections taking place at that time or found ways to accept Johnson's statements without protest. An Ohio paper objected that "a very large class" believed Johnson was wrong and could require Black suffrage, but at least he had made it clear that he personally favored suffrage now for army veterans. If "southern statesmen adopt this policy," they would do much to resolve a very "troublesome question." Another Ohio editor agreed that Johnson should not "force" Black suffrage "on the white people of the South" but believed that "they will ere long concede this privilege to the freedmen." The *Ebensburg Alleghanian,* a reliably Republican paper in Pennsylvania, printed Stearns's account in full. Then it referred to the 1864 incident in which Johnson pledged to be Black people's "Moses" and argued that his assertion that "if he were in Tennessee, he would be an advocate of negro suffrage, is in strict accord with this former record." Another Republican editor in Pennsylvania argued that "the true spirit of Republican institutions" required extending the right of suffrage "without regard to race or color" but conceded "that it is only to be reached by gradual approaches." Attaining "ideal republican perfection . . . at a single stride" was unrealistic and "has never been advocated." A Kansas editor who admitted that his faith had been "very much shaken" focused on the idea that Johnson was making "an experiment" and that he or Congress would rectify errors. Another editor in that state believed that "loyal blacks" must have "the same rights at the polls as the rebel whites." But he estimated that "a majority of the people of every State are opposed to negro suffrage," and therefore it was sensible to defer action.[33]

To some Republicans Johnson's positions on Black suffrage and on the acceptability of the new constitutions in the South might have remained a bit unclear. Radical Republicans by now had been disabused of their hopes for Johnson. But they and others took it for granted that Congress naturally would have a major influence on policy once it reconvened. During the fall's elections in the North, few Republicans wanted to precipitate conflict with the titular head of their party. Nevertheless, the tension between Johnson's positions and those of many Republicans was evident and growing. When Alexander McClure, a prominent editor and state politician in Pennsylvania, interviewed the president, he came away sobered and disapproving. He learned that Johnson was "averse to confiscation . . . has not much hope that the Negroes will vindicate their right, by works to be recognized as the equals of the White men," and was flattered by the approval and attentions of the Democratic Party. McClure wrote, "*I feel warranted in saying,*" that Johnson would "*adhere to the political fortunes of the Southern States, without regard to political consequences.* This may, or may not, sever him from the party that sustained and cherished him in the darkest days through which he passed, and that won him the highest honors of the nation through a flood of obloquy." Clearly, however, Johnson "*means above all other things, to compass the admission of the Southern members,* and the complete restoration of power of those States," despite the deficiencies in their conduct. McClure wondered "where in all this . . . the nation shall see that 'treason is the greatest of crimes and must be punished.'" A break between Johnson and Republicans seemed ever more likely, and the reconvening of Congress in December was well suited to bring it into the open.[34]

12

Toward the Return of Congress

B y November many articles in the northern press focused on the return of Congress in December, but international events also received persistent coverage. A violent internal conflict had broken out in Jamaica, and given the racial character of the suffrage issue in the United States, the two topics converged. Democratic newspapers seized on Jamaica as a means to warn of racial dangers in the United States and to promote their agenda for Reconstruction. Republicans rejected that connection and prepared their own proposals. Despite being aware that the chance for Black suffrage in 1865 had passed, Republicans were determined to improve on the results of Andrew Johnson's initiatives. African Americans and their most committed white allies continued to advocate for suffrage and to demand equal rights. Racial issues thus continued to be central to the issues of Reconstruction.

Jamaica's Morant Bay Rebellion occurred in a climate of poverty, crop failures, drought, and epidemic disease. Although the island's slaves had been freed in 1834, fewer than one-half of 1 percent could vote, due to high poll taxes, and most islanders were suffering. A protest march led by a Black preacher met with gunfire from the militia, and over the next few days rebellion blossomed. The growing resistance triggered brutal repression by the government, which was still under British colonial control. There were hundreds of deaths and hundreds of arrests leading to prison sentences and whippings. Although many details about the events are still debated, Democratic newspapers in the North believed that the lessons for the United States were crystal clear.

Jamaica's "Negro Rebellion," said a Pennsylvania newspaper, demonstrated "incontestably that the natural antipathieo existing between the two races render it impossible for them to live together in harmony on terms of equality." It was a "perversion of natural laws" to attempt to legislate equality, for "negroes are naturally savage. Their instincts are all barbarian." The *New York World* warned that if violence could break out in Jamaica "over petty questions of local administration," the United States must recognize its "peril" and establish firm control "at the South." In unsettled conditions "ignorant" and "untutored" southern Blacks might give free rein to "a storm of insurgent passions, which the imagination shudders from contemplating." Another Pennsylvania paper feared "The War of Races," while Ohio's *Cadiz Sentinel* called the "scenes of barbarous cruelty" in Jamaica "the most horrible known to modern history." A newspaper colleague in Ohio misleadingly claimed that the island's Blacks had enjoyed "equal political rights" for twenty-seven years and had repaid "the effort to make them the equal of the White race, by taking the high road to barbarism."[1]

The *Indianapolis Daily Herald* declared that "Republican Freedom in Jamaica" had shown "What We May Fear in the United States." Another Democratic newspaper in Indiana deplored the murder of "innocent and helpless white men, women and children . . . cruelly butchered" by Blacks whose "religious orgies" encouraged them to believe they were entitled to land. A few weeks later the *New York World* raised similar fears, seeing "a singular accordance between the dreams and vision of the revolting negroes in Jamaica" and desires for land that were "now agitating the negro populations in many parts of the South." The *World* cited rumors of planned uprisings in Louisiana, Virginia, Arkansas, and Georgia and deplored the "savage traits" of Blacks, who were being encouraged by Republicans. As evidence of "savage traits," a Pennsylvania editor relied on the claim by a Mobile, Alabama, newspaper that the freed people practiced Voodoo rites, including "human sacrifice."[2]

To Democratic editors the events in Jamaica made clear what the Republicans and abolitionists must not be allowed to accomplish in the United States. Democrats used the conflict to intensify a variety of racist attacks and validate their rejection of Republican goals for Reconstruction. Calling Jamaica "one of those Edens which Mr. H. Greeley and Wendell Phillips are laboring to establish in this country," an Illinois newspaper warned that equal rights for Blacks meant suffrage and "marry[ing] the white man's sister and daughter." Blacks had turned Jamaica "from a first-class productive country . . . into nothingness." What else could be expected of the abolitionist's "gentle African" who "makes a hash of his own children for breakfast"? The *Indianapolis Daily State Sentinel* revived the prediction that Blacks "turned loose in the South . . . will pour in upon us by the thousands," and soon "little American citizens of African descent will be as thick among us as the frogs were in Egypt." The Black man must never be allowed to gain a position "where he can vent his hostility of race against us by exercising his power over us." To allow that "*inferior race*" to vote would "make our elections confused mobs" and destroy the republic, as supposedly occurred when Rome enlarged the suffrage.[3]

When Republican newspapers commented on the violence in Jamaica, they either treated it as a foreign event irrelevant to Reconstruction in the United States or they showed that Democrats were distorting facts for political advantage. The *Chicago Tribune* was frank—"the Copperhead and rebel press" was "lying about" the Morant Bay Rebellion. It cited the *New York Herald* for numerous errors in its reporting, errors that amounted to "mingled ignorance, cunning, duplicity and intentional falsehood." The powerless, heavily taxed masses on that island had reacted against what a London publication admitted was "notoriously the worst governed dependency of Great Britain, and nothing but the law-abiding docility of the negro and his warm loyalty to the British crown has preserved a severely oppressed people in a state of peaceable endurance." A Pennsylvania editor agreed that Democrats were "misrepresenting the negro and endeavoring to prejudice the white race against him." Violence had erupted in Jamaica not because Blacks were savage but because they struck for "manhood and liberty." *Harper's Weekly* judged that "morbid hostility to the colored race" had tainted all the Copperhead reporting about Jamaica.[4]

Many Democrats, unshaken by defeat in recent elections, also defended the South and affirmed their past claims about an unjustifiable abolition war and Republican violations of civil liberties. The result of the "Black Republican four years' war 'for the African and his race,'" insisted one editor, was "four billions of money squandered . . . hundreds of thousands of valuable lives wasted in battle," and freed Blacks who were starving in the South. He declared, "*We would rather be defeated upholding the rights of white men* than triumphant" through abandonment of the party's principles.

Wisconsin's *La Crosse Democrat* blasted the "psalm-singing, hypocritical skin-flints" of New England who were breaking down "white liberties." Poor whites there would have to "paint their skins black" and "kink their hair" to get any help, since the region's puritanical Republicans cared only for African Americans.[5]

Ohio's *Ashland Union* stuck by its wartime charge that negotiation would have ended the war more quickly and deplored cruel mistreatment of southern whites. This paper declared that white southerners were being treated with "no justice, no honor, no humanity." Supposedly "'the poor whites' are dying of *starvation* by the hundreds!" while "indolent Negroes are provided with the necessaries of life by the Freedmen's Bureau." The *Daily Ohio Statesman* protested that if Congress were to make "further demands" on the South or "inflic[t] additional humiliation upon the people . . . such demands will be made and enforced in violation of the Constitution of the United States." New York's prominent former governor Horatio Seymour agreed that the nation had "deviated from the principles of the Constitution" and declared, "Our soldiers did not risk their lives on the battle-field to hold a section of the country in military enslavement." Another Ohio editor commended Montgomery Blair, who now charged Republicans with being a "gang of scoundrels" trying to give Blacks "dominion" in the South. This paper condemned "The Conspiracy against the Whites of the South."[6]

Several Democratic newspapers even defended the idea of paying the rebels' war debt, an idea with little support in the North. The *Chicago Times* took the lead, claiming, "There is no ground of justice upon which we can expect the Southern people to submit willingly to the situation unless we recognize the same value in their funded obligations as our own." The *Hartford Times*, observed papers in New York and Connecticut, also "had declared the assumption of the rebel debt a duty." The *North American and United States Gazette* added the names of the *Cincinnati Enquirer* and the *Buffalo Courier* to the list—"all leading northern Democratic papers . . . advocating the assumption of the confederate debt." The *North American* warned that if southerners were seated in Congress, "every one" of them "would vote for assumption of the debt" and be supported by northern Democrats. The Democratic press was in a fighting mood.[7]

But if Democrats were not going to withdraw from the political battle, neither were Radical Republicans and African Americans in both the North and South. Despite the rejection of Black suffrage in three northern states and the territory of Colorado—events that arrested progress on the issue—advocates for Black suffrage and equal rights pressed on. Senator Charles Sumner published a letter in the New York *Independent* that was copied elsewhere. Sumner commended that paper for taking "sure ground" for "equal rights" and declared that "never was a duty plainer.... If the country fails to do justice now, it will commit a crime," for Blacks had earned full citizenship. All the future good of the country—in security, commerce, agriculture, and national credit—depended on "justice" and a "new order of things." Asserting that "every pretended government organized by recent rebels" must be treated as a "nullity," Sumner said it was impossible to "measure the mischief which has already ensued from the 'experiment'" the president began. Congress would have to act and "apply the remedy." Even among Republicans who were less devoted to Black rights than Sumner, the conviction had hardened that changes must be made. As one Kansas editor put it, Johnson's "experiment . . . has not proved satisfactory in most respects." He hoped that Johnson would alter it, but in any case, "accursed be that Northern man who would vote in Congress—or out of it—to restore [the rebel states] to their forfeited rights in the Union." Another Kansas newspaper asked why Johnson would not make an "experiment" of Black suffrage and complained he was giving all power "into the hands of rebels."[8]

The *Ebensburg Alleghanian* agreed that "the masses" would not stand for any "system of reconstruction" that allowed "those who were instrumental in precipitating the country into rebellion and in upholding and prolonging that rebellion" to participate in legislation or "hold offices of honor or trust under the government." Yet the *Cincinnati Gazette* reported that twenty members of North Carolina's constitutional convention vowed to accomplish exactly that. The delegates had met in secret and pledged to give their support solely to candidates who were loyal Confederates. Another Republican paper in Pennsylvania rejected "The President's Plan," saying, "We never had much faith in the President's theory of reconstruction." It was certain that "more will be required and made known . . . either by the President or Congress." From Kansas came an editor's judgment that southern whites "are still rebels at heart, and that all their professions of loyalty are hollow and deceitful." The *New York Tribune* warned that conventions and elections in the South showed "a spirit of defiance," and the *Cleveland Leader* rendered a similar verdict when 47 percent of the delegates in Georgia's convention voted against repudiation of the rebel debt.

Even the conservative but independent *New York Herald* speculated that southern behavior in Georgia, Mississippi, and South Carolina had been so bad that Johnson would not decree "a general amnesty" for those states.[9]

African Americans were not waiting for Republicans to fight for Black suffrage. In both the North and South Black people organized and spoke out strongly for their rights. The "colored citizens of Vicksburg" led the way in the fall by assembling to "warn the North" about "the sort of reconstruction inaugurated by the white Convention of that State." Mississippi's white convention had called on the subsequent legislature "to guard the State against any evils that may arise from sudden emancipation." The system of "warranteeism" the convention advocated, in which freedmen might be handed over "to the unchecked control of the Board of County Police," could prove to be "but another name for slavery." The Blacks who assembled in protest put their "firm conviction" on record that, if Mississippi gained readmission to the Union, its legislature would "pass such proscriptive class laws against the freedmen as will result in their expatriation from the State, or their practical re-enslavement." Congress should block that possibility.[10]

South Carolina Blacks spoke out for their rights in a Convention of Colored People that met at Zion Presbyterian Church in Charleston from November 20 to November 25. Fifty-one delegates attended and heard from two sympathetic U.S. Army officers and a white South Carolinian before passing resolutions calling for "good schools" and urging Black progress through "industry and economy." In resolutions aimed at whites, they declared they had "no hatred or malice" toward former slaveholders, denied that there was any danger of "an insurrection by the 'Negroes,'" and explained that their desire was for "fellowship" with all people of the state. But the Black South Carolinians also knew that "we are not freemen till we attain to all the rights and privileges of freemen," and that the Freedmen's Bureau needed to continue its work until state laws would "fully" protect "our persons and property." The convention would accept "qualifications" for the suffrage, but "we reject discriminations because of color."[11]

In an address to the people of South Carolina, the convention cited the Declaration of Independence, the Constitution, and religious principles and then declared, "We ask only for *even-handed Justice*" that would allow a fair path to progress. The delegates were not reluctant to list the wrongs they suffered—denial of rights of citizenship, testimony in courts, suffrage, education, or the opportunity to buy land and engage in business. They "simply desire[d] that we shall be recognized as men" so that they could "acquire homesteads," enjoy "equity and justice," and contribute to "the prosperity and growth" of South Carolina by elevating themselves. A Declaration of Rights and Wrongs was eloquent on the practical denial of truths in the Declaration of Independence. Prejudice had nullified their "natural" and "inalienable rights," deprived them of "political rights," and closed "the avenues of wealth and education," while Black bodies had been "outraged with impunity." Although the Black population had "bled and sweat[ed]" to enrich "those who have degraded us, and still continue to oppress us," the wrong of "taxation without representation" continued.[12]

Finally, the Black South Carolinians addressed both the state legislature and Congress. To the legislators the delegates argued for repeal of laws applied "on account of our color" and asked for "the right of suffrage and the right of testifying in courts of law," two things "necessary to our welfare and elevation." Their appeal was based on "justice" but also on hopes of "*generosity*," and the common sense that the legislature's actions would determine "whether we shall become useful citizens or dissatisfied subjects." From Congress they asked not only for "law and order" in South Carolina but also "that a fair and impartial construction be given to the pledges of government to us concerning the land question." In addition, they wanted "the school, the pulpit, [and] the press" to be "as secure in South Carolina as in Massachusetts," and "that equal suffrage be conferred upon us, in common with the white men of this State." Laws such as a recent effort "to deprive us of arms" should be forbidden as well as any code of Black laws different from "the same laws that control other men."[13]

In Arkansas a Convention of Colored Citizens met in Little Rock from November 30 through December 2. One of the speakers promptly argued that the ballot should be available to Blacks everywhere and quoted Frederick Douglass that "it was the Negro thrown into the scale on the side of the nation that broke the back of the rebellion and saved the nation." Therefore, "the Government of the United States is pledged to secure our rights; we wrote the contract in blood." An unusual scene occurred when "Mr. Cobb, a returned Southron," came forward "reluctantly" but spoke "with feeling, and finally resorted to tears (though they may have been hypocritical ones)" to assert "the love he has ever had for the Negro." He "implored his colored brethren to forgive him" for his efforts to destroy the Union and oppress Blacks. The delegates, addressing their most important concerns, proceeded to show that they needed "the protection of law" to guarantee their emancipation. They asked the state legislature for "equality before the law and the right of suffrage." Like other Black conventions, this assembly cited the Bible and the principle of no taxation without representation, and appealed to southern whites to help the state prosper by "provid[ing] for the education of our children." The quantity of cotton "produced by the freedmen of Arkansas, under the most disadvantageous circumstances," refuted claims that Black laborers were indolent, and therefore they asked also for just and equitable treatment of labor.[14]

These initiatives, unfortunately, were sure to be scorned in the South and met with a mixed reception in the North. But the former slaves had committed allies. Radical Republicans took note of the memorials, appeals, and resolutions, and some Republican newspapers in the North did so also. The *Vermont Watchman and State Journal*, for example, published the "Memorial of the South Carolina Freedmen" to Congress, as did a neighboring paper in Burlington, Vermont. However, most Republican papers outside the major cities had limited space for detailed accounts from the South. It was more likely that Republican editors in the North would cover the actions of Blacks and abolitionists in their own states.[15]

There was much to cover, for northern Black leaders were very active in the fall, almost everywhere that a convention had not been held during the first part of the year. Prominent Black abolitionists spoke out at the Twenty-Ninth Annual Meeting of the Pennsylvania Anti-Slavery Society at the end of October. The *Philadelphia Press* and the *Liberator* printed a long report from the meeting. The group recognized that "the spirit of slavery was still violent in many parts of the country" and that Pennsylvania needed to do more to "secure the freedom of the black man." The society's Executive Committee proposed resolutions declaring that equal suffrage was essential, that southern whites remained hostile, and that the posture of Andrew Johnson and the Republican Party merited strong criticism. Compromise with wrong, the committee declared, was always a disaster. Speakers like Robert Purvis and Wendell Phillips called on members to work harder because antislavery work was not done. Even if the Thirteenth Amendment were successfully ratified, the southern states were sure to erect barriers to freedom if they gained readmission to Congress.[16]

Michigan's Colored Men's Convention assembled in mid-September to work for rights and to reorganize that state's chapter of the Equal Rights

League. Angry that officers of the original state league had ignored the wishes of elected representatives, these delegates reorganized and refounded the Equal Rights League. After concluding that matter, the delegates denounced Andrew Johnson's policy of Reconstruction as "unwise, [and] unfaithful to the colored American." All means must be pursued to reconstruct the Union on "the basis of Universal Suffrage." Some speakers declared with feeling that the Black man "will submit no longer to his own degradation," and that experience taught that racial elevation depended not on whites but "upon the black man." An *Address to the People of Color* in the state called on them to give active support to the reorganized Equal Rights League.[17]

In Indiana 150 Black men met in Indianapolis's African Methodist Church late in October. Complaining that their rights had been "flagrantly, wickedly, and most inhumanly violated," they called on federal and state governments to repeal "tyrannical laws." Like other conventions of "colored men," they dedicated themselves to elevating the race and vowed to petition the state legislature at its next session to gain access to school funds and the right to testify in court cases. Proud of their role in suppressing the rebellion, they claimed "equal rights with other men before the laws." In Iowa U.S. Army veterans organized a Convention of Colored Iowa Soldiers, where the group's president promptly called for political rights. Republicans had won the recent state elections, so now it was time for "the legislature to do its duty" and open the path "to the ballot box." Resolutions declared that the troops had earned that right. The conventioneers then appealed to their "white friends" to do justice and honor the Declaration of Independence.[18]

In Wisconsin leaders of the Black community called for a state convention in Milwaukee near the end of October. That same month African Americans in Kansas met and called for the right to vote. The state needed to strike the word "white" from its laws governing suffrage in order to recognize the legitimate claims of the Black population. In addition, this convention demanded the "securing [of] negro equality in the reconstruction of the southern states, in order to give the balance of power to the Union party of the north in its efforts to reconstruct the government." New York had its own State Convention of Colored Men, which decided to send spokesmen to Washington "to urge upon the members of Congress the importance of having the status of the colored Americans so fixed in the land" that color would not impair "the enjoyment of all rights that appertain to citizenship." The New Yorkers designated a committee whose work would be "to urge the franchise" and other measures for the rights of Black citizens.[19]

Far to the west in California Black men began their convention by hearing the meeting's president call immediately for the right to vote. The more than three dozen delegates wanted more primary schools for Black children, or "if they were not to have a separate school, let them be admitted to those already established." Calling also for secondary education and advances in morality, temperance, and wealth, they demanded "Equality before the Law" in addition to the "political franchise." To demonstrate their contributing role in the state, they compiled statistics on their population, churches, businesses, professions, and wealth. "The country is only half saved," they declared, and "slavery only half abolished and the war but half ended, until all of the disabling laws which were the natural fruits of slavery are repealed, and universal suffrage exist in every State in the Union." By publishing an address to the people of California they made these demands known.[20]

The northeast also had its New England Regional Convention of Colored People in Boston at the beginning of December. Renowned figures such as William Wells Brown, George T. Downing, and Fredrick Douglass took part, with Douglass saying that the war had ended too soon. "Peace for the Southern white man," he said, "now meant war against the negro." The group decided to send a representative to Washington to lobby Congress and urge "equality before the law for all Americans." One resolution declared that Congress must not allow any privileged class in the returning states or any exclusive right to vote for whites. Another condemned the "many cases" of "whipping, scourging and murdering" of freed people in the South, as well as "the oppressive laws which have been enacted by the provisional legislatures of the Southern States." Hailing "the efforts of Charles Sumner and his co-workers in Congress," the body named George Downing as its representative to go to Washington and undertook to raise ample money to support his work.[21]

These Black protests bolstered Republicans' support for equal rights. Meanwhile party leaders in Congress were not sitting idly by as the reconvening of Congress approached. The *Cleveland Leader* reported that "an important suffrage meeting was to be held in Washington" in the middle of October. It was known that General Benjamin Butler and Senator Henry Wilson of Massachusetts, two leading Radicals, were scheduled to speak. Other congressional leaders undoubtedly shared correspondence or spoke together where face-to-face meetings were possible. Thaddeus Stevens received mail expressing dismay over Johnson's policies. One correspondent complained that the "great principles involved in the recent struggle are lost sight of entirely," and that around the White House one heard "vehement denunciation of the Radicals." Another supporter arranged to send two hundred copies of one of Stevens's speeches to Union senators and representatives. Stevens himself made plans to speak at an anniversary celebration for the Pennsylvanian Anti-Slavery Society while he considered what would be needed in Congress.[22]

Benjamin Butler sent Stevens his ideas for a bill to fight "southern injustice to the Negro." Butler aimed to exclude from Congress the formerly rebellious states, and he wanted legislation to make clear that the second section of the Thirteenth Amendment—giving Congress the power to enforce the end of slavery—was indeed able to give "life and effect" to emancipation "and in favor of liberty and equal rights." Although his legislation would not mention "the rights of suffrage," he felt that anyone who might vote against the bill and "against equality of rights" thereby supported "the black code of the south with its whipping of women and hunting of men with guns and hounds." Butler feared southern Black codes that would make vagrancy a crime for which "the negro shall be sold in servitude as a punishment" by some "petty magistrate or Justice of the Peace." He proposed a jury trial as a means to block such results and was ready to consult with Stevens on similar measures.[23]

Stevens and others were steadily receiving more troubling information about the unreconstructed attitudes of defiant white southerners. For example, a former slaveholder who now declared that he favored both Black rights and the Republican Party wrote to Stevens from New Albany, Mississippi. Leaving the freed people in the hands of prejudiced southerners, he said, would be "barbarous. Look at the character of the legislation already carried out and proposed"—its aim was to continue the "wrongs and oppression" of the past. Mississippians believed that "the president intends to sustain such a course; and hence the south is encouraged" and "the hatred . . . against the freedman" is "intensified." He warned that "traitors" were being sent to Congress to play a role in "the very government" they had been "attempting to destroy." Illinois's Elihu Washburne received a similar letter from S. S. Panfield, a Mississippian who was originally from New York and who described himself as a "*true* Union man." Any "real expression of union sentiment," said Panfield, "is even now not tolerated in this state of unrepentant rebels. We are so afraid that you will be all deceived by the interested *policy* of the South. *Pray be careful.*"[24]

The *New York Tribune* chronicled a succession of discouraging events in the South. South Carolina's affection for Wade Hampton and the actions of the convention in Georgia revealed that "a spirit of defiance is pervading the South." In North Carolina the Union candidates for Congress were all beaten; Alabama likewise defeated its Union candidates. With such election results, what would become of the Union victory? The *Tribune* asked, "Has the South Any Statesmen Still Living?" A Republican newspaper in Pennsylvania noted that South Carolina's convention repealed the act of secession without denying its "right" to break up the Union. The words of Mississippi's newly elected governor, in the view of a Maryland paper, amounted to "a threat of future rebellion" if the South did not get its way. Even the *New York Herald's* correspondent reported that "a majority" of Mississippi's former slaveholders hoped that warranteeism would allow them "to compel the negroes to work for stipulated wages and stated lengths of time." The *Cincinnati Gazette* carried reports that outside of Tennessee the South "will not elect loyal men to Congress," and the *Chicago Tribune* reported that Johnson's appointments in Alabama were all disloyal men.

Senator Henry Wilson of Massachusetts introduced a bill to emancipate slaves in the District of Columbia and fought with determination for Black rights after the war. (Julian Vannerson, photographer, *McClees' Gallery of Photographic Portraits of the Senators, Representatives, and Delegates of the Thirty-Fifth Congress* [Washington, D.C.: McClees and Beck, 1859]; Library of Congress, Prints and Photographs Division)

"There is not," said this correspondent, "an unconditional loyal politician or newspaper in all of the recently seceded States."[25]

As Radical Republicans looked toward the actions of Congress, they had the support of many of the North's serious magazines. *Harper's Weekly* wrote that Alabama's convention "adhere[d] to the right of secession" and politically outlawed "half the population of the State." The outlawed half consisted of those who showed "unswerving fidelity to the Union during the darkest hour of the war." Such evidence meant that the clerk of the House of Representatives should not seat newly elected southerners because they were not "regularly elected in accordance with the laws of their States respectively, or the laws of the United States." In subsequent articles it declared that "it is not so necessary that the disorganized States should resume their relations in the Union speedily as that they should resume them safely." The South was still displaying a spirit of "hostility to the Union," and "any truly loyal man" would have to condemn "the course of the Administration." Military control of the defeated Confederacy should continue. *Littell's Living Age* published an analysis by the *Economist* that Johnson's policy featured "great clemency" for whites but only "a very limited definition" of freedom for Blacks. Evidently "Johnson has made up his mind to reconstruct the Union by pushing the principle of State rights to its logical conclusion without any guarantees for the coloured population other then [sic] the bare prohibition of legal slavery." The *Atlantic Monthly* believed that "the great mass of the free people" need to have "the right to vote" and worried that Congress might ignore the fact that many of Johnson's southern governors "by an explicit law of Congress are ineligible."[26]

Indiana's Representative Schuyler Colfax was the incumbent Speaker of the House, and it was expected he would win reelection to that powerful post. Therefore, it was significant that Colfax took a series of strong positions toward Reconstruction. These signaled his intentions and, at least in his judgment, the will of most Republicans as they prepared to return to Washington. There had been no "voluntary submission" to end the war, said Colfax, only a complete military victory by Union forces. Now some "members of the so-called Confederate Congress, who . . . last March were struggling to blot this nation from the map of the world, propose . . . to enter Congress on the opening day of its session . . . and resume their former business of governing the country they struggled so earnestly to ruin. They say they have lost no rights." But Colfax could not agree. He was sure Congress would exercise its right to judge "the qualifications of the election returns of its members." It was unacceptable that some southern states, contrary to President Johnson's policy, had "merely repeal[ed]" their ordinances of secession. Congress would insist, Colfax predicted, on ratification of the Thirteenth Amendment and repudiation of the "Rebel debt." Also, "the Declaration of Independence must be recognized as the law of the land, and every man, alien and native, white and black, protected" in his inalienable rights. Lincoln had proclaimed that "the Government would maintain" the freedom of the slaves, and "we cannot abandon them and leave them defenseless at the mercy of their former owners." Colfax specified that the rights to sue and to testify in court were essential for them to be "freemen of the Republic."[27]

He went on to declare that amended southern constitutions, which many conventions had adopted only "reluctantly, under the pressure of dispatches from the President . . . should be ratified by a majority of their people." Otherwise there was a danger that rebels might later assert that the improved constitutions were "adopted under duress by delegates elected by a meager vote under Provisional Governors and military authorities" and thus without legitimacy. Colfax further declared that Johnson could insist on the election of congressmen able to take "the oath prescribed by the act of 1862," an act that required officials to swear that they had never engaged in disloyal conduct. "In defiance of this, and insulting the President and the country, they have, in a large majority of instances, voted down mercilessly Union men who could take the oath, and elected those who boasted that they could not, and would feel disgraced if they could." The nation, Colfax insisted, had a right to insist on "earnest and cheerful loyalty." The danger lay "in too much precipitation." Therefore, "Let us rather make haste slowly" and reconstruct "on the basis of indisputable loyalty." With these powerful and comprehensive declarations, Colfax signaled that Congress would not seat the southern representatives and that the legislative branch, dominated by Republicans, was going to have a major influence on Reconstruction policy.[28]

Colfax was not ready to break openly with President Johnson. Neither, according to all indications, was the majority of Republican congressmen, for most had refrained from harsh criticism, focused on favorable statements or actions, or assumed he would cooperate with the Republican Congress. But Colfax's final comments made clear what kind of executive conduct should be the basis of cooperation. Claiming to have "unshaken confidence" in the president, Colfax recalled Johnson's 1864 speech to Blacks in Nashville, in which "he declared that all men should have a fair start and an equal chance in the race of life." Colfax also cited the president's "speech to the colored regiment of the District of Columbia, where he repudiated that stereotyped declaration that this 'is a white man's country alone,' and insisted that it was theirs also." To a South Carolina delegation Johnson had said "that the only right system was to protect 'all men, both white and blacks.'" Colfax also recalled that Johnson had nullified the Richmond elections "when a disloyal Mayor and Common council were chosen, and that he has signed the death warrant of every one who has been convicted of conspiracy" in Lincoln's assassination. Schuyler Colfax wanted policies that prioritized loyalty over leniency, inclusion over racial domination, and progress toward racial justice.[29]

Equality before the law remained a central goal for many Republicans, even if Black suffrage was not currently attainable. The *Cleveland Leader* announced that Colfax's speech proved "a new plan of reconstruction will

As Speaker of the House, Representative Schuyler Colfax of Indiana led his northern Republican colleagues into opposition to President Andrew Johnson's racist policies. (ca. 1855–65; Brady-Handy Photograph Collection, Library of Congress, Prints and Photographs Division, LC-DIG-cwpbh-01935)

be adopted." President Johnson's "experiment, has failed." The *Leader* even claimed that "the President himself has been among the first to recognize this fact," as he saw loyal candidates defeated in southern elections and the reluctance of constitutional conventions to make necessary changes. "Congress, fairly representing the people," said the *Leader*, "will insist that the war shall not have been fought in vain." The former rebels would be required to prove their loyalty, repudiate state debts, and "render the fullest justice to their former slaves" by "annihilation of every vestige of slavery . . . every obstacle in the way of the perfectest freedom of that long-oppressed race. . . . Perfect equality of the freedmen in courts will be made essential" and the Declaration of Independence made real.[30]

But Andrew Johnson had given many indications that he had different priorities and aims, and consequently suspicions had grown on both sides. Radical Republicans believed that Johnson's approach to Reconstruction must be altered, and if moderate Republicans still hoped for a cordial relationship with the president, members of the Cabinet had no such expectations. Hostility that had not openly or frequently surfaced was seething below the surface. For more than a month Secretary of the Navy Gideon Welles had believed that "the Radicals of Massachusetts are preparing to make war upon the President," and on December 1 his irritation grew. Schuyler Colfax arrived in Washington that day and gave a speech that Welles noted "was telegraphed over the country and published the next morning. It is the offspring of an intrigue," Welles believed, "and one that is pretty extensive. The whole proceeding was premeditated." When Congress took up its work, the fissure between Johnson and the Republican majority was sure to appear, and advocates for Black rights and Black suffrage would defy Johnson by continuing their efforts.[31]

❖ 13 ❖

Congress Reconvenes—The Effort Continues

W hen Congress reconvened in December, some things were clear to observers but others were matters of intense speculation. After the rejection of Black suffrage by three northern states and the territory of Colorado, no one expected any version of impartial suffrage to be enacted in 1865. Still, it was clear that the commitment to it had grown in the Republican Party. Radical strength among congressional Republicans had grown from 20 or 25 percent to roughly 46 percent.[1] The Radicals planned to push onward for Black rights, and if President Johnson became more hostile, they could expect to receive growing sympathy from others in the party. What the relationship between President Johnson and congressional Republicans would be, however, was uncertain. Some Republicans professed to have confidence in the president; others were critical of his Reconstruction policy but believed that he respected the right of Congress to modify it; Radicals had concluded that he was untrustworthy and that wise laws would have to be made without him. As for the northern Democrats, they had varying degrees of optimism that the president might block the radical elements in his party, break with the Radicals, or align himself fully with the Democrats.

Democratic newspapers had found much to commend in Johnson's policies since May or June. By the fall Pennsylvania's *Franklin Valley Spirit* was encouraged by the burgeoning relationship between Johnson and the Democratic Party. The *Daily Ohio Statesman* believed that Democrats would stand by Johnson to enforce the Constitution, follow conservative economic policies, and uphold white supremacy. The *New York World* hoped

Johnson would "discomfit the radicals," stand firm, and "appeal to the country in the Congressional elections of next year, when he is morally certain of a victory." In Illinois the *Ottawa Free Trader* praised Johnson's tolerance of southern resistance and then asserted that the nation—including one-third of the Republicans—favored his policies. Johnson should "throw himself upon the country" and "make his issue" against the Radicals "in the election of the next congress." An Indiana paper was ready for southerners elected under Johnson's plan to take their seats in Congress, although Republicans planned to keep them out "for thirty years to come." The *Louisville Journal* spoke for virtually all Democrats when it wrote, "The less confidence the radicals have in him and his Administration, the more the true and enlightened friends of the country will have." The actions of Congress and Johnson would bring some clarity to both sides.[2]

Attention focused first on the clerk of the House of Representatives—how would he treat the newly elected men from the South? Democratic editors feared "the scrutiny and revision" of Johnson's "whole reconstruction policy" by "an unscrupulous and fanatical majority," so naturally they wanted these individuals to be seated. But they feared that the clerk, Edward McPherson, a former Republican representative from Pennsylvania, would "usurp" authority. If he were "not reproved, but commended" in such "arrogant presumption," it would reveal "the degeneracy of the times" and prove McPherson to be a "puppet." Many Republican leaders and newspapers had taken the position that no southern states should be admitted, given their behavior to date. As a Kansas newspaper put it, no southern state merited representation "unless far different guarantees are given than any yet made manifest."[3]

There was discussion and controversy during November over McPherson's future action, even though his course had become known at the beginning of the month. McPherson wrote a letter that was reported and analyzed by the *Chicago Tribune* on November 4. He based his decision on statute law as well as the Constitution. By federal law the clerk was to make a roll and call upon "all the persons, and . . . such persons only, whose credentials show that they were regularly elected, in accordance with the law of the States." No federal law authorized their election, and McPherson's letter pointed out that "no law in any of the States authorizes an election held at the call of a 'Provisional Government,' and from which large numbers of legally recognized voters [the unsworn rebels] are excluded." President

Johnson's whole policy was to set aside Confederate officials and establish provisional governments. His proclamations referred to "laws that were in force immediately prior to" the ordinances of secession. Thus McPherson felt that southern aspirants for seats in Congress had not been elected "in a manner 'authorized' by any State laws, but in a manner authorized solely by President Johnson." The clerk had no duty to seat them.[4]

McPherson adhered to that reasoning when Congress met in December, overruling test efforts to seat an aspirant from Tennessee. As a result, the South's future was in the hands of northern legislators alone. Republicans held their party's caucus on a Saturday evening and agreed that Schuyler Colfax would be their nominee for Speaker. On Monday he won that important post by a vote of 139 to 35. Contrary to the hopes of some Democratic editors, the House Republicans voted in a completely unified manner. There was "no sign of the split Copperheads have been predicting," wrote George Templeton Strong. The New York Tribune commented sarcastically: "The great split and faction-fight between the 'conservative' and the 'radical' Republicans . . . whereof the public has heard so much through The Herald and other veracious channels, would seem to have been indefinitely postponed." Analyzing the result, the Washington correspondent of the New York Evening Post blamed the result on the South's decision "to insult the President and Congress by returning the most offensive rebels." The New York Sun pointed to southerners' "mistake . . . in selecting ineligible representatives" and to the fact that Republicans had "been impressed with the popular anxiety concerning the hasty method of reconstruction which has been tried by the President." When the South "began to throw off the mask of contrition . . . the whole North became convinced of the necessity of less haste."[5]

Republicans in the House set to work. Speaker Colfax challenged the representatives to legislate for "enduring justice" and "to afford what our magna charta, the Declaration of Independence, proclaims is the chief object of Government, protection to all men in their inalienable rights." Applause greeted the news that the Thirteenth Amendment had been ratified. The House's first and most important action came on a proposal from Thaddeus Stevens. At the Republican caucus Stevens had proposed to his colleagues "that a joint committee of 15 members shall be appointed" to "inquire into the condition" of the formerly rebellious states. This joint committee, composed of nine representatives and six senators, would also report whether any southerners should be admitted to Congress, and "until such report shall have been made and finally acted on by Congress, no member shall be received into either House from any of the so-called Confederate States." Stevens's colleagues adopted his proposal, and he introduced it promptly after the Speaker's remarks. Nine days later the Senate agreed with the House on the idea.[6]

Republican representatives immediately introduced measures to safeguard the Union victory and promote the rights of African Americans. Pennsylvania's William Kelley proposed the right of suffrage for Blacks as well as whites in the District of Columbia, and Ohio's John Bingham proposed a constitutional amendment to secure liberty and equal protection to all persons. Representative John Farnsworth of Illinois introduced a resolution "declaring it to be unjust to deny colored persons the right of suffrage who have contributed to the support of the Government and periled their lives in its defence." To encourage Black suffrage and limit the power of former slaveholders, Ohio's Robert Schenck introduced a resolution to amend the Constitution by basing representation not on population but on the number of voters in each state. The House received resolutions from the legislature of Vermont that declared the federal government should act "to secure equal rights, without respect to color." A committee was established to consider parts of the president's message, or other reports, that referred to the freedmen, and a resolution proposed amending the Constitution to forbid payment of the rebel debt.[7]

In the Senate Republicans promptly introduced a series of bills designed to benefit the freed people. Ohio's Benjamin Wade introduced "a bill for universal suffrage in the District of Columbia," and a proposal by Vermont's Justin Morrill would prohibit officials in the territories from enacting laws that made a distinction on the basis of color. Charles Sumner proposed legislation to safeguard trial by jury and require "the admission of colored persons on grand juries . . . where one-sixth of the population" was Black. He also put forward an oath that would bind officials to safeguard the national debt and "resist any laws making any distinctions of color or race." To enforce the Thirteenth Amendment Sumner proposed a fine and imprisonment of up to ten years for anyone who continued to control the services of any person. This bill specified that its provisions would annul any state law in conflict with it.[8]

The Democratic and conservative press reacted harshly to the exclusion of southerners and sprang to the defense of white supremacy. The *New*

York Herald argued that Congress's "only business" should be "the admission of the Southern Representatives," for that was the way to make the "Union stronger." The Philadelphia Daily News condemned the Republican "extremists" and denounced Senator Sumner for proposing five "social equality" bills in the first three days. An irritated Ohio editor added that the torrent of bills from Sumner was "all for the negro." A Maryland paper complained that "the negro worshippers" did not wait to "commenc[e] their work of negro glorification and equality." "The first days proceedings of Congress . . . related entirely to the nigger," said an Indiana paper, and the Chicago Times added, in disgust, "the proceedings open and close with the negro."[9]

On December 6 President Johnson sent his message to Congress. He spoke of his efforts to carry on after the deplorable loss of Abraham Lincoln and praised the Union and the Constitution, including its supremacy clause. States, however, were important, and he explained how he endeavored to bring military rule to a close and restore their vitality, which had only been "suspended." He claimed to have used his pardoning power carefully and said that adoption of the Thirteenth Amendment would give "evidence of sincerity in the future maintenance of the Union." This "heals the wound" and "re-unites us beyond all power of disruption." After recognizing Congress's power to decide on the qualifications of its members, he asserted that he could not make the freedmen voters, as that was a power left to "each State." He claimed that "the freedmen, if they show patience and manly virtues, will sooner obtain a participation in the elective franchise through the States than through the General Government, even if it had power to intervene." Meanwhile, he defended their right to liberty, property, and the "right to claim the just return of their labor." The "experiment" he spoke of was now an experiment of having "the two races . . . live side by side." It should be made "in good faith," Johnson said, and therefore he did not "advise their forced removal and colonization." He then moved on to review other departments of government and praised the future of the United States.[10]

The reaction to his message was generally favorable, from both Republican and Democratic newspapers. A Democratic editor in Indiana, for example, admired "how much like a Democrat he talks" on subjects such as taxation and the need to pay off the debt. Another Democratic paper was pleased to see "the apparently conservative desires and policy of the President," as opposed to the "trouble and danger" the Republicans would bring. The *New York World* said that Johnson's duty now was to "push on vigorously the work of restoration, by him so well begun." He could count on the support "of every Northern Democrat" so long as he did not "pusillanimously" surrender to "the Radical crew." Johnson's address gave the *New York Daily News* hope that a coalition of "conservative Republicans and Democrats" might emerge that would be powerful enough "to check the malignant spirit of the Radicals." The president should be "firm as a rock," said the *New York Express*, for "thus far he has behaved admirably." This paper was pleased that Johnson's private sentiments, as revealed in conversations, "express his unqualified condemnation of the northern radicals."[11]

The Republican Chicago *Tribune* called Johnson's message "moderate and careful" and observed that "nothing" in it "commits him to oppose" the extension of the suffrage, "though he would prefer that . . . [it] should come from the rebel States." Republican editors in Vermont likewise chose to focus on areas of agreement and noted that it had been generally well received. The *New York Tribune* was glad that the message avoided direct conflict with Congress, but a rival paper in the city noted that Johnson "impl[ied] that he favors the admission of the Southern members elected from such States as have adopted the [Thirteenth] amendment."[12]

It was a Democratic editor, however, who identified most clearly the reason that dissent and protest had not been the reaction of Republicans. The "Abolition Press," wrote the *Daily Ohio Statesman*, seemed satisfied with the president's message largely because it did not see "an emphatic avowal of maintaining" his views; rather the abolitionists and Republicans saw a willingness to "tur[n] the whole subject over to Congress." Even the *New York Times*, which supported Johnson's plans, said "he makes no effort to force those plans upon Congress." In fact, most Republican newspapers continued to assume that Congress would have a major role in Reconstruction, and they rejected Johnson's claim that he could not require Black suffrage. As the *Cleveland Leader* put it, for example, his claim ignored "entirely the fact of the rebellion" and was "transparently illogical and baseless." Or, as the *New York Tribune* and other papers reasoned, if Johnson had the power to depose governors and bring provisional governments into being, he equally could require Black suffrage.[13]

The gap between Johnson's views and those of most Republicans soon came into sharper focus. Radical Republicans like Senator Henry Wilson made new proposals, such as a bill to invalidate laws in the "insurrectionary

States, whereby any inequality of civil rights and immunities" was established "on account of race or color." Illinois's Senator Lyman Trumbull declared that he would introduce a bill to continue the Freedmen's Bureau and strengthen its ability to "protect every individual in the full rights of person and property and furnish them with means for their vindication." Then, responding to a request from the Senate, the president submitted on December 19 his view of "the condition of the States lately in rebellion," along with two investigative reports, one by General Ulysses Grant and the other by General Carl Schurz. Johnson "transmitted" Schurz's report without comment. By contrast, he "invited . . . the attention of the Senate" to the report "of Lieut. Gen. Grant, who recently made a tour of inspection through several of the States whose inhabitants participated in the rebellion." Johnson's own words and his preference for Grant's report signaled how far the president stood from the Radicals or from the majority of Republicans in Congress.[14]

Johnson's assessment of conditions in the South was very favorable. He informed the Senate that, under his measures, eight of the Confederate states were demonstrating their allegiance "with more willingness and greater promptitude than, under the circumstances, could reasonably have been anticipated." Florida and Texas were "making commendable progress" and "no doubt" would be ready to rejoin the Union "at an early period." (Virginia was considered to have the loyal restored government under Pierpont.) Everywhere "the aspect of affairs is more promising than, in view of all the circumstances, could well have been expected." Johnson had an "abiding faith" in the former rebels' professions of loyalty and felt little concern about violence toward freed people. "Occasional disorders . . . are local in character, not frequent in occurrence, and are rapidly disappearing," he claimed. The "great and sudden change in the relations between the two races" had "naturally" produced "perplexing questions . . . but systems are gradually developing" that would give the freedman "the protection to which he is justly entitled" and enable him to become "a useful and independent member of the community." Johnson declared himself confident that "sectional animosity" was rapidly "merging itself into a spirit of nationality."[15]

Support for these rosy views could be found in Grant's report, which was a letter of two pages. To learn "the feelings and intentions" of southerners "toward the general government," Grant had very recently spent five days visiting just four cities in three states—Raleigh, North Carolina; Charleston, South Carolina; and Savannah and Augusta, Georgia. He pronounced himself "satisfied that the mass of thinking men of the south accept the present situation of affairs in good faith." Southern whites were "possibly" not ready to "yield that ready obedience to civil authority" that was normal and expected. But "small garrisons" could remain in place until "civil authority is fully established." He recommended that troops stationed in any area where there were many freedmen should be white, because "the presence of black troops, lately slaves, demoralizes labor" through advice from the troops and the presence of army camps to which Blacks could "resort." He admitted that some "ignorant" persons might attempt violence against the troops, and he said that "the late slave" seemed to think that "the property of his late master should, by right, belong to him." But Grant agreed that "the citizens of the southern States" were eager to rejoin the Union. They were ready to fulfill requirements "not humiliating to them as citizens." Although Grant admitted that he did not have abundant time to study the Freedmen's Bureau, he made a few recommendations for efficiency and economy. He also repeated southerners' charge that many Blacks felt that freedom meant living without care or foresight.[16]

The Schurz report was quite different. It was forty-four pages long and appended sixty pages of documents and reports from army officers and officials of the Freedmen's Bureau. In July President Johnson had asked Schurz to tour the South, and before departing Schurz had asked, "Am I to understand, Mr. President, that your policy is not yet fixed?" Johnson then gave Schurz assurances that his policy was "not settled" and that he wanted to "know better how the present experiment [was] working before settling upon any definitive scheme with regard to the franchise question." Following written instructions, Schurz undertook an extensive visit to a majority of the former Confederate states, omitting Virginia, North Carolina, Texas, Arkansas, and Tennessee. In three months he stopped in twenty-one cities as well as in the Teche country of Louisiana, and he talked with all classes of southerners and with U.S. troops.[17]

Schurz described four categories of southern whites, and in at least three of them loyalty was problematic or conditional. Many, including the politicians, wanted to regain "absolute control of their home concerns." They praised Johnson, clamored for withdrawal of troops, and sought the "abolition of the Freedmen's Bureau." A second group consisted of "incorrigibles" who still wanted independence and incited passions and prejudices. A third, large body of less informed or educated whites had strong prejudices and passions and were "apt to be carried along by" the incorrigibles. There was only one group, whose members had mature age and good economic standing, that knew change was inevitable. Whites in this group tried to accommodate themselves to the new reality, although they were prejudiced. Schurz warned that "this kind of loyalty" had been produced only by force, consisted merely in not actively rebelling, and was "of a negative character." It was not a good sign that representatives of the United States often were unsafe and sometimes had been shot. Southern whites felt an enmity toward all northerners, in comparison to which northern criticisms of southerners were mild and affectionate. As a result of such feelings the position of southern Unionists was "precarious." Even Governor William Sharkey of Mississippi admitted that Unionists "would not be safe" if U.S. troops left, and for all Blacks the situation would be "intolerable."[18]

The governments thus far established, said Schurz, had "the forms of civil government" but not the real "spirit." Strong Unionists could not be elected. There was "an *utter absence of national feeling*" among the old leaders who were "crowding into places of trust and power." That lack of national feeling was characteristic even of Louisiana, which had had a loyal government in occupied areas during the war. "Order and security" remained unsatisfactory, with much robbery and opposition to paying the U.S. debt. Many former slaveholders wanted "compensation for their emancipated slaves" and for damages caused by the war.[19]

On racial questions, Schurz remarked, "it frequently struck me that persons who conversed about every other subject calmly and sensibly would lose their temper as soon as the negro question was touched." Nineteen of twenty whites asserted that compulsion was needed to make Black people work. Violence against the freed people was common and often "of a particularly atrocious nature." Near Atlanta "bands of guerillas were prowling about . . . making it dangerous for soldiers and freedmen to show themselves outside of the immediate reach of the garrison." Small numbers of U.S. troops, concentrated at a few points, had little control over the interior of the country. Whites in Alabama were holding Blacks in servitude, and the provost marshal at Selma reported that twelve were killed by whites for "trying to come to town or to return to the plantation after having been sent away." White patrols boarded boats in southwestern Alabama, and if they found Blacks aboard, "they hang, shoot, or drown the victims. . . . All those found on the roads or coming down the rivers are almost invariably murdered."[20]

In Mississippi Schurz found the same patterns, with Blacks in various sections of the country "kept in the most abject slavery." Where southern whites recognized that "slavery in the old form" had to end, they introduced "corporal punishment" and "as much as possible of the traditions of the old system" into labor contracts. Formerly non-slaveholding whites also "are possessed by a singularly bitter and vindictive feeling against the colored race," and "the maiming and killing of colored men seems to be looked upon by many as one of those venial offences which must be forgiven to the outraged feelings of a wronged and robbed people." South Carolinians hoped to succeed in establishing a system of debt peonage or "to make free labor compulsory by permanent regulations." In Louisiana local ordinances quoted by Schurz gave force to "the idea that although the former owner has lost his individual right of property in the former slave, 'the blacks at large belong to the whites at large.'" Another force blocking all hope of change was a "popular prejudice . . . almost as bitterly set against the negro's having the advantage of education as it was when the negro was a slave." Education, whites believed, would "spoil the nigger for work" and any "elevation of the blacks will be the degradation of the whites." Some schools and churches had been burned in Alabama.[21]

By contrast whites in Charleston told Schurz that the conduct of the emancipated slaves was "surprisingly good" or "admirable." There were no acts of "revenge" and the predicted "'horrors of St. Domingo' proved utterly groundless." Southern whites complained that "the negroes would not work," but Schurz found that "the negro generally works well where he is decently treated and well compensated." The number of Blacks on relief was "remarkably small and continually decreasing." Both Blacks and whites needed to learn more about following labor contracts. There were some "rare" instances of "insolence" from young Black men, but "on the whole, the conduct of the colored people is far more submissive than anybody had a right to expect." There was very little violence against whites, and "insolence" to southern whites simply meant conduct different "in any manner from what a southern man was accustomed to when slavery existed." Schurz concluded, "The negro is constitutionally docile and eminently good-natured. Instances of the most touching attachment of freedmen to their old masters and mistresses have come to my notice." But he reasonably worried that "if the persecution and the denial of their rights as freemen continue, the resentments growing out of them will continue and spread." Nevertheless, whites' fears of insurrections were "uniformly" found to be "unwarranted by fact." Evidence indicated that some of these "apprehensions were industriously spread for the purpose of serving as an excuse for further persecution."[22]

It was clear to Schurz that once military power was removed, there would be "a general attempt . . . to restore slavery in its old form." Black codes in Louisiana and South Carolina had already given evidence of this goal. A General W. L. Brandon in Mississippi told Schurz that whites' idea was to "accept the situation as it is, *until we can get control once more of our own State of affairs.*" The movement was in the direction of "peonage of the Mexican pattern, or serfdom of some European pattern," and Schurz warned that "there are a hundred ways of framing apprenticeship, vagrancy, or contract laws, which will serve the purpose" of the southern whites. Some politicians had supported allowing Black testimony in courts but mainly as a way "for getting rid of the jurisdiction of the Freedmen's Bureau." Although southern whites would ratify the Thirteenth Amendment "as a *conditio sine qua non* of readmission" after receiving a telegram demanding that action, no telegram could obliterate their prejudice or "prevent those prejudices from making themselves seriously felt in the future."[23]

The viewpoint advanced by Schurz was similar overall to that of Thaddeus Stevens or Charles Sumner. He stated that the necessary goal was not just readmittance of southern states into the Union but reconstruction of "the whole organism of southern society," or "rather reconstruct[ing it] anew, so as to bring it into harmony with the rest of American society." The government had "commenced a great social revolution in the south" and should not leave the task to those who always were "hostile." Nor would it be right to leave "the class in whose favor it was made completely without power to protect itself and to take an influential part in that development." He opposed letting the southern states organize militias, which would support white interests only, and urged a firm and clear announcement by the federal government that it would "not . . . give up the control of the free-labor reform until it is finally accomplished." The Freedmen's Bureau was "very unpopular" because it was "a barrier to reactionary aspirations." In fact, it had done good work and should be continued. Schurz added that "nothing is more foreign to my ways of thinking in political matters than a fondness for centralization or military government." But "we are living under exceptional circumstances" that require unusual but practical measures due to the rebellion.[24]

Schurz made clear that he favored Black suffrage because "the feelings of the colored man are naturally in sympathy with the views and aims of the national government," and African Americans' loyal participation would speed the solution of the "free labor problem" and protect the "national debt." Possession of the ballot would protect the freed people from "oppressive class-legislation" and from "persecution" and could encourage political parties to take an interest in their votes and welfare. Moreover, "it is idle to say that it will be time to speak of negro suffrage when the whole colored race will be educated, for the ballot may be necessary to him to secure his education. It is also idle to say that ignorance is the principal ground upon which southern men object to negro suffrage, for if it were, that numerous class of colored people in Louisiana who are as highly educated, as intelligent, and as wealthy as any corresponding class of whites, would have been enfranchised long ago." Schurz restricted himself from discussing the "moral merits" of extending the suffrage, but he added that southern whites would not grant it and that it should be made "a condition precedent to 'readmission.'" He rejected deportation of Blacks as impractical, wrong, and undesirable but speculated that if some freed people voluntarily migrated along the line of the Pacific railroad, that might cause white landowners to value their labor more.[25]

In his concluding paragraphs Schurz repeated several of his early findings and then advised that the former rebels "be not permitted to build up another 'peculiar institution' whose spirit is in conflict with the fundamental principles of our political system." The "popular spirit" in the South was contrary to the nation's principles, and as long as that remained the case, "their loyalty to the Union will always be uncertain." He emphasized also that he had been careful not to exaggerate his findings or "to use stronger language" than was justified: "A comparison of the tenor of the annexed documents with that of my report, will convince you that I have studiously avoided overstatements." He urged President Johnson to ask Congress to conduct further investigations "before final action is taken" on readmitting southern states, and he advised the president "to take no irretraceable step towards relieving the States lately in rebellion from all national control, until such favorable changes are clearly and unmistakably ascertained."[26]

Reactions to these three documents by Johnson, Grant, and Schurz showed that conflict lay ahead. A Republican newspaper in Indiana wanted to avoid hostility to President Johnson, whose purposes probably were "laudable." But his message "complacently" claimed that all was functioning again in the South and was based on "a rose-colored view of affairs." It was clear that white southerners were not showing "great willingness to comply with conditions imposed on them." This editor also noted that Grant's "hurried" trip to the South "was a flying one" which gave him few opportunities to discern "authoritatively what ought to be done." A Republican editor in Kansas completely dismissed Grant's report, saying, "It is absurd to think the General could learn *much* in so short a time." His views ought not to be the foundation for legislation or policy. Grant evidently had become important to Johnson because the president found "a strong current running against his re-construction policy," but this "is not exactly the way for Mr. Johnson to 'make treason odious,' or to 'hang traitors.'" The president's message on southern affairs "is not much of a document . . . and is only distinguished for great faith in recent rebels on the smallest foundation." Democratic papers predictably praised Johnson and emphasized Grant's negative comments about freed people. If Democratic editors charged the Republicans with "building up an intense and perpetual hatred in the South against the North," Republican journals reminded their readers that 186,057 Black men had fought for the Union and 68,178 had died. "Let us think of this and be just."[27]

The cursory treatment that Johnson gave to Schurz's detailed and thorough report, compared to his warmer words for Grant's short letter, clearly indicated where Johnson stood. In addition, the comments in his opening message to Congress about the "sincerity" of the white South's desire to reunite were unconvincing and, at best, willfully naive in view of Schurz's report and much news from the South. Charles Sumner promptly denounced the president's handling of these reports, saying that Johnson's message "was like the whitewashing message" that Franklin Pierce had once delivered on the violent events in Bleeding Kansas. The *Chicago Tribune* observed that Johnson's message had "deeply offended some of the members when it was read to the Senate."[28]

Other recent actions by the administration, said the *Tribune*, were setting it against Congress. In its previous session Congress had required that all federal officials swear that they had not voluntarily participated in the rebellion, and the House insisted by a vote of 126 to 32 that the test oath for anyone holding federal office was still in force. However, this new Congress learned from Secretary of the Treasury Hugh McCulloch that "no persons have been appointed to office not authorized by law" but that some could not take the oath. In other words, McCulloch was claiming that some were "authorized" to hold an office "notwithstanding the act of Congress to the contrary." Secretary of State William Seward also had notified the provisional governor of Alabama that "in the judgment of the President" the time had come for him to transfer his papers to the new governor-elect, even though Congress disagreed on the state of things in Alabama. Most members believed that "LAW is required to create a State, not the mere will of the President." The "Administration versus Congress" was becoming a reality.[29]

It now was clear that conflict between the Republican Congress and President Johnson would center on protection for African Americans and the loyalty or disloyalty of southern whites. Black suffrage and legal equality were crucial for a large and growing number of Republican lawmakers. The idea of a "white man's government" was "political blasphemy," said Thaddeus Stevens. He and many of his colleagues felt a moral and patriotic duty to press on. A racial concept of government, Stevens declared, was a violation of "the fundamental principles of our gospel of liberty," a repudiation of the epochal achievement of the founders, and an offense against God: "If we have not yet been sufficiently scourged for our national sin to teach us to do justice to all God's creatures, without distinction of race or color, we must expect the still more heavy vengeance of an offended Father."[30]

Advocates of Black suffrage, like Stevens, recognized that they lacked the support to reach their goal in 1865, but they were determined to carry on the fight. The dynamic of events, in fact, was one that would aid and inspire them. As dissatisfaction with Andrew Johnson's version of Reconstruction grew, the importance of Black suffrage would become more salient. Black suffrage would become more necessary both as a means for former slaves to protect themselves and as a way to increase loyalty and Unionism in the South. As Carl Schurz expressed it in his report, "The feelings of the colored man are naturally in sympathy with the views and aims of the national government." This was true for "all questions concerning the Union, the national debt, and the future social organization of the South." The "natural impulse" of the freedman "in all the important issues" would lead him "to forward the ends of the government," and his influence as a voter could "tell upon the legislation of the States" and "render the interference of the national authority less necessary."[31]

A sign of the reviving pressure for Black suffrage came in the form of yet another surprising reversal by Henry Ward Beecher, the famed orator and renowned minister of the Protestant North. On the evening of December 13, "the largest audience ever gathered" in the House chamber came to hear Beecher speak. Chief Justice Salmon Chase presided over the evening's program, and the opening prayer was delivered by Reverend Henry Highland Garnett, an African American abolitionist and educator who in February had been the first Black man to give an address in the nation's legislative chambers. Beecher now returned to his original advocacy of Black suffrage, which he had abandoned two months previously when he praised Johnson unreservedly. A newspaper account gave this summary of Beecher's new convictions: "He argued that the emancipation promised by Lincoln would not be complete till the freedmen were given all the rights which liberty means in this land to any other free man. He scouted the idea that suffrage was not a natural right. It is. If it was not, then liberty was not; for it was absurd to talk of giving liberty without all the rights by which that liberty is to be maintained. But going beyond this, he insisted that not only all men, but all women had the right to vote." Beecher's demand for Black rights sparked "loud applause, mingled with a very few hisses," but his advocacy of suffrage for women met with laughter and then silence.[32] Before the war Black suffrage too would have been ridiculed, but now northern society was moving toward realization of the values of the Declaration of Independence. The continued controversy over Reconstruction would benefit Black suffrage greatly but do far less for women's rights.

Another sign came just before Christmas when the *New York Herald*, reliably conservative though not officially Democratic, made a proposal that returned in large measure to Abraham Lincoln's last goal. To reach an "adjustment in the supreme law" that would be "satisfactory to all parties," the *Herald* supported a constitutional amendment which it understood was to be brought before Congress. This amendment would restore the rights of southern whites through a universal amnesty, an idea consonant with Lincoln's preference for leniency. It also would confirm that each state had exclusive jurisdiction over the right of suffrage, "provided, however, that no person shall be excluded from the elective franchise on account [of] color, race or religion." That formula for an impartial suffrage was not too different from Lincoln's preference, which was to give voting rights to "very intelligent" Blacks and those who had served in the military. After many months and a multitude of confusing developments, part of the spirit of Lincoln's goal remained alive.[33]

Much more controversy and conflict between North and South would be necessary to bring about sufficient support for Black suffrage, and that conflict would materialize in 1866 and 1867. By 1868 freedmen would be voting in the South, as the northern Congress imposed a new policy on intransigent southern whites. Two years later the Fifteenth Amendment—forbidding denial or abridgement of the right to vote "on account of race, color, or previous condition of servitude"—would become part of the Constitution. The debates over Black suffrage in 1865 helped to prepare the ground for these developments.

Patterns in the Civil War Era

T he cause of Black suffrage failed in 1865 for many reasons. The most important reason was obvious: racism in the North was extremely widespread and was socially and politically powerful, even among some Republican officeholders. Emancipation was a monumental achievement, but it occurred because the existential crisis of the Union required unprecedented and controversial measures. Still, the evils of racism and white supremacy remained. For many years histories of the Civil War era minimized that fact in favor of a far more celebratory story. Leading scholars as well as popular writers often depicted the Civil War as the triumph of an exceptional nation advancing human liberty. Despite the measure of truth in that viewpoint, one might have assumed that a bloody internecine conflict that fractured the polity and claimed as many as 750,000 lives revealed a failure of the democratic system. Only recently, as citizens and scholars have paid more attention to shortcomings in the nation's history, has northern racism gained more recognition.

Perception depended, as it always does in collective memory, on what was emphasized. There *was* enormous progress in the Civil War era—precisely because slavery, racism, and white supremacy were deeply rooted. These malignancies were intimately entwined with people's daily lives and had long ago become a part of "normal" reality. As I argued in a previous book, what William Lloyd Garrison called "the worst passions of human nature" nurtured white racism during the war years and made what was achieved even more important. Those racist passions did not evaporate of course on the day Lee surrendered to Grant. It was to be expected that racism and white supremacy would throw up a strong barrier to Black suffrage in the remaining nine months of 1865.[1]

The fountainhead of racist propaganda in 1865, as during the war years, was the Democratic Party. Dominant portions of that party had not shed their devotion to white supremacy, their hostility to what they condemned as an unnecessary abolitionist war, or their defense of southern slaveholders and secessionists. Popular opposition to Black suffrage in the North was strongest in the southern portions of states bordering the Ohio River, such as Ohio, Indiana, and Illinois, as well as in neighboring Kentucky. In these places and elsewhere there was an angry rejection of New England's calls for equal rights and its tacit claim to moral leadership. Racism played a smaller but significant role in the Republican Party. The refusal of some prominent Republicans to support Black suffrage and the failed suffrage initiatives in 1865 were seriously damaging.[2] But they did not negate the fact that support was growing in the Republican Party or that the previously unthinkable was gaining more acceptance in northern society as a whole.[3]

A second key reason was the power that Andrew Johnson inherited and the role that he played. Before his death Abraham Lincoln and his advisors had looked forward happily to the adjournment of Congress, which would give the president eight months to shape Reconstruction on his own terms. When that opportunity fell to Andrew Johnson, a stubborn man and a southerner more steeped in society's racism than Lincoln, the chances for Black suffrage declined further. In a meaningful sense, they suffered a premature and partial eclipse under Johnson's leadership.

A third reason for the failure of Black suffrage was an aspect of white supremacy—the mentality among northern whites that southern rebels, though traitors to the Union, were an essential and valuable part of the political community. Those rebels continued to be seen as "brothers and sisters," even if they were sometimes called "erring" brothers or sisters. Democrats advocated most strongly for the former rebels, but even some of the leading Republicans continued to regard them as members of the family to be brought inside the circle, not relegated to the status of outsiders or even to be punished meaningfully. Only a minority found such attitudes strange. "Nothing is more striking," commented a writer in the North American Review, than "the tenacity with which the theories of the erring brother and the prodigal son were clung to, despite all evidence of facts to the contrary." Freed slaves and African Americans in the North, however, did not enjoy the same cultural and social status, due to the nation's racist heritage and practice.[4]

The scant power that African Americans wielded in that era was another important reason. In the free states of the North the Black population was only a little more than 1 percent of the population.[5] Most white citizens had little or no contact with African Americans or knowledge of them, and no matter how impressive leaders from the Black community were, they had an enormous challenge to make themselves heard. Beyond the influence of racism, this is fundamentally a problem inherent in any majoritarian democracy. Democratic decision-making carries the danger that a preponderant majority will assume its perspectives are right, while small minorities are overlooked or ignored entirely. When northerners thought of the South, where almost all the Black people had been enslaved, they assumed that the former slaves were not merely illiterate but also ignorant of the basic principles of American government and life. That assumption was false but it was widespread, and the vigorous efforts of abolitionists to denounce the slave system had, ironically, reinforced images of a hopelessly degraded, oppressed people.

A further important reason was the exhaustion caused by four years of war and the understandable desire of ordinary northern citizens to return to a more normal life. The wartime emergency brought revolutionary measures but not an enduring revolutionary mentality. Energy would be required to confront the challenge of equal rights, to take it up seriously, and to advance toward the long-delayed fulfillment of the nation's ideals. Many did not welcome that additional challenge as peace arrived. Instead they wanted conflict to end and the nation to resume its accustomed patterns through reunion. In northern states that rejected Black suffrage, fewer people voted on the suffrage question than on other ballot issues. That reflected both war-related weariness and a deficit of reforming energies, especially where Republican leaders were divided on Black suffrage.[6]

National ideals and morality had not been sufficient to end slavery before the Civil War, and they also proved insufficient to establish Black suffrage and equal rights in 1865. Stating that fact should not minimize or discount the progress that did occur and was evident in magazines, many newspapers, and especially in the Republican Party. Significant numbers of northerners recognized that the revolutionary period of war should continue until national laws conformed more closely to national ideals. Those who organized, spoke out repeatedly, and distributed pamphlets and speeches fought courageously for a good cause and furthered the North's gradual acceptance of Black suffrage. But their efforts were not enough in 1865. The bold, persistent, determined protests and demands by African Americans, north and south, demonstrated both their belief in American values and fitness for inclusion, though they had not yet enjoyed success.

Ironically, Black suffrage would come about—as emancipation had come about—through necessity. Secession, rather than idealism, had opened the road to emancipation, and southern resistance to Black freedom would enable Black suffrage. Racism remained strong during the next two years, as initiatives for Black suffrage failed in the Nebraska Territory, Kansas, Minnesota, and Ohio.[7] But Reconstruction politics revealed to a majority of northerners and to the Republicans they elected that white southerners were intransigent and that the South was determined to win the peace.[8] The supposed benefits of northern victory were being nullified or were disappearing, and in a short time that unpalatable reality compelled a stronger, more determined congressional reaction. Although northern racism remained strong, empowering southern Black men with the right to vote became a means to secure the Union victory. The continuation of war in the realm of politics brought progress that morality and national ideals alone was not able to achieve.

These facts remind us how few Americans, north or south, were able to embrace Lincoln's final vision of a redeemed nation that would go forward with "malice toward none; with charity for all" *and* with the right to vote for at least some African Americans. Lincoln's final goal was ambitious. What he desired was a measure of his quality as a human being and a testament to how far human beings in the collective generally fall short of such a high standard.

Finally, the fate of Black suffrage in 1865 and its realization in 1868 and 1869 are part of a longer, repeated story, a story of progress and regression, of progress that again and again has to be renewed. The ideals enunciated by the founding fathers, who were themselves flawed and imperfect, have been a goal repeatedly sought but never fully realized. The gains of the Civil War era and the regression to decades of Jim Crow disfranchisement and segregation replicated a longer pattern of progress and retreat in U.S. history. Lincoln understood this dynamic. Before the war he spoke of "the eternal struggle . . . between right and wrong" and praised the ideals of the Declaration of Independence as "a standard maxim for free society, which should be familiar to all, and revered by all; constantly looked to, constantly labored for, and even though never perfectly attained, constantly approximated, and thereby constantly spreading and deepening its influence."[9] The men and women who worked for Black suffrage in 1865 made vital contributions to progress in that continuing struggle.

❖ NOTES ❖

PREFACE

1. Key portions of Stephens's "cornerstone" speech of March 1861 may be found in Durden, *The Grey and the Black,* 7–9.
2. Escott, *"What Shall We Do with the Negro?"*; Escott, *Lincoln's Dilemma*; Escott, *"The Worst Passions of Human Nature."*

INTRODUCTION

1. Welles, *Diary,* 2:272–73.
2. *New York Anglo-African* quoted in Hodes, *Mourning Lincoln,* 217.
3. See Escott, *"What Shall We Do with the Negro?"*
4. The quoted words are from Lincoln's first annual address to Congress and may be found in Gienapp, ed., *This Fiery Trial,* 89.
5. Lincoln, *Collected Works,* 5:48; Freehling, *The South vs. the South,* 111. Before January 1, 1863, Lincoln sent envoys into occupied parts of the South and urged elections in which only "the largest number of people possible" might vote. For greater detail on Lincoln's actions, see important studies such as Donald, *Lincoln,* and Freehling, *The South vs. the South.* A more compact coverage is in Escott, *Lincoln's Dilemma.*
6. Lincoln's annual address to Congress, December 3, 1861, in (for example) Barnes and Noble, comp., *Abraham Lincoln: Selected Writings* (New York: Barnes and Noble, 2013), 648; Magness and Page, *Colonization after Emancipation*; Gienapp, ed., *This Fiery Trial,* 132, 188, 192, 215. Few African Americans were interested in leaving the United States, and governments in Central America, where Lincoln's allies proposed colonization, were opposed.
7. Escott, *Lincoln's Dilemma,* 107, 135; Gienapp, ed., *This Fiery Trial,* 193.
8. See works cited in Preface, note 2, above. Lincoln had long and consistently argued that gradual emancipation was best for all concerned.

9. Gienapp, ed., *This Fiery Trial*, 220–21.
10. Donald, *Lincoln*, 572–74.
11. Ibid., 576, 577, 580. 584.
12. Escott, *Lincoln's Dilemma*, 196–97, 208.
13. Gienapp, ed., *This Fiery Trial*, 223–27.
14. Ibid., 105.

1. SHOCK, GRIEF, DISORIENTATION

1. Escott, *Lincoln's Dilemma*, 214–15. See also Welles, *Diary*, 2:286–87.
2. Sherman, *John Sherman's Recollections*, 1:355; Escott, *Lincoln's Dilemma*, 215–16; Hodes, *Mourning Lincoln*, 170; Lodge, *Early Memories*, 129.
3. *Vermont Watchman and State Journal*, April 21, 1865, 1; *New York Tribune*, April 17, 1865, 1; *Chicago Tribune*, April 19, 1865, 1 (two headlines); *White Cloud Kansas Chief*, April 20, 1865, 5; *Ashtabula Weekly Telegraph*, April 22, 1865, 1; *Delaware State Journal and Statesman*, April 21, 1865, 2; *Bedford Inquirer*, April 21, 1865, 2; *Civilian and Telegraph*, April 20, 1865, 2; Cimbala and Miller, *The Northern Home Front*, 150.
4. *Ottawa Free Trader*, April 22, 1865, 2; *Franklin Valley Spirit*, April 19, 1865, 3; *Columbia Democrat and Bloomsburg General Advertiser*, April 22, 1865, 2; *Daily Ohio Statesman*, April 17, 1865, 2; *Jasper Weekly Courier*, April 22, 1865, 2.
5. *Daily Ohio Statesman*, April 17, 1865, 2; *New York Tribune* quoted in *Cadiz Sentinel*, April 26, 1865, 1; *Independent* (Oskaloosa), April 22, 1865, 2; *Ottawa Free Trader*, April 22, 1865, 2; Cimbala and Miller, *The Northern Home Front*, 150; Charles Francis Adams, Diary, March 30, April 26, 1865, Massachusetts Historical Society, Boston, https://www.masshist .org/publications/cfa-civil-war/. Adams also commented that "the just doubts about his capacity for reconstruction are scattered to the winds in the solemnity of the termination."
6. *New York World* quoted in *Chicago Tribune*, April 20, 1865, 1; *Philadelphia Bulletin* quoted in *Bedford Inquirer*, April 28, 1865, 2; *Cincinnati Gazette* quoted in *Wisconsin State Register*, April 29, 1865.
7. *Burlington Free Press*, April 21, 1865, 2; *Hillsdale Standard*, April 25, 1865, 2; *Caledonian*, April 21, 1865, 2; *Franklin Valley Spirit*, April 26, 1865, 2; *Vermont Watchman and State Journal*, April 28, 1865, 2.
8. *Chicago Tribune*, April 19, 1865, 2; Welles, *Diary*, April 15, 1865, 2:289; *Vermont Watchman and State Journal*, April 28, 1865, 2.
9. *Evansville Daily Journal*, April 21, 1865, 1; Chandler and Wright quoted in Hodes, *Mourning Lincoln*, 91, 224; *Daily Ohio Statesman*, April 22, 1865, 2; *Burlington Free Press*, April 21, 1865, 2.

10. Clarke quoted in Hodes, *Mourning Lincoln*, 251.

11. *New York Sun*, April 18, 1865, 2; *Harper's Weekly*, May 20, 1865, 206; *Chicago Tribune*, April 20, 1865, 2; June 13, 1865, 2; *New York Herald* quoted in *Chicago Tribune*, April 20, 1865, 1.

12. *Chicago Tribune*, May 10, 1865, 2.

13. *Evansville Daily Journal*, April 25, 1865, 1; *Bedford Inquirer*, April 28, 1865, 2; *Civilian and Telegraph*, April 20, 1865, 2; May 4, 1865, 2; *New York Tribune*, April 21, 1865, 2.

14. The Crittenden Compromise had several parts, but its key provision would have divided all territory, owned then or in the future, along the Missouri Compromise line, with slavery permitted to spread below that line. Lincoln opposed the westward expansion of slavery and additionally worried about the possibility that pro-slavery forces would press for new territory (for example in the Caribbean) not then owned by the United States.

15. *Columbia Democrat and Bloomsburg General Advertiser*, April 22, 1865, 2; *Urbana Union*, April 19, 1865, 2.

16. *Daily Ohio Statesman*, April 17, 1865, 2; *Dayton Empire* quoted in *Ashtabula Weekly Telegraph*, April 22, 1865, 2; *New York World* quoted in *Cadiz Sentinel*, April 26, 1865, 1; *Jasper Weekly Courier*, April 22, 1865, 2.

17. *Independent* (Oskaloosa), May 6, 1865, 2; *Evansville Daily Journal*, May 17, 1865, 1; Cimbala and Miller, *The Northern Home Front*, 153; *New York Sun*, May 18, 1865, 1.

18. *Independent* (Oskaloosa), May 6, 1865, 2; *Columbia Democrat and Bloomsburg General Advertiser*, May 6, 1865, 2; *New York Herald* quoted in *New Hampshire Statesman*, June 2, 1865, 3; *New York World* quoted in *Urbana Union*, May 24, 1865, 1.

19. The text of this agreement may be found at "Surrender Negotiations," Bennett Place State Historic Site, Durham, N.C., https://www.bennett placehistoricsite.com/history/surrender-negotiations/.

20. *Burlington Free Press*, April 28, 1865, 2; *Chicago Tribune*, April 25, 1865, 2; *Ottawa Free Trader*, April 29, 1865, 2.

21. *Ottawa Free Trader*, May 6, 1865, 2; *Columbia Democrat and Bloomsburg General Advertiser*, May 13, 1865, 2; *Daily Ohio Statesman*, May 4, 1865, 2; *New York World* quoted in *Ashtabula Weekly Telegraph*, April 29, 1865, 2; *Cadiz Sentinel*, May 10, 1865, 2.

22. *New York Herald* quoted in *Ashtabula Weekly Telegraph*, May 13, 1865, 2; *Franklin Valley Spirit*, April 26, 1865, 2; *Republican* (Springfield) quoted in *Cadiz Sentinel*, May 10, 1865, 2; *Aegis and Intelligencer*, April 21, 1865, 2.

23. *Daily Ohio Statesman*, April 22, 1865, 2; *Columbus Crisis* quoted in *Cadiz Sentinel*, April 26, 1865, 1; *Urbana Union*, May 24, 1865, 1; *Philadelphia Ledger* quoted in *Ottawa Free Trader*, May 13, 1865, 2; *Albany Evening Journal* quoted in *Ottawa Free Trader*, May 27, 1865, 1.

2. HOPEFUL SIGNS

1. Massachusetts, Maine, Vermont, and New Hampshire allowed Blacks to vote on the same basis as whites. New York had property and residency requirements. Blacks had voted in some parts of Pennsylvania until 1837, when a constitutional convention took away that right. See Litwack, *North of Slavery*, 75, 84.
2. *New York Herald* quoted in *Bedford Inquirer*, May 12, 1865, 2. See also quotations from the *New York Herald* in the *Cleveland Daily Herald*, May 12, 1865, 2. During the previous winter some "important Republican newspapers such as the *New York Tribune* and the *Boston Journal* endorsed the principle of equal suffrage," as James M. McPherson pointed out in *The Struggle for Equality*, 310.

   Gary W. Gallagher has argued that "at the end of the war, with the Union salvaged and emancipation accomplished, most loyal citizens believed they had taken care of everything. There was no groundswell of support for doing more, for pursuing equal social and political rights for freedpeople, for maintaining a massive military presence in the former Confederacy." In other words, he concluded, "emancipation marked the end of a story . . . not the beginning of a story that would move on to achieve full racial equality." Gallagher, "The Civil War at the Sesquicentennial," 301. There is substantial truth in his declaration, and much of my own work has been devoted to laying bare the deep-rooted racism that limited progress in the Civil War era. Yet there was determined advocacy for Black suffrage, if not a groundswell, and in the days after victory support appeared in some surprising places. To better understand the reasons why Black suffrage failed in 1865, as well as the extent to which a basis was laid that aided its success by 1868 and 1869, a closer look at the dynamics of debate is necessary.
3. *New York Herald* quoted in *Cleveland Daily Herald*, June 19, 1865. See also *New York Herald*, June 15, 1865, 4.
4. *New York World* quoted in *Bedford Inquirer*, May 12, 1865, 2; Strong, *Diary*, June 29, 1865, 14. For examples of the fact that other newspapers noted the position of the *New York World* and the *New York Herald*, see *Bangor Daily Whig and Courier*, May 19, 1865, 2, and *Scioto Gazette*, May 23, 1865.

5. *Bedford Inquirer,* May 12, 1865, 2; *New York World* quoted in *Liberator,* May 5, 1865, 3; *New York Tribune,* May 3, 1865, 4; April 17, 1865, 1; and quoted in *Cadiz Sentinel,* May 17, 1865, 2. Staff members of the *New York World* had written the *Miscegenation* pamphlet that inflamed fears of racial equality in the 1864 electoral campaign. Croly and Wakeman, *Miscegenation.*

6. *Chicago Tribune,* April 27, 1865, 2; May 17, 1865, 2; *White Cloud Kansas Chief,* May 25, 1865, 2.

7. *North American Review,* April 1865, 549, 551, 553, 559, 554.

8. *Atlantic Monthly,* May 1865, 623, 624, 625.

9. *Harper's Weekly,* April 22, 1865, 242; May 13, 1865, 289; June 3, 1865, 338.

10. *New Englander,* January 1865, 119, 122, 124, 151; October 1865, 756, 758, 773.

11. *Littell's Living Age,* July–September 1865, 44–46.

12. Quoted in *New York Tribune,* May 16, 1865, 4.

13. Quoted in *Liberator,* April 28, 1865, 1. See also *Jasper Weekly Courier,* May 6, 1865, 1.

14. *Liberator,* May 12, 1865, 3.

15. *Daily Ohio Statesman,* May 9, 1865, 2.

16. Quoted in *Ottawa Free Trader,* May 20, 1865, 2; *Burlington Free Press,* June 16, 1865, 2.

17. Frederick Douglass, "What the Black Man Wants," April 1865, Uncle Tom's Cabin and American Culture, African American Responses, Later Assessments, http://utc.iath.virginia.edu/africam/afspfdat.html.

18. *Liberator,* May 26, 1865, 1. Most of the debates appear in *Liberator,* May 26 and June 2, 1865.

19. *Liberator,* May 26, 1865, 1.

20. Ibid.; *Liberator,* June 2, 1865, 1, 2, 3. Edmund Quincy of Massachusetts was an important abolitionist editor who often took charge of the *Liberator* when William Lloyd Garrison was absent.

21. *Liberator,* June 2, 1865, 2–3.

22. *Liberator,* May 5, 1865, 4; June 2, 1865, 3.

23. *Cadiz Sentinel,* May 3, 1865, 1; *Jeffersonian Democrat,* May 5, 1865, 1.

24. Chase quoted in Hodes, *Mourning Lincoln,* 219; *Jeffersonian Democrat,* May 5, 1865, 1; *Hillsdale Standard,* June 6, 1865, 1; *Daily Ohio Statesman,* June 28, 1865, 1; *Cleveland Leader,* July 26, 1865, 2.

25. *New York Tribune,* April 22, 1865, 4; May 3, 1865, 4.

26. *Civilian and Telegraph,* May 18, 1865, 2.

27. Quoted in *Bedford Inquirer,* May 19, 1865, 2.

28. *Ashtabula Weekly Telegraph,* June 17, 1865, 2.
29. *Chicago Tribune,* April 25, 1865, 2; May 17, 1865, 2.
30. *Chicago Tribune,* May 17, 1865, 2.
31. *Boston Commonwealth* quoted in *White Cloud Kansas Chief,* June 1, 1865, 2.
32. *Caledonian,* May 2, 1865, 1.
33. *Madison Capitol* quoted in *Milwaukee Daily Sentinel,* May 26, 1865, 1.
34. *Vermont Watchman and State Journal,* July 21, 1865, 1.
35. Ibid.; *Burlington Free Press,* June 30, 1865, 1.
36. *New York Evening Post,* quoting the *New York News,* printed in the *Hillsdale Standard,* July 25, 1865, 2.

3. DEMOCRATIC OPPOSITION

1. For more on the wartime Democratic Party, see Escott, *"The Worst Passions of Human Nature,"* especially chapters 2 and 6.
2. "Franklin Pierce's Letter to Jeff Davis," January 6, 1860, Duke University Libraries, Repository Collections and Archives, https://repository .duke.edu/dc/broadsides/bdsnh11250; "Franklin Pierce and Jefferson Davis," Presidential History Geeks, January 25, 2014, https://potus-geeks .livejournal.com/440347.html.
3. Vorenberg, *Final Freedom,* 99, 138, 165, 142. See also Escott, *"The Worst Passions of Human Nature."*
4. *Daily Ohio Statesman,* April 17, 1865, 2; April 19, 1865, 3; April 22, 1865, 2; May 4, 1865, 2; *Jasper Weekly Courier,* May 27, 1865, 1; *Louisville Journal* quoted in *Jasper Weekly Courier,* May 13, 1865, 1.
5. *Rock Island Evening Argus,* May 10, 1865, 2 (with words quoted from the *New York Tribune*); *Ottawa Free Trader,* May 13, 1865, 2 (quoting the *Philadelphia Ledger*); May 20, 1865, 2; *Columbus Crisis* quoted in *Cadiz Sentinel,* April 26, 1865, 1; *Cadiz Sentinel,* May 3, 1865, 2; *Plymouth Weekly Democrat,* May 4, 1865, 2; May 11, 1865, 1.
6. *Plymouth Weekly Democrat,* June 1, 1865, 1, quoting the *Malone Gazette* and the *New York Evening Post; Columbia Democrat and Bloomsburg General Advertiser,* June 3, 1865, 1; *Ashland Union,* May 17, 1865, 2.
7. *Jasper Weekly Courier,* July 8, 1865, 1, quoting the *New York Evening Post; Ashland Union,* May 3, 1865, 1, quoting the *Holmes County Farmer;* May 24, 1865, 2; May 10, 1865, 1, quoting the *Urbana Union.*
8. *Urbana Union,* April 26, 1865, 2; *Franklin Valley Spirit,* April 26, 1865, 2.
9. *Jasper Weekly Courier,* May 6, 1865, 2; May 13, 1865, 1; June 10, 1865, 1. See also *Ashland Union,* May 10, 1865, 1.
10. *Ashland Union,* May 31, 1865, 1; June 7, 1865, 1.

11. *Jasper Weekly Courier,* July 22, 1865, 1; *Cadiz Sentinel,* June 21, 1865, 1; *Chicago Times* quoted in *Daily Ohio Statesman,* August 22, 1865, 1; September 1, 1865, 2.

12. *Daily Ohio Statesman,* May 25, 1865, 2; May 30, 1865, 1, 2, which includes its quotation of the *Cincinnati Commercial; Plymouth Weekly Democrat,* May 4, 1865, 1, quoting the *Nashville Press,* April 10, 1865, 1.

13. *Hartford Times* quoted in *Plymouth Weekly Democrat,* June 8, 1865, 1; *Plymouth Weekly Democrat,* June 8, 1865, 1.

14. *Mount Vernon Banner* quoted in *Ashland Union,* June 7, 1865, 2; *Cincinnati Enquirer* quoted in *Ashtabula Weekly Telegraph,* July 8, 1865, 1.

15. *New York Express* quoted in *Franklin Valley Spirit,* June 28, 1865, 2; *Daily Ohio Statesman,* June 20, 1865, 2; *Plymouth Weekly Democrat,* June 29, 1865, 1; *Chicago Times* quoted in *Plymouth Weekly Democrat,* July 13, 1861, 1.

16. *Chicago Times* quoted in *Plymouth Weekly Democrat,* July 13, 1861, 1; *Jasper Weekly Courier,* July 8, 1865, 1, quoting the *Boonville Enquirer; Philadelphia Bulletin* quoted in *Columbia Democrat and Bloomsburg General Advertiser,* June 10, 1865, 2; *Ottawa Free Trader,* May 27, 1865, 2.

17. *Cadiz Sentinel,* April 26, 1865, 2; *Grand Haven News,* May 17, 1865, 1; *Plymouth Weekly Democrat,* May 11, 1865, 1.

18. *Columbia Democrat and Bloomsburg General Advertiser,* May 6, 1865, 2.

4. JOHNSON ANNOUNCES HIS POLICY ON RECONSTRUCTION

1. *Ashtabula Weekly Telegraph,* May 27, 1865, 1; *Delaware State Journal and Statesman,* May 19, 1865, 2; May 26, 1865, 2 (quoting the *Philadelphia Press*). Davis had thrown his wife's shawl over his shoulders as he tried to slip away from approaching U.S. troops, and various reports ridiculed him for supposedly disguising himself as a woman.

2. *Ashtabula Weekly Telegraph,* May 6, 1865, 2; May 13, 1865, 1; *Cincinnati Gazette* quoted in *Milwaukee Daily Sentinel,* May 3, 1865, 2; *Delaware State Journal and Statesman,* May 26, 1865, 2; *Chicago Tribune,* May 15, 1865, 2.

3. *Cleveland Leader,* May 24, 1865, 1; *Chicago Tribune,* May 17, 1865, 2; *Scioto Gazette,* May 23, 1865, 2; *Vermont Watchman and State Journal,* May 26, 1865, 4; May 5, 1865, 2; *Burlington Free Press,* May 26, 1865; *Hillsdale Standard,* May 23, 1865, 2.

4. *Philadelphia Ledger* quoted in *Aegis and Intelligencer,* May 12, 1865, 2; *Frederick Union* quoted in *Aegis and Intelligencer,* May 19, 1865, 2; *Pittsburg Post* quoted in *Daily Ohio Statesman,* May 10, 1865, 2.

5. *Urbana Union,* May 24, 1865, 1; *Daily Ohio Statesman,* May 15, 1865, 2; *Jasper Weekly Courier,* May 27, 1865, 1; *New York Sun,* May 18, 1865, 2.

6. *Ottawa Free Trader,* May 13, 1865, 2; May 20, 1865, 1; *Rock Island Evening Argus,* May 8, 1865, 2; May 13, 1865, 2.

7. *New York Herald* quoted in *Evansville Daily Journal,* May 20, 1865, 1.

8. Welles, *Diary,* May 9, 1865, 2:301–4. Some of Welles's excessive and confusing punctuation has been removed.

9. Ibid.

10. Ibid.

11. Ibid.

12. Crofts, "Ending Slavery and Limiting Democracy," 39, 51–52.

13. The text may be found at Andrew Johnson, "Johnson's Proclamation of Amnesty and Reconstruction," May 29, 1865, Teaching American History, Documents, https://teachingamericanhistory.org/library/document /proclamation-of-amnesty-and-reconstruction-2/.

14. The full text may be found at Andrew Johnson, "Message Reestablishing Governments in Former Confederate States," May 29, 1865, Miller Center, University of Virginia, Presidential Speeches, Andrew Johnson Presidency, https://millercenter.org/the-presidency/presidential-speeches/ may-29-1865-message-reestablishing-governments-former.

15. Ibid. Martha Hodes also believes that Lincoln, unlike Johnson, would have "listened to, absorbed, and responded to the demands of African Americans." Frederick Douglass declared in December 1865 that "had Abraham Lincoln been spared to see this day, the negro of the South would have more than a hope of enfranchisement and no rebels would hold the reins of Government in any one of the late rebellious states." Hodes, *Mourning Lincoln,* 273.

16. Hodes, *Mourning Lincoln,* 245; McPherson, *The Struggle for Equality,* 321–22.

17. *Bedford Inquirer,* June 2, 1865, 2; June 9, 1865, 2.

18. *Civilian and Telegraph,* June 8, 1865, 2; June 22, 1865, 2.

19. *White Cloud Kansas Chief,* June 1, 1865, 2; *Ashtabula Weekly Telegraph,* June 17, 1865, 2.

20. *Cleveland Leader,* June 1, 1865, 2; June 9, 1865, 1; *Vermont Watchman and State Journal,* June 23, 1865, 2; *Caledonian,* June 16, 1865, 2; June 23, 1865, 2.

21. *Burlington Free Press,* June 3, 1865, 2; *Aegis and Intelligencer,* June 23, 1865, 2; *Independent* (Oskaloosa), June 3, 1865, 2.

22. *Chicago Tribune,* May 31, 1865, 2; *New York Times,* May 30, 1865, 1; *New York Times* quoted in *Chicago Tribune,* June 22, 1865, 2. The *Tribune* said the message of Johnson's policy was, "in effect, 'Go away, nigger; you have no rights that a white President is bound to respect!'"

23. Adams quoted in Hodes, *Mourning Lincoln*, 242.

24. *Republican* (Springfield) quoted in *Caledonian*, June 16, 1865, 2.

25. Ibid.

26. Ibid.

27. Welles, *Diary*, May 10, 1865, 2:304.

28. *Boston Commonwealth* quoted in *Caledonian*, June 23, 1865, 1; *Harper's Weekly*, May 27, 1865, 322.

29. *New York Tribune*, June 17, 1865, 1; *Ashtabula Weekly Telegraph*, June 17, 1865, 2.

30. Sherman, *John Sherman's Recollections*, 1:362; *New York Times* and the Philadelphia correspondent cited in *Ashland Union*, July 5, 1865, 1.

31. Samuel May to William Lloyd Garrison, quoted in *Liberator*, June 23, 1865, 98.

32. *Urbana Union*, May 31, 1865, 1, 2; see also June 7, 1865, 2, and June 14, 1865, 2.

33. *Urbana Union*, June 21, 1865, 2.

34. *New York World* quoted in *Milwaukee News*, June 5, 1865; *Ottawa Free Trader*, June 10, 1865, 1; *Joliet Signal* quoted in *Rock Island Evening Argus*, June 8, 1865, 2; *Columbia Democrat and Bloomsburg General Advertiser*, June 10, 1865, 2.

35. *Columbia Democrat and Bloomsburg General Advertiser*, June 17, 1865, 1; June 24, 1865, 2; *Ashland Union*, June 21, 1865, 2; June 28, 1865, 2; *New York World* quoted in *Daily Ohio Statesman*, June 13, 1865, 2. Wendell Phillips agreed with the *Daily Ohio Statesman* that "the admission of a single State without negro suffrage would settle the whole question, and slavery would exist in reality, but not in name." See his words quoted in *Cadiz Sentinel*, June 14, 1865, 1.

36. *Ottawa Free Trader*, June 17, 1865, 1; *Cadiz Sentinel*, June 7, 1865, 2; June 14, 1865, 1; June 21, 1865, 2; *Wheeling Register* quoted in *Cadiz Sentinel*, June 21, 1865, 1; *Jasper Weekly Courier*, June 10, 1865, 1; June 24, 1865, 1; *New York World* quoted in *Milwaukee Daily Sentinel*, June 12, 1865, 2.

37. *Daily Ohio Statesman*, May 31, 1865, 2. Eleven of fourteen Democratic journals for which a complete or substantial run of issues has survived demonstrated this support. The views of other Democratic newspapers encountered in research were similar.

5. REPUBLICANS ADVOCATE FOR BLACK SUFFRAGE

1. *Ashland Union*, July 19, 1865, 2; *Cleveland Leader*, June 19, 1865, 1. The rebellion in Haiti against Spanish control resulted in the establishment of

a second Dominican Republic independent of Spain. On the rest of the island, Haiti remained under Spanish control.

2. Hodes, *Mourning Lincoln*, 229, 264, 257; Strong, *Diary*, July 6, 1865, 4:15–16.

3. Strong, *Diary*, June 20, 10, 1865, 4:12, 7.

4. Hodes, *Mourning Lincoln*, 12–16, 236–37.

5. Stearns's printed appeal, Stevens, Papers, May 26, June 10, 1865; McPherson, *The Struggle for Equality*, 319.

6. Charles Schulz (?) to Thaddeus Stevens, June 19, July 12, 1865, Stevens, Papers.

7. Cornelius Cole to Thaddeus Stevens, July 31, 1865, Stevens, Papers.

8. James Harlan to Elihu Washburne, June 12, 1865, Washburne, Papers.

9. J. Wildon (?) to Elihu Washburne, August 19, 21, 1865, Washburne, Papers.

10. *Liberator*, June 16, 1865, 3.

11. *Cleveland Leader*, June 20, 1865, 2.

12. Ibid.

13. Ibid.

14. *Cleveland Leader*, June 19, 1865, 1; June 23, 1865, 2.

15. *Liberator*, June 30, 1865, 2, 4.

16. *Caledonian*, July 7, 1865, 2.

17. *Liberator*, July 21, 1865, 1.

18. *Bedford Inquirer*, July 14, 1865, 2; *Cleveland Leader*, July 8, 1865, 2.

19. *Bedford Inquirer*, July 14, 1865, 2; *Cleveland Leader*, July 8, 1865, 2.

20. J. W. Dwinelle quoted in *Liberator*, August 18, 1865, 1.

21. *Jeffersonian Democrat*, July 21, 1865, 1; July 28, 1865, 2.

22. *Jasper Weekly Courier*, July 22, 1865, 1.

23. *Jeffersonian Democrat*, July 21, 1865, 2.

24. *Liberator*, August 18, 1865, 1, copying an article from the *Philadelphia Inquirer*.

25. *Liberator*, August 25, 1865, 4; Kelley, "Safeguards of Personal Liberty," 5, 10–11, 13–14; Brown, "William D. Kelley and Radical Reconstruction," 322.

26. *Liberator*, August 4, 1865, 1; September 15, 1865, 1.

27. *New York Tribune*, June 7, 1865, 4; *Cleveland Leader*, June 9, 1865, 2; *White Cloud Kansas Chief*, June 22, 1865, 2; *Liberator*, June 30, 1865, 1.

28. *Jeffersonian Democrat*, July 14, 1865, 2; *Civilian and Telegraph*, June 29, 1865, 2.

29. *St. Cloud Democrat*, June 29, 1865, 2; *Vermont Watchman and State Journal*, July 7, 1865, 2, quoting "Agate," the D.C. correspondent of the *Cincinnati Gazette*, July 1, 1865.

30. *New York Tribune*, May 27, 1865, 4.

31. *New York Tribune* quoted in *Ashtabula Weekly Telegraph,* July 1, 1865, 1.
32. *New York Tribune* quoted in *Ashtabula Weekly Telegraph,* May 27, 1865, 4; June 7, 1865, 4; June 3, 1865, 4; May 30, 1865, 4; August 5, 1865, 4.
33. *New York Tribune* quoted in *Ashtabula Weekly Telegraph,* June 3, 1865, 4; July 31, 1865, 4.
34. *Boston Traveller* quoted in *Liberator,* July 28, 1865, 1.
35. *Boston Journal* quoted in *Caledonian,* July 7, 1865, 2; *Independent* (New York) quoted in *Caledonian,* July 28, 1865, 2; *New York Evening Post* quoted in *Bedford Inquirer,* July 14, 1865, 1.
36. *Chicago Tribune,* June 17, 1865, 2; June 20, 1865, 2.
37. *Chicago Tribune,* July 11, 1865, 2; July 13, 1865, 2; August 5, 1865, 2; August 8, 1865, 1.
38. *Hillsdale Standard,* June 27, 1865, 2; July 4, 1865, 1, 2; July 25, 1865, 2; August 1, 1865, 2; *Delaware State Journal and Statesman,* August 4, 1865, 2.
39. *Chicago Tribune,* July 11, 1865, 1; *Hillsdale Standard,* July 4, 1865, 1.
40. *Vermont Watchman and State Journal,* June 16, 1865, 2; June 23, 1865, 1; July 14, 1865, 1; August 11, 1865, 2; August 25, 1865, 2.
41. *New York Times,* September 14, 1865, 1; July 13, 1865, 4; July 8, 1865, 4.

6. BLACK AND WHITE ABOLITIONISTS ADVOCATE

1. *Cadiz Sentinel,* June 14, 1865, 1; *Liberator,* June 16, 1865, 2.
2. *Jasper Weekly Courier,* June 17, 1865, 1; June 24, 1865, 1; *Liberator,* June 16, 1862, 2–3.
3. *National Anti-Slavery Standard* quoted in *Jasper Weekly Courier,* June 24, 1865, 1.
4. *Ottawa Free Trader,* June 17, 1865, 1. See also *Rock Island Evening Argus,* June 17, 1865, 2.
5. *Franklin Valley Spirit,* July 19, 1865, 2; *Liberator,* July 14, 1865, 4.
6. *Liberator,* July 14, 1865, 4.
7. McPherson, *The Struggle for Equality,* 323.
8. *Liberator,* August 11, 1865, 4.
9. See Escott, "The Worst Passions of Human Nature." The white abolitionist press enjoyed a healthier financial condition than the Black press. Frederick Douglass's newspaper, for example, was perennially short of funds and struggled to gain more subscribers.
10. *Proceedings of a Convention of the Colored Men of Ohio,* 2, 13–14.
11. Ibid., 15–16.
12. *Proceedings of the State Equal Rights Convention of the Colored Men of Pennsylvania,* 13, 31, 32.

13. Ibid., 19, 32, 46, 47.
14. *Proceedings of the Connecticut State Convention of Colored Men*, 6–8, 9, 10.
15. *Proceedings of the State Convention of Colored Men of the State of New Jersey*, 11–15.
16. *Proceedings of the Annual Meeting of the Pennsylvania State Equal Rights' League*, 133, 137.
17. Ibid., 138–39.
18. Ibid., 139–40, 144, 145.
19. *State Convention of the Colored People of Louisiana*, 247, 252, 249, 251, 242.
20. *Liberator*, June 30, 1865, 2.
21. *Boston Transcript* quoted in *Liberator*, June 16, 1865, 3; *Liberator*, June 30, 1865, 3; *Bedford Inquirer*, June 23, 1865, 1.
22. *Equal Suffrage*, 10–12. For information on some of the leaders of the Norfolk assembly, see Varon, *Appomattox*, 197–98.
23. *Equal Suffrage*, 1–2, 3–4, 6–7, 8.
24. *Liberator*, June 16, 1865, 2.
25. *Delaware State Journal and Statesman*, July 4, 1865, 2; *Liberator*, July 28, 1865, 3.
26. *Proceedings of the Convention of the Colored People of VA.*, 9–11.
27. Ibid., 12, 16, 17–18, 20.
28. Ibid., 21–22, 19, 24; *Liberator*, August 18, 1865, 3; *Vermont Watchman and State Journal*, August 18, 1865, 2; *New York Tribune*, August 11, 1865, 5.
29. *Proceedings of the State Convention of Colored Men of the State of Tennessee*, iii, 6, 12.
30. Ibid., 12–15, 18, 21–22, 23–27.
31. *State Convention of the Colored People of North Carolina*, 180; account drawn from *Christian Recorder*, October 28, 1865.
32. *Address by a Convention of Black North Carolinians to the Constitutional Convention of North Carolina and the Legislature to Assemble Thereafter*, in Andrews, *The South since the War*, 128–30.
33. Ibid.
34. *Liberator*, September 15, 1865, 3; October 6, 1865, 3, quoting the *Boston Journal*.

7. NORTHERN DEMOCRATS ATTACK

1. "The Murder of Mrs. Surratt," *Ashland Union*, July 26, 1865, 2.
2. *Harper's Weekly*, August 12, 1865, 502; *Caledonian*, July 21, 1865, 2; August 25, 1865, 2; *New York Tribune*, August 5, 1865, 1.

3. *New York World* quoted in *New Haven Daily Palladium,* July 21, 1865, 2; *New York World* quoted in *Franklin Valley Spirit,* August 2, 1865, 1; August 16, 1865, 1; *Aegis and Intelligencer,* July 7, 1865, 2.

4. *Urbana Union,* July 5, 1865, 2; *Chicago Times* quoted in *Ashland Union,* July 5, 1865, 1; *Ottawa Free Trader,* July 8, 1865, 2; *New York Herald* as copied in *Daily Mississippian,* July 26, 1865, 2.

5. *Cincinnati Enquirer,* August 21, 1865, quoted in *Cleveland Daily Herald,* August 22, 1865, 1; *New York Evening Post* quoted in *Jasper Weekly Courier,* July 8, 1865, 1; *Cadiz Sentinel,* August 16, 1865, 1; *Bedford Inquirer,* September 8, 1865, 2; *Urbana Union,* August 9, 1865, 2. Pennsylvania Democrats were blaming the Republican Party for a quotation taken from William Lloyd Garrison. The prewar Republicans always denied, of course, that they were abolitionists.

6. *Franklin Valley Spirit,* August 23, 1865, 2; August 30, 1865, 2; September 6, 1865, 2. For more on the Democratic Party's dedication to white supremacy, see Escott, "*The Worst Passions of Human Nature.*"

7. *Columbia Democrat and Bloomsburg General Advertiser,* August 26, 1865, 2; September 2, 1865, 1; September 30, 1865, 1, quoting the *Philadelphia Age; Ashland Union,* June 7, 1865, 1; July 12, 1865, 2.

8. *Mount Vernon Banner* quoted in *Ashland Union,* August 9, 1865, 1; *Philadelphia Inquirer* quoted in *New Haven Daily Palladium,* July 31, 1865, 2.

9. *Holmes County Farmer* quoted in *Ashland Union,* August 2, 1865, 2; *Daily Ohio Statesman,* July 1, 1865, 2; *Cadiz Sentinel,* July 12, 1856, 1.

10. *Jasper Weekly Courier,* July 29, 1865, 2; *New Albany Ledger* quoted in *Jasper Weekly Courier,* July 22, 1865, 1; *Vermont Watchman and State Journal,* July 7, 1865, 1.

11. *Columbia Democrat and Bloomsburg General Advertiser,* August 5, 1865, 2; *Ashland Union,* August 2, 1865, 2.

12. One exception among Democratic newspapers was the *New York News,* which late in June came out in favor of Black suffrage. Regarded as prorebel by many, the *News* now reasoned that former slaves were "imitative creatures" who would vote with their old masters and that President Johnson looked toward "negro suffrage as an element of Democratic supremacy." These words from the *News* are quoted in *Evansville Daily Journal,* June 30, 1865, 1.

13. *Franklin Valley Spirit,* July 19, 1865, 2; July 26, 1865, 2; *Urbana Union,* July 19, 1865, 1; August 16, 1865, 1; *Jasper Weekly Courier,* September 2, 1865, 2.

14. *Chicago Times* quoted in *Plymouth Weekly Democrat,* July 13, 1865, 1; *Franklin Valley Spirit,* September 13, 1865, 1; September 20, 1865, 2; *Columbia*

Democrat and Bloomsburg General Advertiser, July 29, 1865, 1–2; September 2, 1865, 1; *Ashland Union,* August 16, 1865, 1; *Fort Wayne Times Sentinel* quoted in *Plymouth Weekly Democrat,* September 7, 1865, 1.

15. An unidentified Connecticut newspaper cited in *Franklin Valley Spirit,* August 9, 1865, 1; *Columbia Democrat and Bloomsburg General Advertiser,* July 17, 1865, 2; *New York Herald* copied by *Franklin Valley Spirit,* August 9, 1865, 1; *Franklin Valley Spirit,* September 20, 1865, 1.

16. *St. Louis Dispatch* quoted in *Plymouth Weekly Democrat,* August 17, 1865, 2; *Jasper Weekly Courier,* August 12, 1865, 2; August 5, 1865, 2; August 19, 1865, 1, quoting the *Louisville Democrat.*

17. *Ashland Union,* August 16, 1865, 2; *Cincinnati Enquirer* quoted in *Ashtabula Weekly Telegraph,* July 8, 1865, 1; *Urbana Union,* August 2, 1865, 2.

18. Quoted in *Franklin Valley Spirit,* September 20, 1865, 1; September 13, 1865, 1; *Columbia Democrat and Bloomsburg General Advertiser,* July 15, 1865, 2; *Cleveland Plain Dealer* quoted in *Daily Ohio Statesman,* July 7, 1865, 2; *Cincinnati Enquirer* quoted in *Evansville Daily Journal,* August 2, 1865, 1; paper perhaps misattributed as *N.Y. Express,* quoted in *Evansville Daily Journal,* August 2, 1865, 1; Croly and Wakeman, *Miscegenation.*

19. *Jasper Weekly Courier,* July 29, 1865, 1, quoting the *Boston Post; Urbana Union,* July 26, 1865, 2; August 16, 1865, 2; *Plymouth Weekly Democrat,* September 7, 1865, 1; *New York Herald* quoted in *Arkansas Gazette,* July 27, 1865, 1; *Cadiz Sentinel,* July 19, 1865, 2.

20. *North American Review,* July 1865, 199–205; *St. Louis Dispatch* quoted in *Plymouth Weekly Democrat,* July 6, 1865, 2; *Philadelphia Age* quoted in *Columbia Democrat and Bloomsburg General Advertiser,* September 30, 1865, 1; *Hartford Times* quoted in *Arkansas Gazette,* July 18, 1865, 1; *Cincinnati Commercial* quoted on Jefferson Davis in *Jasper Weekly Courier,* August 5, 1865, 1.

21. *New York World* quoted in San Francisco *Daily Evening Bulletin,* August 1, 1865, 1; *New York Tribune,* August 5, 1865, 4.

22. *Philadelphia North American* quoted in *Daily National Intelligencer,* August 21, 1865, 2; *New York World* quoted in *Franklin Valley Spirit,* July 26, 1865, 2; *New York Journal of Commerce* quoted in *Daily National Intelligencer,* August 21, 1865, 2; *Chicago Times* quoted in *Daily Mississippian,* August 26, 1865, 2; *Memphis Bulletin, Richmond Commercial Bulletin, Memphis Commercial,* and *New York Commercial Advertiser,* all quoted in *Daily National Intelligencer,* August 21, 1865, 2.

23. *Urbana Union,* August 30, 1865, 1; *Daily Ohio Statesman,* July 24, 1865, 1.

24. *Jasper Weekly Courier,* August 5, 1865, 2; *New York Day Book* quoted in *Plymouth Weekly Democrat,* August 31, 1865, 1; *New York World* quoted in *Milwaukee Daily Sentinel,* August 18, 1865, 2.

8. REPUBLICANS SEEK A PATH FORWARD

1. For example, see *Bedford Inquirer,* August 18, 1865, 2.
2. *New York Times,* December 29, 1864, 4. See also October 18, 1863, 4; December 27, 1864, 4; January 15, 1865, 4; and February 9, 1865, 4, for other examples.
3. *New York Times,* July 8, 1865, 4; July 13, 1865, 4; August 14, 1865, 4; September 14, 1865, 4; September 15, 1865, 4.
4. *Evansville Daily Journal,* June 30, 1865, 1, including quotations from the *New York News.*
5. *New York Sun,* July 27, 1865, 2.
6. *Columbia Democrat and Bloomsburg General Advertiser,* July 29, 1865, 1, quoting an article in the *Easton Argus;* McPherson, *The Struggle for Equality,* 332; *Chicago Tribune,* August 8, 1865, 1; September 9, 1865, 1. The latter report actually dealt with "the interior of North Carolina," not South Carolina.
7. Browne and Hawks quoted in Hodes, *Mourning Lincoln,* 258, 260; correspondence to the *New York Tribune* reproduced in *Boston Advertiser,* August 9, 1865, 4; *Ashtabula Weekly Telegraph,* August 26, 1865, 2, quoting the *Raleigh Progress,* August 16, 1865. For information from Freedmen's Bureau reports on North Carolina, see Escott, *Many Excellent People,* chapter 5.
8. *Delaware State Journal and Statesman,* August 15, 1865, 2; August 22, 1865, 2; *Evansville Daily Journal,* July 11, 1865, 1; August 5, 1865, 2; *New York Tribune,* August 31, 1865, 4.
9. *Ottawa Free Trader,* August 19, 1865, 2; *Vermont Watchman and State Journal,* September 8, 1865, 1, 2.
10. Carter, *When the War Was Over,* 148.
11. *Caledonian,* July 7, 1865, 2; *Philadelphia Press* quoted in *New Haven Daily Palladium,* June 23, 1865, 2; "African Peonage" quoted in *Liberator,* August 25, 1865, 1.
12. *New York Herald* quoted in *Vermont Watchman and State Journal,* August 4, 1865, 1; *Vermont Watchman and State Journal,* September 8, 1865, 1; *Ashtabula Weekly Telegraph,* September 30, 1865, 2.
13. *Liberator,* August 4, 1865, 3; July 28, 1865, 1, quoting the *New York World;* *New York World* quoted in *Lowell Daily Citizen and News,* July 7, 1865, 2; *New York World* quoted in *Bangor Daily Whig and Courier,* July 21, 1865,

3; *Memphis Commercial* quoted in *Evansville Daily Journal*, August 15, 1865, 1.

14. *Ebensburg Alleghanian*, September 21, 1865, 2; *Harper's Weekly*, July 29, 1865, 466; *Independent* (Oskaloosa), July 29, 1865, 2; August 5, 1865, 2; *New York Tribune*, August 5, 1865, 4.

15. *Ashtabula Weekly Telegraph*, September 9, 1865, 1, quoting the *Colored Tennessean*; *Cleveland Leader*, August 8, 1865, 2.

16. *Bedford Inquirer*, August 4, 1865, 2, quoting the *Philadelphia Evening Telegraph*; *Civilian and Telegraph*, July 27, 1865, 2; August 17, 1865, 2; *Hillsdale Standard*, August 15, 1865, 2, including its reprinting of an article from the *Kalamazoo Telegraph*.

17. *White Cloud Kansas Chief*, August 3, 1865, 2; *Ashtabula Weekly Telegraph*, August 5, 1865, 1; *Boston Advertiser* quoted in *Jeffersonian Democrat*, August 4, 1865, 2; *Chicago Tribune*, July 4, 1865, 2; August 21, 1865, 1.

18. *Independent* (Oskaloosa), July 15, 1865, 2; *White Cloud Kansas Chief*, July 13, 1865, 2; *Ashtabula Weekly Telegraph*, August 5, 1865, 1, 2; *Evansville Daily Journal*, July 31, 1865, 2; September 2, 1865, 2; *Delaware State Journal and Statesman*, September 1, 1865, 2.

19. *Vermont Watchman and State Journal*, September 29, 1865, 1; *White Cloud Kansas Chief*, August 3, 1865, 2.

20. Kilpatrick is quoted in an article of the *Philadelphia Ledger* copied by *Franklin Valley Spirit*, September 9, 1865, 1, and also in *Vermont Watchman and State Journal*, August 25, 1865, 2; *Civilian and Telegraph*, July 20, 1865, 2; *Evansville Daily Journal*, July 17, 1865, 1.

21. *Civilian and Telegraph*, August 3, 1865, 2; *Cleveland Leader*, July 1, 1865, 2; *Caledonian*, August 18, 1865, 1, 2; *Harper's Weekly*, August 5, 1865, 482; *Evansville Daily Journal*, August 24, 1865, 1, quoting George W. Curtis's essay in *Harper's New Monthly Magazine* in July.

22. *Syracuse Journal* quoted in *White Cloud Kansas Chief*, September 7, 1865, 1; *White Cloud Kansas Chief*, September 7, 1865, 2.

23. Statement of the Vermont Union Party quoted in *Daily Ohio Statesman*, July 1, 1865, 2; *Evansville Daily Journal*, July 27, 1865, 1, including text of the "Negro suffrage" letter to the *Indianapolis Journal* of July 23, 1865.

24. *New York Tribune*, August 5, 1865, 4; *Chicago Tribune*, July 11, 1865, 2; August 5, 1865, 2; September 13, 1865, 2.

25. *Liberator*, August 18, 1865, 1.

26. *Atlantic Monthly*, August 1865, 238–47, especially 238, 242, 244, 246, 247.

27. *Vermont Watchman and State Journal*, August 25, 1865, 2.

28. *New York Times*, September 10, 1865, 2.

29. *Vermont Watchman and State Journal,* September 1, 1865, 2.
30. *Philadelphia Inquirer* quoted in *Vermont Watchman and State Journal,* September 29, 1865, 2; *Independent* (Oskaloosa), August 5, 1865, 2.
31. *Jeffersonian Democrat,* July 7, 1865, 2.
32. Ibid. quoting the *Frankfort Commonwealth.*
33. *Cincinnati Commercial* quoted in *Hillsdale Standard,* July 18, 1865, 1.
34. *White Cloud Kansas Chief,* August 17, 1865, 1.

9. TOWARD ELECTIONS

1. *Littell's Living Age,* July–December 1865, 559; *Harper's Weekly,* August 12, 1865, 502; September 2, 1865, 560. Wirz was tried and then hanged on November 10, 1865.
2. *New York Tribune,* August 23, 1865, 1.
3. *New York Tribune,* August 28, 1865, 1; *Burlington Free Press,* August 18, 1865, 1, 2, including a report from the *New York Herald; Harper's Weekly,* September 23, 1865, 603–4.
4. *Vermont Watchman and State Journal,* July 14, 1865, 1; *Caledonian,* July 7, 1865, 1.
5. Quoted in *Cleveland Leader* (morning edition), August 11, 1865, 1.
6. *New York Tribune,* September 15, 1865, 1; *Vermont Watchman and State Journal,* September 22, 1865, 1.
7. Escott, "What Shall We Do with the Negro?" 228–29; *New York Tribune,* September 9, 1865, 4.
8. *New York Tribune,* September 9, 1865, 4; Escott, "What Shall We Do with the Negro?" 236.
9. G. Galin Berrier, "The Negro Suffrage Issue in Iowa—1865–1868," *Annals of Iowa* 39 (1968): 241–61; *Chicago Tribune,* August 24, 1865, 1.
10. Sam Kauffelt to Thaddeus Stevens, September 4, 1865, Stevens, Papers; *Chicago Tribune,* September 20, 1865, 1; *New York Tribune,* August 18, 1865, 1; *Franklin Valley Spirit,* September 27, 1865, 2; September 20, 1865, 2.
11. *Big Blue Union,* October 7, 1865, 1; *White Cloud Kansas Chief,* September 7, 1865, 2; *Independent* (Oskaloosa), September 9, 1865, 2; October 21, 1865, 2.
12. Escott, "What Shall We Do with the Negro?" 233–34; *Cleveland Leader,* October 4, 1865, 2.
13. *New York Times,* July 13, 1865, 4; October 15, 1865, 2; resolutions of the New York Republican State Convention are quoted in *Cleveland Leader,* September 22, 1865, 1.

14. *Cincinnati Gazette* quoted in *Wisconsin State Register,* August 5, 1865, 2; *Ashtabula Weekly Telegraph,* August 12, 1865, 2.
15. *Cleveland Leader,* August 16, 1865, 2; *Scioto Gazette,* September 26, 1865.
16. *Cleveland Leader,* August 16, 1865, 2; August 17, 1865, 2.
17. *Ashtabula Weekly Telegraph,* August 12, 1865, 2; August 19, 1865, 2, including comments on the *New York Tribune,* the *Albany Journal,* and the *Chicago Tribune; New York Tribune,* August 22, 1865, 2; *Cleveland Leader,* October 5, 1865, 2; August 14, 1865, 2; August 11, 1865, 2.
18. *Cleveland Leader,* August 23, 1865, 2; *Urbana Union,* August 23, 1865, 2; August 16, 1865, 2.
19. *Cleveland Leader,* September 4, 1865, 2; September 16, 1865, 2; *Cleveland Daily Herald,* September 2, 1865. At Savannah, before Sherman started northward into the Carolinas, he met with local Black leaders, almost all of whom agreed with Reverend Garrison Frazier that it would be best for Blacks to live away from hostile, prejudiced whites.
20. *Ashtabula Weekly Telegraph,* August 19, 1865, 2; *Jeffersonian Democrat,* August 25, 1865, 2; *Aegis and Intelligencer,* August 25, 1865, 2.
21. *Cleveland Leader,* August 25, 1865, 1; August 18, 1865, 1; *Cadiz Sentinel,* August 30, 1865, 2.
22. *Urbana Union,* August 30, 1865, 1.
23. *Urbana Union,* August 16, 1865, 2; August 23, 1865, 2; September 27, 1865, 2; *Daily Ohio Statesman,* September 16, 1865, 1; September 21, 1865, 2; *Ohio State Journal* quoted in *Cadiz Sentinel,* August 9, 1865, which draws its quotation from the *Daily Ohio Statesman,* 2; *Ashland Union,* September 20, 1865, 1, 2.
24. *New Hampshire Statesman,* October 13, 1865, 1, reprinting an article from the *Cincinnati Gazette; Liberator,* October 13, 1865, 1, reprinting an article from the *Cincinnati Gazette; Cleveland Leader,* August 22, 1865, 1; August 24, 1865, 2.
25. *Ashtabula Weekly Telegraph,* September 16, 1865, 2; September 30, 1865, 2; October 21, 1865, 2; *Jeffersonian Democrat,* September 15, 1865, 1; September 8, 1865, 2.
26. *Jasper Weekly Courier,* September 23, 1865, 1; *Indianapolis Daily Herald,* November 10, 1865, 2; *Evansville Daily Journal,* October 13, 1865, 2.
27. *Chicago Tribune,* September 20, 1865, 2; *White Cloud Kansas Chief,* November 23, 1865, 2.
28. *White Cloud Kansas Chief,* August 31, 1865, 1; McPherson, *The Struggle for Equality,* 318.

29. White Cloud Kansas Chief, September 28, 1865, 1; Bates, Diary, September 2, 1865, 504; Chicago Tribune, October 26, 1865, 2; Evansville Daily Journal, October 20, 1865, 1; Cincinnati Gazette quoted in Bangor Daily Whig and Courier, November 11, 1865, 2.

30. Welles, Diary, August 21, 1865, 2:364–65; September 28, 1865, 2:373–74; October 21, 1865, 2:382–83.

10. ELECTIONS SETTLE TWO QUESTIONS

1. Twenty-three Republican newspapers in eleven states offered an uninterrupted or very substantial run of issues for thorough study. Of these twenty-three papers, 70 percent reported frequently on mistreatment of the freed people; 57 percent emphasized the danger of a rebellious South regaining power; half documented laudable progress among the ex-slaves; and about one-third expressed great fear for the national debt. Thirty-nine percent were willing to accept some form of qualified suffrage for the freedmen, or in a few cases a delay of the right to vote.

2. New York Herald quoted in Cleveland Daily Herald, September 4, 1865, 2.

3. Franklin Valley Spirit, September 6, 1865, 2; resolutions of the state convention quoted in Bedford Inquirer, September 8, 1865, 2; New Jersey resolutions quoted in White Cloud Kansas Chief, September 28, 1865, 2; October 26, 1865, 2; New York World quoted in Cadiz Sentinel, September 6, 1865, 2.

4. Urbana Union, September 6, 1865, 2, 1; "Democratic Platform" quoted in Ashland Union, September 13, 1865, 1; Ohio Democrats' resolutions quoted in Daily National Intelligencer, copied in Detroit Free Press, September 5, 1865, quoted in Delaware State Journal and Statesman, October 2, 1865, 2.

5. Jasper Weekly Courier, September 16, 1865, 1; Plymouth Weekly Democrat, October 5, 1865, 2; October 12, 1865, 1.

6. Daily Ohio Statesman, August 18, 1865, 2; Cincinnati Enquirer, November 11, 1865.

7. New York World quoted in New Haven Daily Palladium, August 12, 1865, 2; Franklin Valley Spirit, September 6, 1865, 2; Jasper Weekly Courier, September 23, 1865, 1; September 16, 1865, 1.

8. Franklin Valley Spirit, September 20, 1865, 1, 2; October 4, 1865, 2; convention resolution quoted in Jasper Weekly Courier, September 16, 1865, 1.

9. Columbia Democrat and Bloomsburg General Advertiser, September 23, 1865, 1; Philadelphia Age quoted in Columbia Democrat and Bloomsburg General Advertiser, September 30, 1865, 1, 2.

10. *Urbana Union,* August 16, 1865, 2; September 13, 1865, 1; September 27, 1865, 2; *Seneca Advertiser* quoted in *Urbana Union,* October 4, 1865, 2.

11. *Cincinnati Enquirer* quoted in *Ashland Union,* August 23, 1865, 2; *Ashland Union,* October 4, 1865, 1; *Daily Ohio Statesman* quoted in *Ashland Union,* October 4, 1865, 1; *Ashland Union,* October 4, 1865, 2.

12. *Daily Ohio Statesman,* August 18, 1865, 2; October 2, 1865, 1; *Dayton Empire* quoted in *Ashland Union,* September 20, 1865, 1; *Cadiz Sentinel,* August 23, 1865, 2; October 4, 1865, 2.

13. *Chicago Times* quoted in *Jasper Weekly Courier,* September 2, 1865, 1; *Jasper Weekly Courier,* September 16, 1865, 2, reprinting the prospectus of the *Indiana State Sentinel; Boonville Enquirer* quoted in *Jasper Weekly Courier,* September 23, 1865, 1; soldiers' convention quoted in *Evansville Daily Journal,* September 16, 1865, 4; *Plymouth Weekly Democrat,* September 14, 1865, 2; October 5, 1865, 1.

14. *Aegis and Intelligencer,* September 22, 1865, 2; *Columbia Democrat and Bloomsburg General Advertiser,* October 21, 1865, 1; *Cadiz Sentinel,* September 13, 1865, 2; *Jasper Weekly Courier,* October 7, 1865, 2.

15. *Chicago Times* quoted in *Milwaukee Daily Sentinel,* September 27, 1865, 2; October 17, 1865, 2; *Ottawa Free Trader,* September 30, 1865, 2; *Grand Haven News,* October 18, 1865, 2; *Louisville Democrat* quoted in *Daily Mississippian,* September 27, 1865, 2.

16. *Chicago Tribune,* September 23, 1865, 2; September 26, 1865, 2.

17. *Chicago Tribune,* October 2, 1865, 2; October 9, 1865, 1, 2.

18. Johnson, "Lincoln and Equal Rights"; *New York Times,* September 26, 1865, 1; *Jeffersonian Democrat,* September 29, 1865, 2; *Chicago Tribune,* October 9, 1865, 1, 2.

19. *New York Tribune,* September 9, 1865, 4; October 2, 1865, 4; September 18, 1865, 4.

20. *Civilian and Telegraph,* September 28, 1865, 2; *Independent* (Oskaloosa), August 26, 1865, 2; *Boston Advertiser,* September 21, 1865; *San Francisco Daily Evening Bulletin,* October 3, 1865; *Cincinnati Gazette* quoted in *Bangor Daily Whig and Courier,* October 18, 1865, 1.

21. *Delaware State Journal and Statesman,* August 4, 1865, 2; November 10, 1865, 2; *Vermont Watchman and State Journal,* September 8, 1865, 1; September 29, 1865, 2.

22. *Ebensburg Alleghanian,* September 21, 1865, 2; *Bedford Inquirer,* September 29, 1865, 2; *Independent* (Oskaloosa), October 21, 1865, 2; *Big Blue Union,* October 14, 1865, 2; *Vermont Watchman and State Journal,* August 18, 1865, 2.

23. *Big Blue Union,* October 7, 1865, 1.
24. *White Cloud Kansas Chief,* October 5, 1865, 1.
25. *Bedford Inquirer,* September 8, 1865, 1.
26. *Proceedings of the First Annual Meeting of the National Equal Rights League,* 14–15.
27. Ibid., 14–15, 37–39, 52.
28. *State Convention of the Colored People of Indiana.*
29. *Proceedings of the California State Convention of Colored Citizens,* 2, 3, 5, 7, 14, 19, 21, 26.
30. *Delaware State Journal and Statesman,* September 8, 1865, 2; *Bedford Inquirer,* October 13, 1865, 2; *Columbia Democrat and Bloomsburg General Advertiser,* October 28, 1865, 1; *Philadelphia Press* quoted in *Vermont Watchman and State Journal,* October 27, 1865, 4; Sawrey, *Dubious Victory; Urbana Union,* October 25, 1865, 2; *Cincinnati Enquirer* quoted in *Cleveland Daily Herald,* October 12, 1865, 1; *Cleveland Leader,* October 17, 1865, 2.
31. *Philadelphia Press* quoted in *New Hampshire Statesman,* October 27, 1865, 2; *Delaware State Journal and Statesman,* October 13, 1865, 2; November 10, 1865, 2; *New York Tribune,* November 9, 1865, 1; *Chicago Tribune,* November 8, 1865, 1; *New York Sun,* October 12, 1865, 2; *Bedford Inquirer,* November 17, 1865, 2.
32. *Norwich Morning Bulletin* and *Hartford Daily Courant,* quoted in Escott, "What Shall We Do with the Negro?" 232.
33. *Argus and Patriot* (Albany, N.Y.) quoted in *Burlington Free Press,* October 13, 1865, 2; *New York Journal of Commerce* quoted in *Liberator,* October 20, 1865, 3; *New York Sun,* October 3, 1865, 1.
34. *Republican* (Springfield) quoted in *Caledonian,* October 6, 1865, 2; *New York Tribune,* October 2, 1865, 4; *New York Tribune* quoted in *Liberator,* October 13, 1865, 2.
35. *Chicago Tribune,* October 12, 1865, 2; Escott, "What Shall We Do with the Negro?" 233–34.
36. Escott, "What Shall We Do with the Negro?" 234–35. The 1865 conflict in Memphis was a prelude to far more extensive anti-Black violence in 1866.
37. Ibid., 235–36.
38. Ibid., 237.
39. Ibid., 237.
40. Clipping in Washburne, Papers, October 20, 1865; *Delaware State Journal and Statesman,* November 17, 1865, 2.
41. *Cleveland Daily Herald,* October 24, 1865, 2.
42. *Daily Ohio Statesman,* November 11, 1865, 2.

11. AN AMBIGUOUS AND DECEPTIVE EXECUTIVE

1. McKitrick, *Andrew Johnson and Reconstruction.*
2. Kenneth Stampp has suggested that Johnson's attitude toward southern leaders may have changed between April and December, as he succumbed to their blandishments. See Stampp, *The Era of Reconstruction, 1865–1877* (New York: Knopf, 1965).
3. *Ashland Union,* June 7, 1865, 2.
4. *Rock Island Evening Argus,* May 3, 1865, 2; May 5, 1865, 2; *Cadiz Sentinel,* September 13, 1865, 2; *Columbia Democrat and Bloomsburg General Advertiser,* July 1, 1865, 2.
5. Quoted in *Liberator,* May 19, 1865, 1; *Daily Ohio Statesman,* April 22, 1865, 2.
6. *Vermont Watchman and State Journal,* May 5, 1865, 2; *Jeffersonian Democrat,* May 12, 1865, 1; *North American Review,* October 1865, 566–69.
7. *New York Tribune,* June 17, 1865, 1.
8. *Jasper Weekly Courier,* June 3, 1865, 1.
9. *Columbia Democrat and Bloomsburg General Advertiser,* May 6, 1865, 2; *Harper's Weekly,* June 10, 1865, 354.
10. *Ashtabula Weekly Telegraph,* June 17, 1865, 2; *Cleveland Leader,* June 26, 1865, 1; *Hillsdale Standard,* June 27, 1865, 2.
11. *Cincinnati Enquirer* quoted in *Plymouth Weekly Democrat,* July 13, 1865, 1; *Ashland Union,* July 12, 1865, 1.
12. *Cincinnati Gazette* quoted in *New Haven Daily Palladium,* July 20, 1865, 2; *Liberator,* July 4, 1865, 4.
13. *Hillsdale Standard,* August 8, 1865, 1.
14. *Chicago Tribune,* August 14, 1865, 1, which cites the *New York Herald.*
15. McPherson, *The Struggle for Equality,* 332.
16. *Liberator,* August 25, 1865, 3; September 1, 1865, 1.
17. *Evansville Daily Journal,* September 2, 1865, 2, reporting a "recent statement" in the *New York Tribune; Hillsdale Standard,* September 19, 1865, 2.
18. *Jeffersonian Democrat,* September 8, 1865, 1; September 15, 1865, 2. See also *Delaware State Journal and Statesman,* September 12, 1865, 2.
19. *New York Times,* September 14, 1865, 4; September 15, 1865, 4; *Jeffersonian Democrat,* September 22, 1865, 2; *Columbia Democrat and Bloomsburg General Advertiser,* September 23, 1865, 2; *Ashtabula Weekly Telegraph,* September 16, 1865, 2; *Hillsdale Standard,* September 26, 1865, 1. Elizabeth R. Varon reviews some of the explanations that scholars have advanced to explain Johnson's support for white southerners. She points, in particular, to his priority of "emancipating the white man." If former slaves

could vote but were controlled by the old planter elite, "the middling white man would continue to be marginalized." Varon, *Appomattox*, 194.

20. *Hillsdale Standard*, September 26, 1865, 1; *Cleveland Leader*, September 16, 1865, 2.

21. *National Anti-Slavery Standard* quoted in *Milwaukee Daily Sentinel*, September 27, 1865, 2; *Chicago Times* quoted in *Milwaukee Daily Sentinel*, September 27, 1865, 2.

22. *Cleveland Leader*, October 12, 1865, 2; Phillips quoted in *Daily Ohio Statesman*, October 19, 1865, 2; *New York Sun*, October 12, 1865, 2.

23. *Ebensburg Alleghanian*, October 19, 1865, 2; *Chicago Republican* quoted in *Big Blue Union*, October 21, 1865. 1.

24. *New York Tribune*, October 23, 1865, 1. Stearns's directory of supporters of Black suffrage had included twenty thousand names, and he had sent fifty thousand copies of a pro-suffrage paper that he founded to every state and territory. *Cleveland Leader*, December 14, 1865, 2.

25. *New York Tribune*, October 23, 1865, 1.

26. Ibid.

27. Ibid.

28. Ibid.

29. Ibid.

30. Ibid.

31. Welles, *Diary*, September 28, 1865, 2:378; Adam Badeau to Elihu Washburne, October 20, 1865, Washburne, Papers; *Daily Ohio Statesman*, November 11, 1865, 2.

32. *New York Tribune*, October 23, 1865, 1; *Chicago Tribune*, October 23, 1865, 2, which refers to the *Cleveland Daily Herald*'s view that Johnson would favor some form of qualified manhood suffrage (such as an intellectual test).

33. *St. Cloud Democrat*, November 2, 1865, 2; *Ashtabula Weekly Telegraph*, October 28, 1865, 2; *Jeffersonian Democrat*, October 27, 1865, 2; *Ebensburg Alleghanian*, November 2, 1865, 1; November 9, 1865, 2; *Bedford Inquirer*, October 20, 1865, 2; *Independent* (Oskaloosa), November 25, 1865, 2; *White Cloud Kansas Chief*, November 23, 1865, 2.

34. *Daily Ohio Statesman*, November 15, 1865, 2.

12. TOWARD THE RETURN OF CONGRESS

1. *Columbia Democrat and Bloomsburg General Advertiser*, November 25, 1862, 2; *New York World* quoted in *Franklin Valley Spirit*, November 29,

1865, 1; *Franklin Valley Spirit,* November 22, 1865, 2; *Cadiz Sentinel,* November 15, 1865, 2; *Daily Ohio Statesman,* November 18, 1865, 2.

2. *Indianapolis Daily Herald* quoted in *Jasper Weekly Courier,* November 18, 1865, 1; *Plymouth Weekly Democrat,* November 30, 1865, 2; *New York World* quoted in *Aegis and Intelligencer,* December 22, 1865, 2; *Franklin Valley Spirit,* October 25, 1865, 1.

3. *Ottawa Free Trader,* November 18, 1865, 2; *Indianapolis Daily State Sentinel,* November 24, 1865, 2; December 20, 1865, 2.

4. *Chicago Tribune,* December 5, 1865, 2; *Bedford Inquirer,* December 1, 1865, 2; *Harper's Weekly,* December 2, 1865, 754.

5. *Columbia Democrat and Bloomsburg General Advertiser,* November 18, 1865, 2; *La Crosse Democrat* quoted in *Urbana Union,* November 1, 1865, 2.

6. *Ashland Union,* November 8, 1865, 2; November 22, 1865, 2; November 15, 1865, 2; *Daily Ohio Statesman,* November 22, 1865, 2; Seymour, *Public Record,* 269, 276; *Cadiz Sentinel,* November 15, 1865, 2, 1.

7. *Chicago Times* quoted in *Bangor Daily Whig and Courier,* October 28, 1865, 3; *New Haven Daily Palladium,* November 8, 1865, quoting the *Albany Evening Journal; North American and United States Gazette,* November 4, 1865.

8. *Cleveland Leader,* November 9, 1865, 2; *Independent* (New York), November 25, 1865, 2; *White Cloud Kansas Chief,* October 12, 1865, 2.

9. *Ebensburg Alleghanian,* November 23, 1865, 2; *Cincinnati Gazette* quoted in *Lowell Daily Citizen and News,* October 18, 1865, 2; *Bedford Inquirer,* November 17, 1865, 2; *Independent* (Oskaloosa), December 2, 1865, 2; *New York Tribune,* November 10, 1865, 4; *Cleveland Leader,* November 9, 1865, 1; *New York Herald* quoted in *Ashtabula Weekly Telegraph,* November 4, 1865, 2.

10. *Liberator,* October 27, 1865, 1.

11. *Proceedings of the Colored Men's Convention of the State of South Carolina,* 6, 8, 9. 11, 13, 19, 20, 21.

12. Ibid., 24, 25, 27.

13. Ibid., 28, 29, 30, 31.

14. *Proceedings of the Convention of Colored Citizens of the State of Arkansas,* 192, 193, 194.

15. *Vermont Watchman and State Journal,* December 15, 1865, 1; *Burlington Free Press,* December 1, 1865, 2.

16. *Liberator,* November 3, 1865, 3, reprinting a report from the *Philadelphia Press.*

17. *Proceedings of the Colored Men's Convention of the State of Michigan,* 13, 7–8, 12–13, 17–18.

18. *State Convention of the Colored People of Indiana*, 185–86; *Convention of Colored Soldiers of Iowa*, 2, 3, 5.

19. *Cleveland Leader*, October 3, 1865, 2; October 6, 1865, 2; November 10, 1865, 1. Unfortunately, I have been unable to find details on the Milwaukee meeting.

20. *Proceedings of the California State Convention of Colored Citizens*, 4, 6, 8, 12, 22, 26.

21. *Convention of the Colored People of New England.*

22. *Cleveland Leader*, October 4, 1865, 2; Thos Shankland to Thaddeus Stevens, September 29, 1865; E. Sherman to Stevens, October 4, 1865, invitation to Stevens, November 4, 1865, Stevens, Papers.

23. Benjamin Butler to Thaddeus Stevens, November 20, 1865, Stevens, Papers.

24. R. W. Flournoy to Thaddeus Stevens, November 20, 1865, Stevens, Papers; S. S. Panfield to Elihu Washburne (included in a letter from Henry Penniman to Washburne), November 14, 1865, Washburne, Papers.

25. *New York Tribune*, November 10, 1865, 4; November 16, 1865, 4; November 24, 1865, 4; *Bedford Inquirer*, October 13, 1865, 2; *Civilian and Telegraph*, November 2, 1865, 2; *New York Herald* quoted in *Bedford Inquirer*, October 13, 1865, 2; *Cincinnati Gazette* quoted in *Boston Advertiser*, November 20, 1865, 1; *Chicago Tribune*, November 11, 1865, 2.

26. *Harper's Weekly* quoted in *Bedford Inquirer*, October 13, 1865, 2; *Harper's Weekly*, November 18, 1865, 706; November 25, 1865, 738; December 2, 1865, 754; December 9, 1865, 770; *Littell's Living Age*, July–December 1865, 624; *Atlantic Monthly*, July–December 1865, 247, 763–64.

27. *New York Tribune*, November 20, 1865, 1.

28. Ibid.

29. Ibid.

30. *Cleveland Leader*, November 24, 1865, 2.

31. Welles, *Diary*, October 12, 1865, 2:381; December 1, 1865, 2:385.

13. CONGRESS RECONVENES—THE EFFORT CONTINUES

1. See Benedict, *A Compromise of Principle*, 26–30. Benedict's impressive and thorough analysis of Congress during this period shows that support for policies deemed Radical grew in step with the intransigence of the white South and its support by Johnson.

2. *Franklin Valley Spirit*, November 22, 1865, 2; *Daily Ohio Statesman*, October 2, 1865, 2; November 11, 1865, 2; *New York World* quoted in *Indianapolis Daily State Sentinel*, November 30, 1865, 2; *Ottawa Free*

Trader, November 25, 1865, 2; December 2, 1865, 2; *Plymouth Weekly Democrat,* November 30, 1865, 2; *Louisville Journal,* quoted in *Arkansas Gazette,* September 29, 1865, 2.

3. *Franklin Valley Spirit,* December 6, 1865, 2; *Big Blue Union,* November 18, 1865, 2.

4. *Chicago Tribune,* November 4, 1865, quoted in *White Cloud Kansas Chief,* November 16, 1865, 2.

5. *Delaware State Journal and Statesman,* December 7, 1865, 2; Strong, *Diary,* December 4, 1865; *New York Tribune,* December 4, 1865, 4; *New York Evening Post* quoted in *Liberator,* December 8, 1865, 3; *New York Sun,* December 4, 1865, 2; December 5, 1865, 2.

6. *New York Tribune,* December 5, 1865, 1; December 4, 1865, 4.

7. *New York Tribune,* December 5, 1865, 4; December 7, 1865, 1; resolutions quoted in *Plymouth Weekly Democrat,* December 21, 1865, 1.

8. *Delaware State Journal and Statesman,* December 7, 1865, 2; *Chicago Tribune,* December 7, 1865, 1; December 5, 1865, 1; *New York Tribune,* December 6, 1865, 1.

9. *New York Tribune* quoted in *Daily Ohio Statesman,* December 5, 1865, 2; *Philadelphia Daily News* quoted in *Franklin Valley Spirit,* December 20, 1865, 2; *Ashland Union,* December 13, 1865, 3; *Aegis and Intelligencer,* December 8, 1865, 2; *Jasper Weekly Courier,* December 9, 1865, 2; *Chicago Times,* December 16, 1865, 2.

10. Text given in *Evansville Daily Journal,* December 7, 1865, 2.

11. *Cadiz Sentinel,* December 20, 1865, 2; *New York World* quoted in *Bangor Daily Whig and Courier,* December 9, 1865, 2; *New York Daily News* quoted in *Daily Ohio Statesman,* December 9, 1865, 2; *New York Express* quoted in *Grand Haven News,* December 6, 1865, 2.

12. *Chicago Tribune,* December 6, 1865, 1; *Vermont Watchman and State Journal,* December 15, 1865, 1; *Caledonian,* December 15, 1865, 1; *New York Tribune,* December 6, 1865, 1; *New York Sun,* December 6, 1865, 1.

13. *Daily Ohio Statesman,* December 9, 1865, 2; *New York Times,* December 8, 1865, 4; *Cleveland Leader,* December 5, 1865, 2; *New York Tribune,* December 6, 1865, 4.

14. *New York Tribune,* December 14, 1865, 1; Summers, *The Ordeal of the Reunion,* 86; *Chicago Tribune,* December 20, 1865, 1.

15. *Report of the President of the United States,* 1–2.

16. Ibid., 106–8.

17. *Cincinnati Gazette* quoted in *New Haven Daily Palladium,* July 20, 1865, 2; *Report of the President of the United States,* 2–3.

18. *Report of the President of the United States,* 5–6, 7, 8, 9.
19. Ibid., 10, 11, 13, 14.
20. Ibid., 17, 15, 18, 19.
21. Ibid., 19, 20, 22, 23, 24, 25, 26.
22. Ibid., 27, 28, 30, 31, 32.
23. Ibid., 34, 35.
24. Ibid., 38, 35, 40, 42.
25. Ibid., 42, 43, 44.
26. Ibid., 45, 46.
27. *Evansville Daily Journal,* December 22, 1865, 2; *Independent* (Oskaloosa), December 30, 1865, 2; *Daily Ohio Statesman,* December 14, 1865, 2; *Ashtabula Weekly Telegraph,* December 30, 1865, 2.
28. *Cleveland Leader,* December 20, 1865, 1; *Chicago Tribune,* December 20, 1865, 1.
29. *Chicago Tribune,* December 22, 1865, 2; *Cleveland Leader,* December 2, 1865, 2.
30. *Congressional Globe,* 39th Congress, 1st session, 74, December 18, 1865.
31. *Report of the President of the United States,* 42–43.
32. *Chicago Tribune,* December 14, 1865, 1.
33. *New York Herald,* December 20, 1865, 4.

EPILOGUE

1. Escott, *"The Worst Passions of Human Nature."*
2. In addition to the failed initiative treated in earlier chapters, the District of Columbia rejected Black suffrage in December 1865.
3. For more on racist propaganda and its strength in the Democratic Party, see Escott, *"The Worst Passions of Human Nature,"* and Stanley, *The Loyal West.*
4. *North American Review,* July 1865, 199–200.
5. Gary Gallagher has pointed this out in *The Union War,* 4. He adds that 96.5 percent of the residents of the loyal states (which included slave-holding Missouri, Kentucky, Maryland, and Delaware) were white.
6. See Summers, *The Ordeal of the Reunion.*
7. Gillette, *The Right to Vote,* 26. In 1868 Missouri rejected Black suffrage and Michigan rejected a proposed state constitution that included Black suffrage. In 1869 New York voters also blocked Black suffrage.
8. The earliest and most important work to demonstrate this point was, of course, Kenneth Stampp's *The Era of Reconstruction.* Among other important studies are Michael Perman's *Reunion without Compromise* and Michael Les Benedict's *A Compromise of Principle.*
9. Gienapp, ed., *This Fiery Trial,* 60, 42.

❖ SELECTED BIBLIOGRAPHY ❖

NEWSPAPERS SYSTEMATICALLY STUDIED

Aegis and Intelligencer (Bel Air, Maryland)
Ashland Union (Ashland, Ohio)
Ashtabula Weekly Telegraph (Ashtabula, Ohio)
Bedford Inquirer (Bedford, Pennsylvania)
Big Blue Union (Marysville, Kansas)
Burlington Free Press (Burlington, Vermont)
Cadiz Sentinel (Cadiz, Ohio)
Caledonian (St. Johnsbury, Vermont)
Chicago Times
Chicago Tribune
Cincinnati Enquirer
Cincinnati Gazette
Civilian and Telegraph (Cumberland, Maryland)
Cleveland Leader
Columbia Democrat and Bloomsburg General Advertiser (Bloomsburg, Pennsylvania)
Daily Ohio Statesman (Columbus, Ohio)
Daily State Sentinel (Indianapolis, Indiana)
Delaware State Journal and Statesman (Wilmington, Delaware)
Detroit Free Press
Ebensburg Alleghanian (Ebensburg, Pennsylvania)
Evansville Daily Journal (Evansville, Indiana)
Franklin Valley Spirit (Franklin, Pennsylvania)
Grand Haven News (Grand Haven, Michigan)
Hartford Times
Hillsdale Standard (Hillsdale, Michigan)
Independent (Oskaloosa, Kansas)

Indianapolis Daily State Sentinel
Jasper Weekly Courier (Jasper, Indiana)
Jeffersonian Democrat (Chardon, Ohio)
Liberator (Boston)
Louisville Democrat
Louisville Journal
New York Tribune
New York Herald
New York Journal of Commerce
New York Sun
New York Times
New York World
Ottawa Free Trader (Ottawa, Illinois)
Plymouth Weekly Democrat (Plymouth, Indiana)
Rock Island Evening Argus (Rock Island, Illinois)
St. Cloud Democrat (St. Cloud, Minnesota)
Urbana Union (Urbana, Ohio)
Vermont Watchman and State Journal (Montpelier, Vermont)
White Cloud Kansas Chief

OTHER NEWSPAPERS ENCOUNTERED

Albany Argus
Albany Evening Journal
Argus and Patriot (Montpelier, Vermont)
Arkansas Gazette (Little Rock)
Bangor Daily Whig and Courier (Bangor, Maine)
Boonville Enquirer (Boonville, Indiana)
Boston Advertiser
Boston Commonwealth
Boston Journal
Boston Post
Boston Transcript
Boston Traveller
Buffalo Express (Buffalo, New York)
Chicago Post
Christian Recorder (Philadelphia)
Cincinnati Commercial
Cleveland Daily Herald
Cleveland Plain Dealer

Crisis (Columbus, Ohio)
Daily Mississippian (Jackson)
Daily National Intelligencer (Washington, D.C.)
Dayton Empire (Dayton, Ohio)
Easton Argus (Easton, Pennsylvania)
Fort Wayne Times Sentinel (Fort Wayne, Indiana)
Frankfort Commonwealth (Frankfort, Kentucky)
Frederick Union (Frederick, Maryland)
Hartford Daily Courant
Holmes County Farmer (Millersburg, Ohio)
Independent (New York)
Indianapolis Daily Herald
Joliet Signal (Joliet, Illinois)
Kalamazoo Telegraph (Kalamazoo, Michigan)
La Crosse Democrat (La Crosse, Wisconsin)
Lowell Daily Citizen and News (Lowell, Massachusetts)
Madison Capitol (Madison, Wisconsin)
Malone Gazette (Malone, New York)
Memphis Bulletin
Memphis Commercial
Milwaukee Daily Sentinel
Milwaukee News
Mount Vernon Banner (Mount Vernon, Ohio)
Nashville Press
National Anti-Slavery Standard (Philadelphia and New York)
New Albany Ledger (Illinois)
New Hampshire Statesman (Concord)
New Haven Daily Palladium (New Haven, Connecticut)
New York Day Book
New York Evening Post
New York Express
New York News
North American and United States Gazette (Philadelphia)
Norwich Morning Bulletin (Norwich, Connecticut)
Philadelphia Age
Philadelphia Bulletin
Philadelphia Evening Telegraph
Philadelphia Inquirer
Philadelphia Ledger

256   SELECTED BIBLIOGRAPHY

Philadelphia North American
Philadelphia Press
Pittsburg Gazette
Pittsburg Post
Republican (Springfield, Massachusetts)
Richmond Commercial Bulletin (Richmond, Virginia)
St. Louis Dispatch
San Francisco Daily Evening Bulletin
Scioto Gazette (Scioto, Ohio)
Seneca Advertiser (Seneca, Ohio)
Toledo Commercial (Toledo, Ohio)
Wheeling Register (Wheeling, West Virginia)
Wisconsin State Register (Portage)

MAGAZINES

Atlantic Monthly
Continental Monthly
Harper's New Monthly Magazine
Harper's Weekly
Littell's Living Age
New Englander
North American Review
Old Guard

OTHER SOURCES, PRIMARY AND SECONDARY

Adams, Virginia M., ed. On the Altar of Freedom: A Black Soldier's Civil War Letters from the Front. Amherst: University of Massachusetts Press, 1991.

Andrews, Sidney. The South since the War; as Shown by Fourteen Weeks of Travel and Observation in Georgia and the Carolinas. Boston: Ticknor and Fields, 1866.

Appendix to the Congressional Globe. 39th Congress. Washington, D.C.: Rives, 1861–65.

Baker, Jean H. Affairs of Party: The Political Culture of Northern Democrats in the Mid-Nineteenth Century. New York: Fordham University Press, 1998.

Bates, Edward. The Diary of Edward Bates, 1859–1866. Edited by Howard K. Beale. Washington, D.C.: Government Printing Office, 1933.

Benedict, Michael Les. A Compromise of Principle: Congressional Republicans and Reconstruction, 1863–1869. New York: Norton, 1974.

Bergeron, Paul H. *Andrew Johnson's Civil War and Reconstruction.* Knoxville: University of Tennessee Press, 2011.

Berlin, Ira. "Who Freed the Slaves? Emancipation and Its Meaning." In *Union and Emancipation: Essays on Politics and Race in the Civil War Era,* edited by David W. Blight and Brooks D. Simpson, 105–22. Kent, Ohio: Kent State University Press, 1997.

Berlin, Ira, et al., eds. *Freedom: A Documentary History of Emancipation, 1861–1867,* series 1, vol. 2, *The Wartime Genesis of Free Labor: The Upper South.* Cambridge: Cambridge University Press, 1993.

———. *Freedom: A Documentary History of Emancipation, 1861–1867,* series 1, vol. 3, *The Wartime Genesis of Free Labor: The Lower South.* Cambridge: Cambridge University Press, 1990.

Berwanger, Eugene H. "Lincoln's Constitutional Dilemma: Emancipation and Black Suffrage." *Journal of the Abraham Lincoln Association* 5 (1983): 25–38.

Blair, Frank P. *Destiny of the Races of this Continent: An Address Delivered before the Mercantile Library Association of Boston, Massachusetts; on the 26th of January, 1859.* Washington, D.C.: Buell and Blanchard, 1859.

Blair, Montgomery. *Letter of Hon. Montgomery Blair, Postmaster General, to the Meeting Held at the Cooper Institute, New York, March 6, 1862.* Washington, D.C.: Congressional Globe Office, 1862.

———. *Speech of the Hon. Montgomery Blair (Postmaster General), on the Revolutionary Schemes of the Ultra Abolitionists, and in Defence of the Policy of the President, Delivered at the Unconditional Union Meeting Held at Rockville, Montgomery Co., Maryland, on Saturday, October 3, 1863.* New York: D. W. Lee, 1863.

Boritt, Gabor S. "Did He Dream of a Lily-White America?" In *The Lincoln Enigma: The Changing Faces of an American Icon,* edited by Gabor Boritt, 1–19. New York: Oxford University Press, 2001.

Brace, Charles L. *The Races of the Old World: A Manual of Ethnology.* New York: Charles Scribner, 1863.

Brasher, Glenn David. *The Peninsula Campaign and the Necessity of Emancipation.* Chapel Hill: University of North Carolina Press, 2012.

Brown, Ira B. "William D. Kelley and Radical Reconstruction." *Pennsylvania Magazine of History and Biography* 85, no. 3 (July 19961): 316–29.

Burlingame, Michael. *Abraham Lincoln: A Life.* 2 volumes. Baltimore, Johns Hopkins University Press, 2008.

Campbell, John Archibald. *Reminiscences and Documents Relating to the Civil War during the Year 1865.* Baltimore: J. Murphy, 1887.

Carter, Dan T. *When the War Was Over: The Failure of Self-Reconstruction in the South, 1865–1867.* Baton Rouge: Louisiana State University Press, 1985.

Carwardine, Richard. *Lincoln: A Life of Purpose and Power.* New York: Knopf, 2006.

Cheever, Rev. George B. *Rights of the Coloured Race to Citizenship and Representation; and the Guilt and Consequences of Legislation against Them: A Discourse Delivered in the Hall of Representatives of the United States, in Washington, D.C., May 29, 1864.* New York: Francis and Loutrel, 1864. Library of Congress, Rare Book and Special Collections Division, African American Pamphlet Collection, http://memory.loc.gov/ammem/aapchtml /rbaapcbibTitles04.html.

Christianity versus Treason and Slavery: Religion Rebuking Sedition. Philadelphia: H. B. Ashmead, 1864.

Cimbala, Paul A., and Randall M. Miller. *The Great Task Remaining before Us: Reconstruction as America's Continuing Civil War.* New York: Fordham University Press, 2010.

———. *The Northern Home Front during the Civil War.* Santa Barbara, Calif.: Praeger, 2017.

Cochin, Augustin. *The Results of Emancipation.* Translated by Mary L. Booth. Boston: Walker, Wise, 1863.

———. *The Results of Slavery.* Translated by Mary L. Booth. Boston: Walker, Wise, 1863.

Congressional Globe. 39th Congress, 1st Session. Washington, D.C.: Rives, 1865.

Convention of Colored Soldiers of Iowa. Muscatine (Iowa) Journal. colored conventions.org.

Convention of the Colored People of New England, Boston, December 1, 1865. coloredconventions.org.

Cox, LaWanda C. F. *Lincoln and Black Freedom: A Study in Presidential Leadership.* Columbia: University of South Carolina Press, 1981.

Crofts, Daniel W. "Ending Slavery and Limiting Democracy: Sidney George Fisher and the American Civil War." *Pennsylvania Magazine of History and Biography* 144, no. 1 (January 2020): 29–60.

———. *Lincoln and the Politics of Slavery: The Other Thirteenth Amendment and the Struggle to Save the Union.* Chapel Hill: University of North Carolina Press, 2016.

Croly, David Goodman, and George Wakeman. *Miscegenation: The Theory of the Blending of the Races, Applied to the American White Man and Negro.* New York: H. Dexter, Hamilton, 1864.

Davis, Hugh. *"We Will Be Satisfied with Nothing Less": The African American Struggle for Equal Rights in the North during Reconstruction.* Ithaca, N.Y.: Cornell University Press, 2011.

Donald, David. *Charles Sumner and the Coming of the Civil War.* New York: Knopf, 1960.

———. *Charles Sumner and the Rights of Man.* New York: Knopf, 1970.

———. *Lincoln.* New York: Simon and Schuster, 1995.

Downs, Jim. *Sick from Freedom: African American Illness and Suffering during the Civil War and Reconstruction.* New York: Oxford University Press, 2012.

Durden, Robert F. *The Grey and the Black: The Confederate Debate on Emancipation.* Baton Rouge: Louisiana State University Press, 1972.

Escott, Paul D. *Many Excellent People: Power and Privilege in North Carolina, 1850–1900.* Chapel Hill: University of North Carolina Press, 1985.

———. *Lincoln's Dilemma: Blair, Sumner, and the Republican Struggle over Racism and Equality in the Civil War Era.* Charlottesville: University of Virginia Press, 2014.

———. *Paying Freedom's Price: A History of African Americans in the Civil War.* Lanham, Md.: Rowman and Littlefield, 2017.

———. *"What Shall We Do with the Negro?": Lincoln, White Racism, and Civil War America.* Charlottesville: University of Virginia Press, 2009.

———. *"The Worst Passions of Human Nature": White Supremacy in the Civil War North.* Charlottesville: University of Virginia Press, 2020.

Equal Suffrage. Address from the Colored Citizens of Norfolk, VA., to the People of the United States. Also an Account of the Agitation among the Colored People of Virginia for Equal Rights. New Bedford, Mass.: E. Anthony and Sons, 1865. coloredconventions.org.

Fisher, Sidney George. *The Laws of Race, as Connected with Slavery.* Philadelphia: Willis P. Hazard, 1860.

———. *A Philadelphia Perspective: The Civil War Diary of Sidney George Fisher.* Edited by Jonathan W. White. New York: Fordham University Press, 2007.

Foner, Eric. *Reconstruction: America's Unfinished Revolution, 1863–1877.* Updated edition. 1988; New York: Harper, 2014.

Frederickson, George. *The Black Image in the White Mind: The Debate on Afro-American Character and Destiny, 1817–1914.* New York: Harper and Row, 1971.

Freehling, William W. *The South vs. the South: How Anti-Confederate Southerners Shaped the Course of the Civil War.* New York: Oxford University Press, 2001.

Furniss, Jack. "States of the Union: The Rise and Fall of the Political Center in the Civil War North." Ph.D. thesis, University of Virginia, 2018.

Gallagher, Gary W. "The Civil War at the Sesquicentennial: How Well Do Americans Understand Their Great National Crisis?" *Journal of the Civil War Era* 3 (2013): 257–65.

————. *The Union War.* Cambridge, Mass.: Harvard University Press, 2012.

Garrison, William Lloyd, *William Lloyd Garrison.* Edited by George M. Frederickson. Englewood Cliffs, N.J.: Prentice-Hall, 1968.

Gienapp, William E., ed. *This Fiery Trial: The Speeches and Writings of Abraham Lincoln.* New York: Oxford University Press, 2002.

Gillette, William. *The Right to Vote: Politics and the Passage of the Fifteenth Amendment.* Baltimore: Johns Hopkins University Press, 1965.

Glatthaar, Joseph T. *Forged in Battle: The Civil War Alliance of Black Soldiers and White Officers.* New York: Free Press, 1990.

Goodheart, Adam. "How Slavery Really Ended in America." *New York Times,* April 3, 2011. Nytimes.com/2011/04/03/magazine/mag-03CivilWar-t .html.

Harris, William C. "The Hampton Roads Conference: A Final Test of Lincoln's Presidential Leadership." *Journal of the Abraham Lincoln Association* 21 (Winter 2000): 31–61.

————. *With Charity for All: Lincoln and the Restoration of the Union.* Lexington: University Press of Kentucky, 1997.

Hay, John. *Lincoln and the Civil War in the Diaries and Letters of John Hay.* Selected and with an introduction by Tyler Dennett. New York: Dodd, Mead, 1939.

Hodes, Martha. *Mourning Lincoln.* New Haven, Conn.: Yale University Press, 2015.

Holt, Michael. *Political Parties and American Political Development: From the Age of Jackson to the Age of Lincoln.* Baton Rouge: Louisiana State University Press, 1992.

Horowitz, Robert F. *The Great Impeacher: A Political Biography of James M. Ashley.* New York: Brooklyn College Press, 1979.

Jimerson, Randell C. *The Private Civil War: Popular Thought during the Sectional Conflict.* Baton Rouge: Louisiana State University Press, 1988.

Johnson, Ludwell H. "Lincoln and Equal Rights: The Authenticity of the Wadsworth Letter." *Journal of Southern History* 32, no. 1 (February 1966): 83–87.

————. "Lincoln's Solution to the Problem of Peace Terms, 1864–1865." *Journal of Southern History* 34 (November 1968): 576–86.

Kaplan, Sidney. "The Miscegenation Issue in the Election of 1864." *Journal of Negro History* 34 (July 1949): 274–343.

Kelley, William D. "Safeguards of Personal Liberty: An Address Delivered at Concert Hall, Thursday Evening, June 22, 1865." Philadelphia: Social, Civil and Statistical Association of Colored People of Pennsylvania, 1865.

Kendi, Ibram X. *Stamped from the Beginning: The Definitive History of Racist Ideas in America.* New York: Nation Books, 2016.

Leech, Margaret. *Reveille in Washington, 1860–1865*. Garden City, N.Y.: Garden City Publishing, 1945.

Lightner, David. "Abraham Lincoln and the Ideal of Equality." *Journal of the Illinois State Historical Society* 75 (Winter 1982): 289–308.

Lincoln, Abraham. *Collected Works of Abraham Lincoln*. 8 volumes and 2 supplements. Edited by Roy Basler, 1953–55, 1974, 1990. University of Michigan Digital Library, https://quod.lib.umich.edu/l/lincoln/.

Litwack, Leon F. *North of Slavery: The Negro in the Free States, 1790–1860*. Chicago: University of Chicago Press, 1961.

Lodge, Henry Cabot. *Early Memories*. New York: Charles Scribner's Sons, 1913.

Magness, Phillip W., and Sebastian N. Page. *Colonization after Emancipation: Lincoln and the Movement for Black Resettlement*. Columbia: University of Missouri Press, 2011.

Manning, Chandra. *What This Cruel War Was Over: Soldiers, Slavery, and the Civil War*. 2007; reprint, New York: Vintage Civil War Library, 2008.

Masur, Kate. "'A Rare Phenomenon of Philological Vegetation': The Word 'Contraband' and the Meanings of Emancipation in the United States." *Journal of American History* 93 (March 2007): 1050–84.

McKitrick, Eric L. *Andrew Johnson and Reconstruction*. Chicago: University of Chicago Press, 1960.

McPherson, James M. *Battle Cry of Freedom: The Civil War Era*. New York: Oxford University Press, 1988.

———. *The Negro's Civil War: How American Blacks Felt and Acted during the War for the Union*. 1965; reprint, New York: Ballantine, 1991.

———. *The Struggle for Equality: Abolitionists and the Negro in the Civil War and Reconstruction*. Princeton, N.J.: Princeton University Press, 1964.

Miscegenation Indorsed by the Republican Party. https://archive.org/details/miscegenationind00newy.

"Mississippi State Colored Convention Held in Vicksburg on November 18." *Liberator*, October 27, 1865. coloredconventions.org.

Neely, Mark Jr. *Lincoln and the Democrats: The Politics of Opposition in the Civil War*. Cambridge: Cambridge University Press, 2017.

Nevins, Allen, and Milton Halsey Thomas. *The Diary of George Templeton Strong: The Civil War, 1860–1865*. New York: Macmillan, 1952.

Nicolay, John G. *With Lincoln in the White House: Letters, Memoranda and Other Writings of John G. Nicolay, 1860–1865*. Carbondale: Southern Illinois University Press, 2000.

Oakes, James. *Freedom National: The Destruction of Slavery in the United States, 1861–1865*. New York: Norton, 2013.

——. *The Radical and the Republican: Frederick Douglass, Abraham Lincoln, and the Triumph of Antislavery Politics.* New York: Norton, 2007.

——. *The Scorpion's Sting: Antislavery and the Coming of the Civil War.* New York: Norton, 2014.

Paludan, Phillip Shaw. *A People's Contest: The Union and the Civil War, 1861–1865.* New York: Harper and Row, 1988.

Perman, Michael. *Reunion without Compromise: The South and Reconstruction, 1865–1868.* New York: Cambridge University Press, 1973.

Proceedings of a Convention of the Colored Men of Ohio, Held in Xenia, on the 10th, 11th, and 12th Days of January, 1865. Cincinnati: A. Moore, 1865. coloredconventions.org.

Proceedings of the Annual Meeting of the Pennsylvania State Equal Rights' League, Held in the City of Harrisburg, August 9th and 10th, 1865. N.p.: The Convention, 1865. coloredconventions.org.

Proceedings of the California State Convention of Colored Citizens, Held in Sacramento on the 25th, 26th, 27th, and 28th of October, 1865. coloredconventions.org.

Proceedings of the Colored Men's Convention of the State of Michigan, Held in the City of Detroit, Tuesday and Wednesday, Sept. 12th and 13th, 1865. Adrian, Mich.: Adrian Times Office, 1865. coloredconventions.org.

Proceedings of the Colored People's Convention of the State of South Carolina, Held in Zion Church, Charleston, November 1865. Charleston: South Carolina Leader Office, 1865. coloredconventions.org.

Proceedings of the Connecticut State Convention of Colored Men, Held at New Haven, June 6th and 7th, 1865. New Haven, Conn.: J. H. Benham, 1865. coloredconventions.org.

Proceedings of the Convention of Colored Citizens of the State of Arkansas, Held in Little Rock, Thursday, Friday, and Saturday, Nov. 30, Dec. 1 and 2, 1865. coloredconventions.org.

Proceedings of the Convention of the Colored People of VA., Held in the City of Alexandria, Aug. 2, 3, 4, 5, 1865. Alexandria, Va.: Cowing and Gillis, 1865. coloredconventions.org.

Proceedings of the First Annual Meeting of the National Equal Rights League, Held in Cleveland, Ohio, October 19, 20, and 21, 1865. Philadelphia: E. C. Markley and Son, 1865. coloredconventions.org.

Proceedings of the State Convention of Colored Men of the State of New Jersey, Held in the City of Trenton, N.J., July 13th and 14th, 1865. Bridgeton, N.J.: J. B. Ferguson, 1865. coloredconventions.org.

Proceedings of the State Convention of Colored Men of the State of Tennessee, Held at Nashville, Tenn., August 7th, 8th, 9th, and 10th, 1865. Nashville, Tenn.: Daily Press and Times Job Office, 1865. coloredconventions.org.

Proceedings of the State Equal Rights Convention of the Colored People of Pennsylvania, Held in the City of Harrisburg, February 8th, 9th, and 10th, 1865. N.p.: The Convention, 1865. Online at coloredconventions.org.

Randall, James G., and Richard N. Current. *Lincoln, the President,* vol. 4, *Last Full Measure.* New York: Dodd, Mead, 1955.

Report of the President of the United States Communicating, in Compliance with a Resolution of the Senate of the 12th Instant, Information in Relation to the States of the Union Lately in Rebellion, Accompanied by a Report of Carl Schurz on the States of South Carolina, Georgia, Alabama, Mississippi, and Louisiana; Also a Report of Lieutenant General Grant, on the Same Subject, December 19, 1865. Senate Executive Document No. 2, 39th Congress, 1st Session. Washington, D.C.: Government Publication Office, 1865.

Richards, Leonard. *Who Freed the Slaves? The Fight over the Thirteenth Amendment.* Chicago: University of Chicago Press, 2015.

Richardson, James D., ed. *A Compilation of the Messages and Papers of the Presidents.* Volume 6. Washington, D.C.: Government Printing Office, 1907.

Ripley, C. Peter, ed. *The Black Abolitionist Papers.* Volume 5. Chapel Hill: University of North Carolina Press, 1992.

Sawrey, Robert D. *Dubious Victory: The Reconstruction Debate in Ohio.* Lexington: University Press of Kentucky, 1992.

Schwalm, Leslie A. *Emancipation's Diaspora: Race and Reconstruction in the Upper Midwest.* Chapel Hill: University of North Carolina Press, 2009.

Seymour, Horatio. *Public Record: The Speeches, Messages, Proclamations, Official Correspondence, and Other Public Utterances of Horatio Seymour, from the Campaign of 1856 to the Present Time.* Edited and compiled by Thomas M. Cook and Thomas W. Knox. New York: I. W. England, 1868.

Sherman, John. *John Sherman's Recollections of Forty Years in the House, Senate, and Cabinet: An Autobiography.* 2 volumes. Chicago: Werner, 1895.

Silber, Nina, and Mary Beth Sievens. *Yankee Correspondence: Civil War Letters between New England Soldiers and the Home Front.* Charlottesville: University Press of Virginia, 1996.

Silbey, Joel H. *A Respectable Minority: The Democratic Party in the Civil War Era, 1860–1868.* New York: Norton, 1977.

Smith, Adam I. P. *"No Party Now": Politics in the Civil War North.* New York: Oxford University Press, 2006.

———. *The Stormy Present: Conservatism and the Problem of Slavery in Northern Politics, 1846–1865.* Chapel Hill: University of North Carolina Press, 2017.

Stanley, Matthew E. *The Loyal West: Civil War and Reunion in Middle America.* Urbana: University of Illinois Press, 2017.

Stanton, William Ragan. *The Leopard's Spots: Scientific Attitudes toward Race in America, 1815–59.* Chicago: University of Chicago Press, 1960.

State Convention of the Colored People of Indiana, Indianapolis, October 24, 1865. coloredconventions.org.

State Convention of the Colored People of Louisiana, Jan. 9th, 10th, 11th, 12th, 13th, and 14th, 1865. coloredconventions.org.

State Convention of the Colored People of North Carolina, Raleigh, September 29, 1865. coloredconventions.org.

Stevens, Thaddeus. Papers. Library of Congress, Washington, D.C.

Stewart, James Brewer. *Wendell Phillips: Liberty's Hero.* Baton Rouge: Louisiana State University Press, 1986.

Striner, Richard. *Father Abraham: Lincoln's Relentless Struggle to End Slavery.* New York: Oxford University Press, 2006.

Strong, George Templeton. *The Diary of George Templeton Strong: Post-War Years, 1865–1875.* Edited by Allan Nevins and Milton Halsey Thomas. New York: Octagon Books, 1974.

Summers, Mark Wahlgren. *The Ordeal of the Reunion: A New History of Reconstruction.* Chapel Hill: University of North Carolina Press, 2014.

Taylor, Nikki M. *Frontiers of Freedom: Cincinnati's Black Community, 1802–1868.* Athens: Ohio University Press, 2005.

Thomas, Benjamin. *Abraham Lincoln: A Biography.* New York: Knopf, 1952.

Trefousse, Hans Louis. *The Radical Republicans: Lincoln's Vanguard for Racial Justice.* New York: Knopf, 1968.

United States. *American Freedmen's Inquiry Commission, Preliminary Report Touching on the Condition and Management of Emancipated Refugees. Made to the Secretary of War, by the American Freedmen's Inquiry Commission, June 30, 1863.* New York: J. F. Trow, 1863.

United States. *Statutes at Large, Treaties, and Proclamations of the United States of America.* Volume 12. Boston: Little, Brown, 1863.

Vallandigham, Clement L. *Speeches, Arguments, Addresses, and Letters of Clement L. Vallandigham.* New York: J. Walter, 1864.

Van Evrie, J. H. *Negroes and Negro "Slavery": The First and Inferior Race: The Latter Its Normal Condition.* New York: Van Evrie, Horton, 1861.

Varon, Elizabeth R. *Appomattox: Victory, Defeat, and Freedom at the End of the Civil War.* New York: Oxford University Press, 2014.

Voegeli, V. Jacque. "A Rejected Alternative: Union Policy and the Relocation of Southern 'Contrabands' at the Dawn of Emancipation." *Journal of Southern History* 69 (November 2003): 765–90.

Vorenberg, Michael. *Final Freedom: The Civil War, the Abolition of Slavery, and the Thirteenth Amendment.* Cambridge: Cambridge University Press, 2001.

Washburne, Elihu B. Papers. Library of Congress, Washington, D.C.

Weber, Jennifer. "Lincoln's Critics: The Copperheads." *Journal of the Abraham Lincoln Association* 32, no. 1 (2011): 33–47.

Welles, Gideon. *Diary of Gideon Welles, Secretary of the Navy under Lincoln and Johnson*. Introduction by John T. Morse Jr. 3 volumes. Boston: Houghton Mifflin, 1909–11.

What Miscegenation Is! New York: Waller and Willetts, n.d. Samuel May Anti-Slavery Collection, Division of Rare and Manuscripts Collection, Cornell University, Ithaca, N.Y.

Whiting, William. *The War Powers of the President, and the Legislative Powers of Congress in Relation to Rebellion, Treason, and Slavery*. 6th edition. Boston: John L. Shorey, 1863.

Williams, David. *I Freed Myself: African American Self-Emancipation in the Civil War Era*. New York: Cambridge University Press, 2014.

Wood, Forrest G. *Black Scare: The Racist Response to Emancipation and Reconstruction*. Berkeley: University of California Press, 1968.

Zietlow, Rebecca E. *The Forgotten Emancipator: James Mitchell Ashley and the Ideological Origins of Reconstruction*. Cambridge: Cambridge University Press, 2018.

Recent books in the series
A NATION DIVIDED: STUDIES IN THE CIVIL WAR ERA